Problematizing
IDENTITY

Problematizing
IDENTITY

Everyday Struggles in Language, Culture, and Education

Edited by
Angel M. Y. Lin
City University of Hong Kong

Montante Family Library
D'Youville College

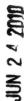

Lawrence Erlbaum Associates
Taylor & Francis Group

New York London

Lawrence Erlbaum Associates
Taylor & Francis Group
270 Madison Avenue
New York, NY 10016

Lawrence Erlbaum Associates
Taylor & Francis Group
2 Park Square
Milton Park, Abingdon
Oxon OX14 4RN

© 2008 by Taylor & Francis Group, LLC
Lawrence Erlbaum Associates is an imprint of Taylor & Francis Group, an Informa business

Printed in the United States of America on acid-free paper
10 9 8 7 6 5 4 3 2 1

International Standard Book Number-13: 978-0-8058-5339-1 (Softcover) 978-0-8058-5338-4 (Hardcover)

Library of Congress Cataloging-in-Publication Data

Problematizing identity : everday struggles in language, culture, and education / [edited by] Angel M.Y. Lin.
    p. cm.
  Includes bibliographical references and index.
  ISBN 978-0-8058-5339-1 (alk. paper)
    1. Sociolinguistics. 2. Identity (Psychology) 3. Language and education. 4. Language and sex. 5. Ethnicity. I. Lin, Angel M. Y. II. Title.

P40.P69 2007
306.44--dc22
                                                2007010584

Visit the Taylor & Francis Web site at
http://www.taylorandfrancis.com

and the LEA and Routledge Web site at
http://www.routledge.com

CONTENTS

PREFACE

Symbolic struggles exist in our everyday lives but we are often not able to become critically aware of and reflect on them, especially when we occupy privileged spaces and positions. This volume aims to provide some of the meta-language and theoretical, analytical tools to embark on such a practice of making the familiar strange, problematizing the taken-for-granted, and uncovering the linguistic, discursive, and cultural processes that serve to subordinate some people while privileging others, locking some people up in essentialized/fixed subject positions and negatively valued identities while creating mobile, fluid, valued, multiple identities and subject positions for the powerful.

In this book, contributors from a range of diverse contexts located in different parts of the world (Hong Kong, Malaysia, Thailand, Australia, United States, United Kingdom, and Sweden) describe and illustrate how different symbolic struggles in the world's different contexts (e.g., in different languages, cultures, societies, institutional, and noninstitutional settings) are being engaged in by different social actors (located in different sociopolitical positions), all using certain forms of symbolic resource as a medium to wage their identity battles (chiefly through language and public, official discourses, as well as through social interactions in different public spheres, educational institutions, or the mass media). As such, this is a textbook about symbolic struggles—who (has the capital to) engage in them, how they do so, and with what consequences for different groups situated differentially with differential capital and resources to forge differential (and hierarchical) identity categories for themselves and others in these struggles.

The chapters are organized around three themes: Identity, Class, and Difference; Gender, Ethnicity, and Education; and Gender, Ethnicity, and Language. The diverse sociocultural contexts in which the data and analyses are situated help to illustrate symbolic struggles and identity politics that are being engaged in by people in different cultures, languages, and societies of the world, offering insights from multidisciplinary, transcultural, and translocal perspectives. It is meant to be a book about the world's symbolic (and political) struggles and their material consequences for different people. The question of how we can deal with these struggles in our own positions in ways that do not help reproduce privilege and essentialized binarism (e.g., ethnicized, racialized, genderized, sexualized "Self and Other") will continue to haunt us and keep us grounded in a continuous search for different ways of constituting a situated postcolonial ethics in our own everyday textual, cultural, and political practices and struggles.

Identity as a term needs to be problematized, not taken for granted—for both the risks and the potential that the concept offers to educators for understanding issues of social inequality and how social inequality is being reproduced; and, for exploring possible alternative ways educators can work with identity de/formation processes to seek to break the social reproduction structures mediated through identity fixing and essentialization. My aim in this book is to contribute to this endeavor by offering a comprehensive integration and clarification/delineation of the different ways identity has been thought about and used in different theoretical traditions, and discussing the implications of different theoretical senses of "identity" for language educators. It is my hope that this volume will be useful to undergraduate and graduate students, researchers, and educators in sociolinguistics, applied linguistics, discourse analysis, sociology, education, gender studies, and cultural and media studies.

1

THE IDENTITY GAME AND DISCURSIVE STRUGGLES OF EVERYDAY LIFE:
An Introduction

Angel M. Y. Lin
City University of Hong Kong, Hong Kong

Introduction

The history of the development and uses of the notion of "identity" has not been an innocent one, if we are alert to the observation that it is usually the powerful who are entitled to and have both more and the right kinds of capital and resources for constructing for themselves advantageous identities. Although people who find themselves in subordinate positions can attempt to construct positive identities for themselves in their struggles to gain recognition, it is often the dominant regimes of the powerful that dictate the identity game to them on the basis of a rigged and stacked text. Very often the subordinated peoples' need to affirm an identity, and thereby construct a hegemonic essentialized structure for one*self* to fit into (in dichotic opposition to an essentialized *Other*), in a specific symbolic and political struggle is somewhat like what postcolonial critic Gayatri Spivak calls the need for "strategic essentialism." There are, therefore, at least 2 driving psychological motivations for identity: *being-for-the-self* and *identity-for-the-other*. As postcolonial critic R. Radhakrishnan observes:

> For too long, oppressed groups have been forced to constantly militarize their sense of identity, (1) as though their identities had no truth or significance beyond the expediency of polemics and strategy (when did we last hear of the practice of "strategic essentialism" by Western white Europeans?), and (2) as though the meaning of their lives has to be

2 ～ ANGEL M. Y. LIN

perennially played out in the context of dominant identities who supposedly have transcended the strategic and the political in the name of their
successful and "natural" history. (1996, p. xxvi)

Identity as a notion therefore needs some more theorizing and problematizing so that it does not easily become neutralized and universalized as
just another chic term (which carries academic capital) in contemporary
academic literature. For different subjects (or social actors) located in differential socioeconomic and sociopolitical positions, the notion of identity
is double-edged and is a weapon with risks and dangers (and often with
far greater risks and dangers for subordinated groups). It can be used by
both sides to reify different positions for different interests, and very often
it is the powerful groups who have more resources and capital to construct
powerful identities for themselves and dictate the rules of the identity game
to subordinated groups. As such, the subordinated groups' engagement in
identity politics seems to be a reaction to or a result of the colonial encounter, and is not necessarily a native form of life or way of being for these
groups (i.e., prior to the colonial encounter). It is in this sense that identity
is forced upon these groups from the Western tradition of possessive individualism (see Beverley Skeggs' argument in chapter 2, this volume). Subordinated peoples often find that they have to *collude in order to resist*—they
have to learn to play along in this game of identity politics in order to resist
and strive to gain recognition, which however might not in the long run
work to their benefit. It is in this sense that "identity" is not innocent and
is problematic—it presupposes certain cultural forms of knowing, acting,
and orientations towards social relations (e.g., Anglo-European possessive
individualism, as argued by Beverley Skeggs in this volume). It is, in short,
not necessarily a universal form of life prior to the colonial or oppressive
encounter.

The collection of chapters in this volume all deal with some form of
symbolic struggle, which is mediated through language (e.g., the Thai
language/lexicon and how it encodes and thus makes available and
culturally acceptable different gender categories including the transgender), discourse, and social interactions. They all bear upon the theme of
language-, discourse-, and interaction-mediated (and hence, *symbolic*)
struggles (*the war of position*—the struggle around positionalities, in
Gramsci's sense), which also have serious *material* (*socioeconomic and
sociopolitical*) consequences (e.g., see Ingrid Harrington's chapter on
"Discourses of Schooling, Constructions of Masculinity, and Boys' Noncompletion of Secondary School in North Queensland, Australia," this
volume). As cultural studies theorist Stuart Hall observes:

My own view is that events, relations, structures do have conditions of existence and real effects, outside the sphere of the discursive; but that it is only within the discursive, and subject to its specific conditions, limits and modalities, that they have or can they be constructed within meaning. Thus while not wanting to expand the territorial claims of the discursive infinitely, how things are represented and the 'machineries' and regimes of representation in a culture do play a constitutive, and not merely a reflexive, after-the-event, role. This gives questions of culture and ideology, and the scenarios of representation—subjectivity, identity, politics—a formative, not merely an expressive, place in the constitution of social and political life. (1996, p. 443)

The symbolic struggles discussed in this book revolve around the linguistic, discursive, institutional, and cultural processes of fixing/essentializing identities and subject positions for subaltern *others* and attributing negative values to those positions while constructing multiple, mobile, fluid, favorable identities and subject positions for *selves*, attributing and reproducing privilege and positive (moral) values to these subject positions. However, these chapters are also about some of the local creative ways of contesting such processes, usually through mobilizing and drawing on other available positive identities and resources to forge more fluid and empowering identities (e.g., as an ethnic minority English faculty member, Joseph Eng draws on his writer identity to re-position himself in the white-dominated academy; see Joseph Eng's chapter, this volume). Albeit often with local, temporary, or limited successes, social actors engage in such symbolic struggles as an unavoidable part of their everyday lives. The degree of success often also depends on what other kinds of capital are available to the social actors. This seems to point to the irony that those subaltern social actors who can achieve some (limited) success in the identity game are not those who are subalterns in most social fields. For instance, a middle-class, well-educated ethnic minority social actor has much more capital than a working-class, less well-educated ethnic minority social actor in playing the game of identity politics. Being academics and/or intellectuals ourselves who are likely to be occupying various both privileged and subordinate positions, we also have a moral responsibility to critically reflect on our own checkered repertoire of positions, and our own implication in processes of essentializing/fixing others' identities in our own privileged positions. What such critical reflexive analyses would lead us towards morally, politically, and educationally is a question on which I would like to ask each of our readers and contributors to continue to think hard and work hard. The anthology is thus meant to be one of the beginnings of many continuing critical explorations; it is not meant to have the last words on issues revolving around the different identity games in our everyday lives.

Overview

Part I: Identity, Class, and Difference, includes three chapters on theoretical issues revolving around the problems with identity fixing/essentialization and liberalist plurality discourses found in Western democratic societies. In chapter 2, Beverley Skeggs conducts a historical excavation (in Foucault's sense) into Western possessive individualism inherent in the political and socioeconomic contexts in which she addresses the practices of assuming, desiring, narrating, and constructing (legally, commercially, and later literarily) a coherent identity and generating a resourceful self (assembled out of otherwise fragmented experiences and affects). "This translation of affect and experience into a social position that relies on history, power, and inscription places the debate within a symbolic economy," Skeggs observes. Drawing on Foucault's notion of technologies of the self and Bourdieu's notion of the symbolic economy of different types of capital, Skeggs aims at showing how the technologies for producing a self become central to how the concept of identity is forged and used, but not equally available to all:

> I want to show how identity is a particular form of inscription, a discursive position that privileges those with access to specific cultural resources to both know and produce themselves. (2003, p. 2)

Chapter 3, also by Beverley Skeggs, goes on to use concrete media and discourse examples taken from the public media and discourses of the United States and United Kingdom to show how global capitalism of our times continues to appropriate and rob the black and white working classes of their cultural experiences and affective energies and how it has re-attached them to white middle-class bodies, thereby commodifying them and selling these new cultural products (images, projected identities, desires, pleasures, and even resentment) back to the working classes (as well as the middle classes). Such cultural exploitation of our postmodernist global capitalism (what Skeggs calls hypercommodification and industrialization of culture) pushes the traditional Marxist sense of labor exploitation into the cultural and affective arenas: not only is their physical labor being exploited but also their experiences, feelings, sexualities, and cultures. On the other hand, these feelings, sexualities, and cultures, when they appear in the working class bodies, continue to inscribe them with "decadent," "hypersexual," and "morally inferior" identities in the dominant discourses of the privileged middle classes.

In chapter 4, Lena Martinsson and Eva Reimers critically examine three specimens of official and religious discourses on social diversity in Sweden and show how these seemingly liberal, multiculturalist discourses obscure inequality and affirm capitalism as a common good. Their analysis shows that these discourses presuppose essential identities as economic resources for business companies and the nation. The authors stress the importance of deconstructing the processes in which essentialized, binarized differences are produced and different subjects (or social actors) are made into fixed positions; and, propose a notion of a self-reflexive deconstructive solidarity that focuses on nonessentialized difference and the conditions under which certain identities and positions are created that induce subordination of other identities and positions. The authors propose the need for a shift from identity politics to a continuous self-reflexive examination and questioning of (one's own as well as others') identity discourses. This echoes with the task that Stuart Hall posed to us:

> This does not make it any easier to conceive of how a politics can be constructed that works with and through difference, which is able to build those forms of solidarity and identification that make common struggle and resistance possible but without suppressing the real heterogeneity of interests and identities, and that can effectively draw the political boundary lines without which political contestation is impossible, without fixing those boundaries for eternity. ... But the difficulty of conceptualizing such a politics (and the temptation to slip into a sort of endlessly sliding discursive liberal-pluralism) does not absolve us of the task of developing such a politics. (1996, p. 444)

Part II: Gender, Ethnicity, and Education includes three chapters that focus on symbolic struggles revolving around gender and ethnicity in educational institutions, which serve as apparatuses for hegemonic production of identity categories and subjectivities. In chapter 5, Joseph S. Eng uses personal narratives to look into his 17 years of experience as a nonwhite, English faculty member in different United States higher institutes and reflect on the different marginal identities and positions he has been locked into. In contesting these imposed positions of otherness, Joseph proposes for himself and us alternative ways of imagining and re-imagining more favorable identities, roles, and positions for non-native, nonwhite English professors:

> Non-native, nonwhite English professors might occupy a rather crucial position that, at the same time they negotiate their nontraditional identities or unimagined roles as English faculty, their own reading and writing could in turn help students develop their marginal voices and further engage their learning interest. ... Claiming a passionate and reflective role in composition instruction, I now seize the opportunity of transforming the pedagogy by admitting that I am, afterall, marginal and marginalized, but meaningfully so. (2003, pp. 1, 7)

So, instead of re-imagining a mainstream faculty member position for himself (which is quite beyond his reach), Eng chooses to remain in the "margins" but also chooses to infuse the margins with different (more empowering) meanings by inscribing such a "marginal" position with pedagogy-transforming practices and enriched cultural meanings, which give both moral and positive social values to his re-imagined marginal position. The extent to which this re-imagining is successful will partially depend on the power circuits through which this re-imagining discourse can successfully circulate, reach, and persuade the desirable audiences. It is in this sense that the present book is in itself both a textual strategy and a political and cultural act of symbolic struggle.

Chapter 6, by Jan Connelly, is about a white female teacher's response to issues in the education of Australian indigenous students; and, it begins with the announcement of the author's own privileged social location: that of a white Australian woman academic with a strong sense of social justice. Jan offers an extract from an inquiry she undertook in a field of difference—an Australian indigenous educational context. The inquiry involves the construction of her own and five other teachers' lived experiences reported via narratives. The inquiry focuses on seeking an answer to the question: How does a white woman respond to a localised indigenous educational setting? Closing her chapter, Connelly writes:

> Through the few snippets of data and narrative analysis I share here, it may be possible to "see" white teachers juggling enormous identity and subject position tensions. These in turn impact on their enacted pedagogy. Mindful of the knowledge created through the discourse of these narratives the educational implications are to ask the question of what now must be done. How can this knowledge generate different understandings and possibilities for the education of Australian indigenous students? In closure in the words of Derrida I ask of government policy makers, teacher educators, indigenous educators and communities who work in fields of difference, 'What now must be thought and thought otherwise?'

While Connelly does not want to mislead us into thinking that there can be easy answers to such difficult questions, she does help us to start thinking hard on how social actors located in relatively more privileged positions (e.g., white Australian teachers) can respond both honestly and morally to the suffering of people in less privileged positions. One step forward is perhaps for people located in relatively more privileged positions to actively engage in dialogues with others and in creative co-explorations of situated ways in which they can help transform some of their institutional structures/policies to enable those in less privileged positions to have more access to the valued resources and capital that they already enjoy. This takes both bold imagination and moral determination—to forge a situated postcolonial ethics and politics.

In chapter 7, Ingrid Harrington looks into the interlinks among discourses of schooling, constructions of masculinity, and Australian school boys' noncompletion of secondary school. Ingrid found that under the distinctive dominant schooling discourses and processes of positioning, most boys were left with little space to express their displeasure with school. Their opposition strategy led them to discourses of anti-authority and oppositional practices not too dissimilar from those studied by Paul Willis (1977). These rural young boys' essentialist, dichotic construction and mobilization of non-school-based working class masculine identities as "Self" in opposition to a school-based "Other" (e.g., teachers, those students who work hard to remain in school) ultimately lead to their noncompletion of school in North Queensland, Australia. Forced into this identity game with little alternative capital, these young boys' essentialist self-other constructions only serve to lock them into further disadvantage and stereotyped working class masculine subject positions. What such an analysis leads us towards, morally, educationally, and politically, is a difficult and troubling question, the answer to which we hope to ask both ourselves and our readers to embark on finding. For instance, what institutional and structural changes in the schooling system and discourses need to happen to make things different? *Who* can contribute to initiating such structural changes and *how* can they do so?

Part III: Gender, Ethnicity, and Language includes four chapters all looking into some aspects of situated language use and the construction, contestation, or reproduction of gendered, ethnicized, or sexualized identities and subject positions. Chapter 8, by Sam Winter, looks into the more flexible and relatively less binary linguistic (and thus social and cultural) space offered in the Thai language and the Thai society for transgenders. Through looking into Thai cultures and Thai (Buddhist) religious values as reflected in the Thai vocabulary referring to different sexes, one can come to appreciate the constructed nature of our existing gender categories, including the deeply naturalized, taken-for-granted, rigid, binary gender system (and the rigidly fixed, binary gender subject positions), found in many languages, cultures, and societies of the world. As Sam Winter puts it, "I am not suggesting here which road is right. For the present I am just trying to suggest that different roads [or different gender subject positions] are offered by different cultures."

In chapter 9, Maya Khemlani David and Janet Yong analyse the linguistic and discursive features of the public responses of 11 successful men and 11 successful women in journalistic interviews conducted and published by both local and international magazines. Distinctive differences are found between the women's and the men's self-representations. The women seem to assert a sense of self, which, however, seems to be dependent on others. The men, on the other hand, seem to project an image under which they inhabit an impersonal milieu where there is little talk about spouse and where the focus is on work, risk-taking, clients, and themselves. The women seem to inhabit a personal world of family and friends. The multiple (traditionally essentialized) roles and identities (e.g., wife, partner, mother, career woman, and homemaker) that the women publicly assign to themselves result in crediting success to these "important others" in their lives and insisting that their priorities are both work and family, properly apportioned. The authors conclude:

> For all the progress women have made in the workforce—and men have made in accepting them there—many people of both sexes are uncomfortable with the outright reversal of gender roles. More and more women are wrestling with gender roles as high-powered jobs come within their reach. The dividends for these working wives—peace of mind, no distractions, the ability to focus single-mindedly on work—are precisely the ones their male counterparts have always had.

It seems that women themselves (and most ironically successful women who occupy important, advantageous positions in circuits of power) do not necessarily want to contest and change the discourses that continue to reproduce traditional gender roles and subject positions. The success enjoyed by this handful of successful women will continue to be restricted to just a privileged few—those with class-based social and cultural capital that facilitates their success despite multiple gender role demands on them. Here we can see that there are problems to an essentialized feminist identity politics: not all women occupy similar socioeconomic positions or have similar interests. The end of the essential feminist subject also entails the recognition that the central issues of gender always appear historically in connection with other categories and divisions and are constantly crossed and re-crossed by the categories of class, race, ethnicity, sexuality, and so on.

In chapter 10, Jette G. Hansen Edwards looks at the occupational trajectories, values, and identities of a Vietnamese husband-and-wife immigrant couple in the United States and what consequences the subject positions and job decisions taken up by each have on their respective English language learning opportunities. As the story of the Tran couple illustrates, gender categorization and identification may be a factor in determining which work roles—and family roles—are available for immigrant husbands and wives. Because of Anh's (the wife) perception that in her role as a filial daughter she had to bear a large part of the responsibility for the financial caretaking of her maiden family, she took a job in a nail salon as this was a relatively easy job to find for Vietnamese women because of Vietnamese social networks in the United States. Although she was unhappy in her job, she stayed in that profession in order to continue earning money to help her maiden family become financially independent. Anh is not happy remaining in the identity of a nail technician. The work context does not give her the opportunities she feels she needs to practice her English so that she can pursue her real dream of becoming a computer programmer. On the other hand, Nhi (the husband) seems to have fairly limited opportunities to practice English if measured time-wise—his only chances are during short breaks and his lunch hour. However, he does have a fairly supportive work environment in terms of English language practice. He has four good friends at work, two American and two Mexican, all men. He talks with them every day during their break times and lunches, and as he says, "they teach English … if I if I speak wrong they correct for me." They teach him job terminology and they often joke during breaks, as he says, "when … break time … we have we talk we talk together funny." He understands everything when he speaks with his friends at work as they tend to speak very slowly so he can follow and join their conversation. The author has led us to ask the question of whether this is simply a matter of luck or systematic social positioning disadvantaging immigrant women. Although both are ethnic minorities, ethnic minority women seem to have fewer opportunities to access a wider range of work types than ethnic minority men. Here are example questions from the author: is it that the kinds of work (and communities and public identities) available to immigrant women provide little access to English (and other important skills) and thus lock these women in their low status jobs and subject positions? And another: do women's self-internalized moral and cultural values/ideologies (e.g., to sacrifice one's aspired career/professional identity to take up the financial burden of her maiden family) lead to their self-limiting job decisions (and role identifications)? These critical questions concern not only socioeconomic structures (e.g., different kinds of jobs for women and men) but also ideological, cultural, and moral value/ideological issues (e.g., are women expected to fit into certain familial identity positions that exert hegemonic/moral expectations of them to sacrifice more for their families in many cultures?).

Chapter 11, by Winnie Cheng, is a discourse analysis of two conversational exchanges on sensitive topics, each between a Hong Kong Chinese and an English-speaking Westerner in Hong Kong. In both exchanges, the Hong

Kong Chinese is seen to be accommodating the prejudiced talk of the English-speaking Westerner. As the talk develops, the Hong Kong Chinese collaborates with the English-speaking Westerner in constructing essentialized, disparaging, ethnic and gender stereotypes of "other less civilized" peoples in Asia, for example, the "traditional" Japanese woman, or the "dog-eating", "horrible" Mainland Chinese. It seems that by *othering* remote (actually not-too-remote) others, the Hong Kong Chinese interactors seem to be clearing for themselves a relatively safe and superior identity space from which to project to the Westerner their more modern Hong Kong identities, as opposed to the traditional Japanese woman identity or the uncivilized dog-eating Mainland Chinese identity. Using such strategies of identity fixing (fixing the remote "Other"), both parties manage to find enough (superior) common ground to establish rapport or a friendly interpersonal relationship in what would otherwise be an anxiety producing situation as a potentially face-threatening, sensitive topic is raised (e.g., women's role in Asian society, dog-eating) by a seemingly self-proclaimed more "modern/civilized" Westerner. As an intercultural communication strategy, this co-constructing of essentialized and denigrated subject positions and identities for "the remote Other" (and simultaneously the superior "Self") seems workable and successful, as can be seen in the exchanges. What the author leads us to think hard on is the question of how we can have interacted differently, how face-threatening topics can be dealt with without adopting such a strategy of *othering* remote others. This seems to be one of the continuous moral and symbolic struggles that many of us will find ourselves faced with in our everyday lives.

Part IV concludes the book with two commentaries—Chapter 12, "Outperforming Identities," by John Erni, and Chapter 13, "Modernity, Postmodernity, and the Future of 'Identity': Implications for Educators," by Angel M. Y. Lin—that seek to integrate themes emerging from the different chapters and to outline future directions for our thinking about identity.

References

Hall, S. (1996). New ethnicities. In D. Morley, & K.-H. Chen (Eds.), *Critical dialogues in cultural studies* (pp. 441–449). London: Routledge.

Radhakrishnan, R. (1996). *Diasporic mediations: Between home and location.* Minneapolis: University of Minnesota Press.

Willis, P. E. (1977). *Learning to labour: How working class kids get working class jobs.* Hampshire: Gower.

2

THE PROBLEM WITH IDENTITY

Beverley Skeggs

Goldsmiths, University of London, United Kingdom

Introduction

I have problems with the term identity on three grounds:

1. Identity is not equally available to all and so operates as an unequal resource that only some can use.
2. The concept of identity is generated from discourses of the self and possessive individualism that were reliant on the conversion and knowledge of experience via practices of telling and representation, which were always about exclusion, authority, and morality.
3. The etymology of identity is from a Western specific colonialist discourse that expresses and authorises the relations of the privileged.

Identity is just one way of thinking personhood, a way that is particularly Western and particularly useful for global capitalism, with a long history through concepts of interest (Adam Smith, 1776/1970), rationality, individuality, self, character, and personality. Identity is one modern variant of speaking personhood that relies upon assumptions about and desires for coherence and completeness. Identity is simultaneously a category, a social position, and an affect.

The translation of affect and experience into a social position that relies on history, power, and inscription immediately places debates about identity within a symbolic economy: This is most obvious at the level of the nation whereby feelings of belonging are produced by and then institutionalised into national identity. There is a difference among inhabiting an identity position, making an identification, being positioned by identity, and experiencing personhood as if it is an identity.

Identity is always underpinned by recognition; "I am" is a recognition of a dialogic relationship in which the way one is being recognised occurs with how one recognises oneself. I'll expand on my doubts about the concept beginning with an outline of why I think identity poses particular problems at this particular historic moment.

In the Western world, identity as a concept and as a subject position from which political claims have been mobilised has increased in significance. The social positions of blacks, women, gays, and lesbians have been used to articulate specific claims for groups previously marginalised. What all these identity claims have in common is that they make their claim on the state and make their presence felt in the public domain. Diverse mechanisms, from consumption to spatial territorialisation, are used to make visible presence known and the claims often take the form of "rights discourse." Moreover, the politics of identity is not just restricted to previously marginalised groups becoming visible, but identity is also now at the heart of workplace politics, labour processes, and the organization of production.

The reorganisation of Western economies through forms of neoliberalism enables the market, global inevitability, consumer sovereignty, and choice to become the dominant symbolic discourses through which new ideas of personhood are formed. This has led political theorists such as Taylor (1994), Honneth (1995), and Fraser (1995) to suggest that the Western world had experienced a shift from the "politics of redistribution" (premised on understandings of class and inequality) to the "politics of recognition" (premised on competing identity-claims). As Fraser argues, the struggle for recognition is fast becoming the paradigmatic form of political conflict of the late twentieth century. Moreover, on a concrete level, identity politics has been institutionalised by what Bower (1997) calls "official recognition," that is, recognition of the law which has been put into effect by marginalised groups on the grounds of transgender, hate crime, and sexuality.

Paradoxically, whilst some spaces for official recognition have been forged, the increased visibility of campaigning groups has also led to their identification by the law enabling different punitive regulations to be simultaneously imposed. So whilst legal claims in the United States for transgendered recognition have been legally instantiated (Bower, 1997), many of the sex-zone spaces of New York have been regulated and closed down (Berlant & Warner, 1998). However, it is not just winners and losers that are significant, but who can play the game of recognition in the first place.

I begin with Foucault (1979) to show how the technologies for producing a self become central to how the concept of identity is forged and used, but not equally available to all. I show how identity is a particular form of inscription, a discursive position that privileges those with access to specific cultural resources to both know and produce themselves.

This chapter is organised into four sections. The first provides a historical background, establishing a frame. The second section explores the techniques necessary for the production of identity. The relationship between affect and resource in the production of the nation is analysed in the third section, and the fourth section examines who is fixed and who is mobile when difference is made via identity. An extended version of this argument, which examines how new forms of cultural property are put to use in the making of self and class relations, can be found in Skeggs (2004).

Possessive Individualism: Generating the Resourceful Self

To understand identity in the contemporary world, we need to know how it draws on different ways of producing personhood. There are very particular features to the development of different forms of Western personhood. For instance, Abercrombie, Hill, and Turner (1986) argue that there are strong reasons for believing that a system of control by the *inner cause of conscience* was a very peculiar development in Western society that led to a uniqueness in the development of the modern personality. The confession, in particular, as Foucault (1979) has shown, was a central technology in the production of a new logic of personhood organised around the key concepts of conscience, consciousness, feeling, and sentiment (Huff, 1981).[1] Foucault's later interest in confession lay in the impersonality of the scene by which personal subjectivities became formed and of how *taxonomies became rationalised* to mark the subject's place within a *categorical typification*.

Abercrombie et al. (1986) show how the techniques for developing the self mutated when they were used differently by different groups. The traditional Catholic confessional was appropriated by Protestant biography, then re-deployed in the modern psychoanalytic confessional and finally reconstituted in bureaucratic forms of inquiry. The confessional technique of telling the inner self became institutionalised as part of the bureaucratic apparatus of the modern state. This discursive development of the self, Abercrombie et al. (1986) argue, was the outcome of intellectual conflicts, competition between groups and classes, and of institutional changes.[2]

The telling of the self that could be known and institutionalised was enhanced by the emergence of new visual technologies. The self that could be told also had to *be seen* to be known fully. This led to struggles around representation.

Those who had access to the techniques for knowing and telling were able to use it as a *resource* for drawing distance and distinction from others. Abercrombie et al. (1986, p. 1) show, for instance, how the self became a resource that could be mobilised for the display of cleverness, as a form of intellectual property. They point out that in representations of the face in the premodern period, the artist's purpose was not to convey a likeness of the individual, but to show his *status and authority* (e.g., depiction of office, patriarchal, and religious status, etc.). So a legacy is established where representation is about power and authority through visualisation.

Evans (1999) shows how later in the 19th century—as a principle of romantic aesthetics—a discourse of a *complete self* that could be told (certainly not the fractal selves described before) was generated through the introduction and repetition of the chronological form. The aim of this telling was to overcome incompleteness, to aspire to full humanity by using techniques of self-cultivation, which aimed to harmonise and reconcile the different, fractured, divisive aspects of personhood (Hunter, 1992). This discursive production of whole and complete selves, cohering in identity, underpins many modern techniques of self-knowing. Historically, the roots of these bounded selves can be found in the discourse of possessive individualism.

Possessive individualism, identified by Macpherson (1962) as the cornerstone of liberal political theory, with a long history dating from the 17th century, was the central political frame through which concepts of personhood, self, and individual became known. The premise of possessive individualism was that you became an individual through owning your own experience. You could evidence that you owned your own experience through particular techniques and create links between disparate experiences. The articulation of experience within a "scientific" or "religious" frame of authority enabled the attribution of moral authority to the story of the self. Moreover, only some groups were seen to be capable of having, telling, and owning their experience. For instance, as Pateman (1988) shows, women were structured out of the category of the individual through ownership rights. "The individual" is defined through *his* capacity to own property in *his* person (it was a he). He is seen to have the capacity to stand outside of himself, to separate "himself" from "his body" and then to have a proprietal relation to himself as bodily property. According to contract theory, the labour power expended in work is detachable from the body of the individual. Therefore, what is said to be sold or exchanged in an employment contract is the individual's capacity to perform labour, rather than the individual himself. The exchange of the man *himself* would count as slavery and run counter to the principle of freedom expressed by contract theory.

Pateman further argues that the contractual relations of the social contract must be constantly repeated in order to reproduce the social system. This is not an act of free will, she argues, but a compulsory reiteration of the category of the individual through the repetition of contracts if the exclusive status and rights of the individual are to be maintained. The legal exchange of recognition (when one is recognised by another as an individual) in turn reinforces the legitimacy of the system of contractual relations. So recognition is structured into the category of the individual as is the ownership of experience by the privileged. The status of "the individual," therefore, does not exist before the moments of contractual exchange or recognition.

By naming someone an "individual," discourse brings into effect that which it names; it is performative. Just as Austin (1962) showed how the marriage ceremony produced a "lawfully wedded husband" through citation, the recognition and naming of another with the status of individual brings them into effect. But this utterance is only effective if it is authorised (in this case before the law). In the performative mode of language, the words are said to do the marriage, to constitute it. So the category individual is produced not only in the exchange of recognition but in the *authorisation* of that recognition.

Moreover, as Pateman shows, the constitution of the category individual is also based on the slave contract and the construction of ideas of the European "self" and the "savage other" developed through colonial encounters and violent domination of indigenous populations of East Africa. This is particularly obvious in the ways in which different forms of property were valued. The owning of experience was converted into value through the category of the individual whereas conversely the owning of objects was seen to be a primitive form of behaviour. Stallybrass, drawing from the work of Pietz (1985, 1987), shows how the fetish as a concept had already been radically inscribed when Marx put it to work and was intimately associated with the formation of European personhood. The fetish was used to demonise the supposedly arbitrary attachment of West Africans to material objects. From this, the European subject was constituted in opposition to this demonised fetishism, seeing the value of "things" only in exchange. Kopytoff (1986) argues that this contrast between individualised persons and commodified things was a central ideological plank of colonialism that served to divorce use from exchange-value, but also significantly associated certain forms of personhood with use and exchange-values. The "civilised" exercised a relationship to things based on a specific perspective on value as always being about experience that could be exchanged. Hence, one's experience becomes a resource to be used in exchange (a point which is significant to the argument developed later).

Strathern (1992a) identifies possessive individualism as one of the ways in which the newly forming bourgeoisie were able to impose themselves, their experience, and their *perspectives* on others. Perspective is a key concept, as it is the way in which some experiences, practices, and objects come to be given value and others are made valueless.

Lury (1998) shows how possessive individualism is being reworked in a contemporary context through advertising, intellectual property rights, and branding as a means of selling the experience of product use back to the consumer as part of their self-formation. Cronin's (2000) recent research shows how, for the French and British middle-classes, the incitement to individuality is produced as a compulsion, in which advertising brands produce their distinctiveness by interpellating people as already possessive individuals, enabling them to recognise themselves as such.

Historically, therefore, as a discourse, possessive individualism provides particular perspectives and vantage points by which a privileged elite group can view and know themselves and establish their moral authority. Necessary to this privilege and authority is the exclusion of those who operated as the constitute limit by which possessive individualism could be bounded.

Cohen (1995) has shown how contemporary understandings of the self create a bounded space in which the principle that each person belongs to himself means that they owe nothing to anybody else. This principle, he argues, is encapsulated in the Marxist critique of exploitation since it is premised on the fact that the employer steals from the worker that which belongs to him—his (sic) labour power. It is the fetishism of the commodity, of course, which hides this labour. Experience and perspective are therefore central components of identity. But whose experience and whose perspective produce identity?

Telling, Technique, and Authorisation

As possessive individualism became woven through different forms of liberal political discourse, its techniques were deployed by the state. The law was used to institutionalise the authority of possessive individuals and de-legitimate others. Steedman (2000) shows how generating a self that could be told, according to recognised techniques, was related to legal and moral decisions about social worthiness. In these characterisations, legally required questions structure the forms of telling and thereby the conditions of possibility for the narration of the self. The accounts produced and recorded are forms in which the interlocutor has been removed and are structured through answers. Steedman (2000) argues:

> By these means, multitudes of labouring men and women surveyed a life from a fixed standpoint, told it in chronological sequence, gave an

account of what it was that brought them to this place, this circumstance now, telling the familiar tale for the justices clerk to transcribe.
(pp. 17–18)

"The knowing self" was thus a subject position always attributed to the
bourgeois perspective and subject. The working-class men and women, as
Steedman (2000) shows, were only offered the position of self to occupy if
they could fit into a particular mode of telling. Marcus (1994) argues that
the autobiographical form historically came to mark and be marked by the
privilege of self-possession. Being the author of one's life rather than the
respondent to another's interlocutions was a significant difference in
the generation of different forms of personhood. In different ways, these
forms of telling a self become institutionalised. Only some are able to have
an experience that can be heard, can be told, and can be converted into
the production of a self.

This becomes apparent when we examine how and which marginalised
groups are able to mobilise around identity politics by using their experience as a resource to make a political claim. Evans (1999, p. 489) shows how
central individualism was to the formation of dissident sexual movements
formed in the 1960s. Evans (1999, p. 489) illustrates how testimonial practices
associated with bourgeois individualism were used to tell "sexual stories" in
which the "coming out" narrative operates almost as a form of redemption.
Telling stories of oneself also makes a claim for social and moral value and
worth; a claim to be recognised by the state. Brown (1995), for instance, has
also demonstrated how the "wounded attachment" is the foundational force
of feminism, enabling women to claim the experience of the moral value of
suffering, pain, wound, and oppression.

Telling stories about self-experience was a central technique in the
formation of identity politics. This became particularly acute within
feminist theory when the categories of woman and women's experience were
disputed as sources of unmediated knowledge. Stories of identity (I am a
man/woman/lesbian/gay/disabled researcher) were shown to replace critical
interrogation into the intricate composites and reifications of the discursive positions that we inhabit and the resources to which we have access.
Being positioned by structural relations (sexuality, gender, race, class) does
not necessarily give access to ways of knowing (although some standpoint
theorists would argue that it helps: see Maynard (1998) and Skeggs (1995a).[3]
As Haraway (1997) argues:

> Location is not a listing of adjectives or assigning of labels such as race,
> sex and class. Location is not the concrete to the abstract of decontextu-
> alisation. Location is the always partial, always finite, always fraught play

of foreground and background, text and context, that constitutes critical inquiry. Above all, location is not self-evident or transparent.... Location is also partial in the sense of being *for* some worlds and not others. (p. 37)

Location is therefore also about perspective and access to resources. We also need to remember that taxonomies and categorisations of persons as Foucault showed were used by the state to know, govern, and control. Those who mobilise around identity become subject to the categorisation that were used to subjugate them in the first place (Miller, 1993). As Said (1991) argues, the value of an emphasis on symbolic systems of identity cannot be allowed to go on for too long, lest they subside into "an ultimately uninteresting alternation of presence and absence" (p. 24). It is this use of surveillant categorisations, as a mechanism for producing subjectivity, that traps identity claims within the law.

For Deleuze and Guattari (1977), the essential social characteristic is to mark and be marked; this is about the articulation and disarticulation of libidinal energies. To inscribe a body or a body part (as bodies are composites), as Deleuze and Guattari argue, is to interrupt a flow of desire. Inscription cuts or scars bodies in the process of assembling them into composite forms, segments, strata, and habitual modes of behaviour. Capitalist semiotisation is one of the ways of achieving inscription; or in Foucault's terms, it is the subjectification of the body to medical and biological discourse that organises the body in particular ways. It is inscription, therefore, that produces the subject via *various* regimes, classification schema, and control of the body. What sociology perceives to be "society," Lingis (1994) argues, for instance, is a product of inscription—that is hierarchy, class, race, sexuality, and gender as forms of classification. Inscription is not just discourse but a complex set of practices for the deployment and coordination of bodies.[4] Bogard (1998) notes that:

> There are modes of social inscription that are exclusive, that separate bodies from what they are capable of doing, that demean their desire and distort their sense; and they are modes that are inclusive and connective, that liberate desire, destroy limits, and draw "positive lines of flight" or escape. (p. 58)

It is important not to confuse inscription with the sign (in a traditional semiotic sense), for as Deleuze and Guattari (1977) argue, there have been many different regimes of signs of which the most recent "representation" is literally that, the most recent. Like Foucault, they argue that the sign is not just representation but power, not just indication, but dividing practice (what they call the cut).

To overcome the forces of subjectification, one, therefore, needs to desubjectify (as well as destratify, deorganify, defunctionalise, desemiotise) (Deleuze & Guattari, 1977). This is why identity represents a conservative politics as it imagines an "I" or a "me" that can make radical desires coherent and representable. Fractal selves, or, as Deleuze and Guattari envisage, fractions of selves, never quite add up to an identity; that is, they never quite fill the space they are allocated. Identity forces a coherence on that which is not. In so doing, it reproduces a model of complete articulable selfhood that is only available for some. Others may not think of themselves as coherent, because the possibility has never been made available to them. The sign of identity is a cut that divides, an inscription that marks out those who can and cannot have a self-produced or an imposed categorisation. This difference is significant in making class.

In the United States and the United Kingdom, middle-class women, partly due to feminism, but also due to the production of "women's culture," which figured heterosexuality and the family as the site for the fulfilment and formation of the complete self (see Berlant, 2001), have been able to enter the space of identity through the techniques of telling, testimony, and trauma in a way in which black and white working class women have not. The stories of daily endurance and survival of black and white working-class women are read as mundane skills, not special or exceptional; their experience is not seen to be of the sort that can be interpreted as a complete coherent identity with value and authority.

Nowhere is this more apparent than in the recent moves to testimony. The concept of testimony comes from the same discursive etymology as possessive individualism: a legal framework whereby witnesses in court bear testimony. As Cosslett, Lury, and Summerfield (2000) show, testimony connects the first-person narrative to truth-telling. It is usually premised upon speaking out about hitherto unheard experiences and testifying to new forms of interpretation.[5] The Western proliferation of testimonial forms involves an extension of the legal domain into other realms of politics and culture.

Berlant (2001) shows how the appropriation of legal rhetoric in tales of testimony highlights a shift in authority claims. The use of legal rhetoric is a discursive ploy to claim the authority of self-evidence as opposed to authority bequeathed by institutions. Berlant has also extensively documented how trauma has become the central mode in testimonial and telling of the self; in which identity is known through the assaults of traumatic experience upon it. Telling becomes a mechanism, she argues, for the already authorised to authorise themselves. Trauma's tautological quality protects the subject by asserting their expertise over the grounds of their claim. Identity claims made through traumatic telling are thus rhetorical claims for power. When repeated over time, they may gain performative power (and hence become institutionalised). The logic of conventional contemporary testimony, she argues, evokes a desire for bigger, insurgent selves in a world whose parameters and value hierarchies are taken for granted. Berlant suggests we ask "For what? Why is the story being told? In whose interests? In what form?" She also shows how trauma has been so significant in the reconstruction of dominant forms of American personhood that it has overridden the everyday suffering of the subaltern and denied them a space in the national imaginary as trauma competes with trauma to be seen, heard, and used by the privileged to authorise themselves.

To recap, it has been shown so far that identity has a long history in the discourse of possessive individualism, which produced particular forms of personhood through not just techniques, but practices and relationships to others and objects that prioritised using experience as a form of property exchange. I have also shown how only a few were offered the subject position of selfhood, of how the experience of others was not considered to be worthy of becoming a coherent identity that could be inhabited with authority. I now want to look at how these legacies are being worked out in the contemporary in the formation of the nation.

Producing National Identity

The space of the national imaginary generates senses of who can and cannot belong to the nation, illuminating a difference between those who in the tradition of possessive individualism own their experience and articulate it as a self-identity and those who have to prove before the law (and culture) that they can occupy personhood.

Ghassan Hage (1998) in *White Nation* argues that in order to make a political claim one needs access to "nationalist practices": practices which assume first, an image of a national space; second, an image of the nationalist himself or herself as a master of this nation; and third, an image of "ethnic/racial other" as a mere object within this space. Nationalist practices are the means by which *value* is attributed to worthy or unworthy citizens. Classifications emphasising "undesirability" cannot be conceived independently of a national spatial background against which persons acquire meaning. A key difference from the historical organisation of the individual is how identity and self is being offered more widely. Taguieff (1991), for instance, notes a shift from the interiorising of the "other" to statements of the absolute, *irreducible difference* of the "self" and the *incommensurability* of different cultural identities. Practical nationality, Hage argues, is a form of national "cultural capital" that represents the sum (the volume) of valued (the right composition) knowledge, styles, social, and physical (bodily) characteristics and practical behavioural dispositions. In short, they are material and symbolic goods constructed as valuable within the national field and specific to it.

> That is, there is a tendency for a national subject to be perceived as just as much of a national as the amount of national capital he or she has accumulated. Thus, a national subject born to the dominant culture who has accumulated national capital in the form of dominant linguistic, physical and cultural dispositions will yield more national belonging than a male migrant who has managed to acquire the dominant national accent and certain national cultural practices, but lacks the physical characteristics and dispositions of the dominant national. (Hage, 1998, pp. 53–54)

To display practical nationality or national belonging, the taxonomies of the state have to be performed. Those who are seen not to belong but who have to make claims on the state are asked to prove their ethnic and raced identities. How can they accumulate and embody certain forms of capital to enable national belonging? As Hage shows, if they have not inhabited the circuits of capital accrual, it is unlikely that they can make up for the loss. For instance, he shows how being Lebanese in Australia operates as a kind of negative capital. It is not convertible into national symbolic belonging but is read instead as an inscribed raced identity. Moreover, he shows, in line with Bourdieu (1992), that regardless of how much national capital one accumulates, *how* one accumulates it makes an important difference to its capacity to be converted to national recognition and legitimacy.

Identity becomes a category that is imposed and inscribed on some who have to perform to it, but doing *so does not give them belonging to the nation but rather separates them from it.* It may, however, give them access to limited resources. It is forced identity and forced recognition. Rouse (1991) expresses concern with the widespread tendency to assume that identity and identity formation are universal aspects of human experience, and also with the dangers of ethnocentrically projecting onto the lives of people who may think and act quite differently what are, in fact, quite culturally specific conceptions of personhood developed in the affluent West in the recent period. The experience of the migrants Rouse studied was not so much one in which people possessing one culturally formed identity had to deal with the pressures to take on or accommodate another identity, different in content. Rather, he argues, more fundamentally, they moved from a world in which identity was not a central concern, to one in which they were pressed with increasing force to adopt a particular concept of personhood (as bearers of individual identities) and of identity as a member of a collective or "community" (rather than as a family), which was quite at odds with their own understandings of their situation and their needs. For these migrants, the taxonomic pressures of various state authorities to enumerate and certify their individual identities was often something to be avoided or neutralised wherever possible, in order to maximise their own flexibility of manoeuvre and action.

Similar critiques of identity have been produced through an analysis of Aboriginal land-right cases, where concepts of coherent and fixed identities are forced on groups, who, in order to become legitimate, have to adopt these identity-categorisations (see Povinelli, 2000). In Sweden, in order to access welfare benefits, immigrants and refugees have to prove that they fit the inscribed racialised identity generated by the state. These state-produced identities have nothing to do with migrant history, background, or culture but are produced, and often inaccurate, state-sponsored reports. But, those who need to make a claim on the state welfare system in order to survive have to learn to perform to these ascribed identities. Also in Sweden, Svensson (1997) shows how, in a strange contemporary echo of Steedman's historical work, the model of ascribed subjectivity through forced telling is employed in Swedish prisons. She shows how the biographical project of the state frames prisoner identity and the morality that is attached to it via the distinction between good and bad selves.

As identity is being extended as a possibility, both through political campaigning, which utilises and reproduces models of possessive individualism, through the development of commercial women's culture and through new forms of culturally essentialised racism that differentiate through culture and experience, identity becomes a category that is made more widely available. As it is opened out, it is cut, divided, and inscribed differently with different forms of value and authority. To make, and know, these differences, identity becomes more visible, more open to differentiation. Identity therefore makes a difference: the difference in value.

The state, the national imaginary, and consumer culture-defined identities are predicated upon visibility and therefore immediately exclude those who choose not to be made visible and not to be recognised. But it is hard to be invisible if the historically visible symbolic economy has colour-coded you and made you always visible. For instance, if you are black in Britain, you have no choice but to be recognised. Moreover, this visibility is always valued and it is the dominant colour-coding systems that negatively evaluate and constantly repeat exclusion from the terms of national belonging (and this is repeated across a range of sites, through immigration law, criminal law, cultural practices, and enforced spatialisation).

But this is not just about colour-coding but about the evaluation of many cultural characteristics, only some of whom are seen to have any value, as we saw in the impossibility of national belonging for those who cannot access and embody the required cultural competences and practices.

When one is recognised and *identified negatively*, it is unlikely that one will happily occupy the categorical positions by which he is located, the signs under which he stands, and the identities that he has been offered. It is also unlikely that one's dispositions will fit positions, as Bourdieu suggests, for this does not happen when misrecognition is generated because the positions available only offer negative values to those who take them up. As my previous ethnographic research (*Formations of Class and Gender: Becoming Respectable*) showed, the forms of inscription (discourse, theory, representation) that produced positions of identity loaded with negative value, are not taken up uncritically. In fact, they are not accepted at all but contested. This contestation means that a political mobilisation around identity cannot take place because it is premised on misrecognition and disidentification. So the identity position of the white working-class woman in the United Kingdom, circulated through the symbolic economy, offers an amalgam of discourses and representations that put together pathology, hypersexuality, fecundity, and degeneracy, inscribed on the body and provide a system of recognition and interpretation for those reading the bodies.

This generation of identity positions that are negatively evaluated becomes clear if we examine the changing evaluation of the white working-class in the United Kingdom, who have become racialised. Haylett (2001), in an analysis of New Labour political discourse, documents how, on June 3, 1997, the British Prime Minister, Tony Blair, made an announcement that was about a mass of people in mass housing. They were identified as people and places who were somehow falling out of the nation, losing the material wherewithal and symbolic dignity traditionally associated with their colour and their class, and becoming an ugly contradiction: abject and white. She shows how this announcement used the white working-class as symbols of a generalised "backwardness" and specifically a culturally burdensome whiteness. The white working-class was represented as the blockage not just to social inclusion, but to the development of a modern nation that can play on a global stage. This is very different to the "White Heat of Technology" debates of the 1970s where white working-class men were positioned at the forefront to the development of the nation. Then, when their colour was normalised, they belonged nationally because they had the resources considered necessary for the nation.

A further example that Haylett notes in the consolidation of this contemporary refiguring can be seen in the speech made by Peter Mandleson (1997) (then a man of some significance in the Blair government and considered to be one of the major architects of New Labour) to launch the Social Exclusion Unit. Here he sets out what he sees to be the "problem" confronting Britain:

> We are people who are used to being represented as problematic. We are the long-term, benefit-claiming, working-class poor, living through another period of cultural contempt. We are losers, no hopers, low life, scroungers. Our culture is yob culture. The importance of welfare provisions to our lives has been denigrated and turned against us: we are welfare dependent and our problems won't be solved by giving us higher benefits. We are perverse in our failure to succeed, dragging our feet over social change, wanting the old jobs back, still having babies instead of careers, stuck in outdated class and gender moulds. We are the "challenge" that stands out above all others, the "greatest social crisis of our times." (Mandleson, 1997, pp. 6–9 in Haylett, 2000)

In defining the "problem," Mandleson reproduces as "empirical reality" the threat to the nation. His rhetoric of social inclusion excludes. The white working-class are forever positioned outside of the nation. This is a significant shift in both class and race terms in Britain. Mandleson uses the discourse of modernity to illustrate the distance between the forward thinking and the low-life no-hopers locked in backward culture: the atavistic and the progressive. Gaps occur within whiteness so that white groups sharing the same skin colour are not "equally white" (Bonnett, 1998). This shift takes us back to emergent conceptualisations where the white working class were seen to be outside of British imperial society, represented as uncivilised, dangerous, a "race apart" (see, e.g., Engels, 1844/1958). So white identity is generated through morally loaded cultural representations in which difference is made between the recognisable dirty white and the normative invisible pure white. The recognised identity is pathologised through negative evaluations of behaviour and spatialisation. But this difference over time from exclusion to inclusion to exclusion is a problem not only of inscription but of how these representations evaluate the worth of the nation and of national personhood.

Haylett (2001) also shows how, in opposition to an atavistic white working-class, the white middle-class is not racialised at all but is instead positioned at the vanguard of "the modern." The "modern" thus becomes a moral category referring to liberal, mobile, cosmopolitan, work, and consumption-based lifestyles and values, and "the unmodern" on which this category depends is the white working-class "other," fixed in place and space, emblematically a throwback to other times and places: They exist to visualise the constitutive limit.

We need to ask why would anybody so positioned by representations and rhetoric so extensively circulated and known, so negatively marked, want to take up that positioning as a form of identity? And, how can anybody mobilise a politics from that which is not just negatively valued but also a negative form of personhood in the nation? What does it mean when identity is seen as a fixed visible cultural characteristic for some groups, but a mobile resource that can be put to use in the identity political-claims of others?

Fixing Identity

Diawara (1998) illustrates the mobilising of identity-loaded dispositions by showing how black (working-class) masculinity can be put to use as a resource, a mobile cultural style that can be used by different characters in film, be they black or white. He shows how in a tradition taken from Baxploitation films, black maleness, coded as cool, can be "transported through white bodies" (p. 52). Moreover, he shows how black characters become fixed into playing "blackness" (Eddie Murphy is probably the most obvious example, even as the donkey in *Shrek!*) whilst white characters who need to achieve "cool" can move between black and white dispositions. Race becomes a resource: fixed and read onto some bodies as a limitation, culturally essentialised, whilst it appears as mobile and transtextual on others (e.g., John Travolta in *Pulp Fiction*). That is, the fixed black character appears to be not acting; they just *are*. Hence, they are culturally essentialised and made authentic. The white self is able to access and resource itself through dispositions initially associated with blackness.[6] But using race, class, or femininity as a resource only exists for those who are *NOT* positioned by it. That is, it does not stick to the body of the one who is able to appropriate; rather it can be attached and detached as a mobile resource.

The issue then, I argue, is not identity but evaluation. The key to understanding difference is not through identity, which actually makes a difference reproducing the authority of the privileged and resourceful, but in understanding how value is attached and sticks to bodies, fixing some in place whilst enabling others to be mobile. This becomes even more acute when we see how some groups are not only forced to perform an inscribed identity, are misrecognised, and negatively evaluated, or whose cultural dispositions are used to enhance the middle-class self, but who are also subject to use in the direct generation of profit.

New studies of workplace organisation have also pointed to the limits of identity, when identity becomes a resource that can be used in the interest of corporate businesses to make profit from what were previously marginalised political identities. Adkins (2000) shows how marginalised identities are mobilised by management to achieve corporate "diversity dividends" such as successful and innovative advertising campaigns, sales pitches, product branding, and customer relations.[7] Diversity management concerns a "new world of visibility" in which identity practices are figured as corporate and occupational resources.

Adkins and Lury (1999) point to a complacency in recent analyses of workplace organization to assume that everybody is in the same position to perform an identity as part of their employment contract. However, they suggest that self-possessing workers with performable identities should not be universalised by theorists of the economic, since a person's relation to self-identity is by no means fixed, and moreover is a key site of workplace contestation. Moreover, some workers may be denied authorship of their workplace identities and the ability to mobilize identity as a workplace resource. Naturalisation is often an issue in regard to women's workplace performances of identity. In many service work organisations and occupations, it is assumed that because women are women they will perform the "emotional labour," which is seen to be a naturalised part of women's selves. It is this use of identity as a resource and also a commodity (gay male identity in particular is often plundered for its user-friendliness [8]) in the workplace that essentialises some, fixing them in place and making their visibility a value for capitalism.

Brown (2001) argues that American identity politics is about a renaturalizing of capitalism:

> Protests about exclusion are premised on a fiction of an inclusive/universalist community, a protest which installs the humanist ideal—it enables the continuation of classificatory regimes in which persons are reduced to observable social attributes and practices which are defined empirically and positivistically as if their existence were intrinsic and factual rather than the effects of discursive and institutional power. (p. 212)

This is exactly what has happened to the white working-class, who are blamed for their own positioning (economically, spatially, culturally, and morally). Identity politics, Brown argues, is locked into liberal discourse, which cannot imagine a future beyond the legitimacy of the state.

Conclusion

Identity reproduces the tradition of possessive individualism, positioning identity as a resource that can be owned and used for political claims-making within a politics of recognition. This fails to recognise that for many identity is a position that is forced, that has to be occupied, for which there is no alternative and which is attributed with no value and hence cannot be mobilised as a resource for enhancing privilege, or a resource to the nation, to belonging.

Identity makes difference rather than simply representing positions. It also reproduces the Western obsession with visibility as the major way of knowing. Nancy Fraser (1995), for instance, in her analysis of what she identifies as the major political shift of modern contemporary politics, completely takes *visibility for granted* (as Mariam Fraser [1999] has shown). In particular, Nancy Fraser does not address either the politics of visibility or the effects of visibility for cultural recognition, assuming that people simply "have" or "own" an identity. This is what Strathern (1992b) and Bourdieu (1992) identify as a particularly bourgeois perspective, in which the positions and experiences of the powerful generate performative "theory effects," in which their own experience is translated into universalising explanations.

Notwithstanding the lack of understanding of inscribed subjectification, forced identification, reliance on those who want to be and can use visibility, another problem with the belief that identity can be used as a politics, is what Brown identifies as the impulse by those who promote identity politics to inscribe in the law and other political registers historical and present pain (a wounded attachment) rather than to conjure an imagined future power to make change. This, she argues, reproduces Nietzsche's (1969) slave morality, which shows how identity is produced in reaction to power, insofar as identity rooted in this reaction achieves its moral superiority by reproaching power and action themselves as evil. Identity structured by this ethos, she argues, becomes deeply invested in its own impotence.

We can see the impotence of the powerful in recent work in the United States, where it is the middle-class who are particularly resourceful at putting the affects of identity (in this case, resentment) to work. McCarthy (2000) shows how the suburban middle-class in the United States is using the discourse of identity politics via resentment in an attempt to articulate its own moral authority (as illustrated in the films *Falling Down* or *American Beauty*). The politics of resentment is a mechanism for using identity as a resource to try to regain authority and to capture back the rhetorical moral high ground of oppression in order to make political claims for those who are in fear of losing their power and privilege.

In this sense, we can see not only how identity makes a difference but how it is used to create the sense of the coherent self, to overcome what Miller (1993) identifies as ethical incompleteness. He argues that in the attempt by the state to overcome the contradiction between capitalism's democratic politics, which requires selfless, community-minded citizens and capitalist economics, which depends on selfish utilitarian consumers, cultural forces are deployed to instill a sense of "ethical incompleteness" in which citizens are then offered the chance to become better, happier, and more fulfilled by using economic, cultural, and political opportunities that encourage political and economic loyalty. Berlant (2001), for instance, argues that the family and hope in heterosexuality are also offered by the state and capitalism to overcome this ethical incompleteness. It is in this gap—in the production of ethical incompleteness—that the foundational claim of identity, experienced and owned by some through the "wounded attachment," that ethical completeness is imagined. The logic of this is that competition is established as groups vie for a position within the nation, claiming their mobile injury in order to achieve their ethical completeness.

To do so, they have to prioritise the symbolic economy and make their visibility both known and valued. Yet, visibility and recognition are not the central issues. As stated earlier, it is the *value* that is given to the visibility that counts: it has to be a valued, authorised visibility. For as Phelan (1993) notes, probably the most visible group in the world is young, white, semi-naked women but they don't carry much power. The very powerful, as Bourdieu (1992) notes, often do not want to be recognised. The powerful only want their authority recognised, not themselves. It is the exchange systems and relationships that establish value that are significant for understanding the production of identity as inequality.

So I would argue that a more politically productive way to think about identity is to think about value and systems of exchange and inscription, where identity is used as a resource for some and a fixed pathology for others. We need to retain the significant political questions about interests: Who can have identity? How can they have it? In whose interests? How do those forced to identify, those misrecognised, and those only attributed negative value to their identity positions mobilise?

The statement "I am" always carries its history, traces, and recognition. It is only through relations with others that identity can be known. Therefore I would argue for a focus outward, towards an inspection of the relations and technologies, the forms of inscription that make identity visible and valued. What are the conditions of possibility that make identity possible? How is exchange established? What are the techniques that produce the knowledge of these relationships and how are they valued? This is not to return to the use of the other in the formation of identity but to examine what makes this type of relationship possible. What makes an identity possible and how do we know and value it as such?

Endnotes

1. Feminist theorists have drawn attention to the impossibility of women becoming persons of conscience (e.g., Pateman, C. 1988. *The sexual contract*. Cambridge: Polity), Goody (1983. *The development of family and*

marriage in Europe. Cambridge: Cambridge University Press) argues that the influence of Christianity did actually enable some women to be seen as worthy of personhood. He argues that because the Church needed converts and bequests, upperclass women who could be part of the property settlement of families, were treated as individuals endowed with reason, will, and independence.

2. Individualism shapes capitalism in that it provides a particular type of economic subject, namely the individual and individual property ownership. Yet capitalism also influences individualism by confirming its discursive dominance and emphasising the positive aspects of individualistic theory.

3. Just as standpoint was something the researcher used to take on behalf of others [Group, 1982 #219], which then became a means of asserting individual and self-authority (see Probyn, E. 1993. True voices and real people: The "problem" of the autobiographical in cultural studies. In V. Blundell, J. Shepherd, & I. Taylor (Eds.), *Relocating cultural studies.* London: Routledge; Skeggs, B. 1995b. Theorising, ethics and representation in feminist ethnography. In B. Skeggs (Ed.), *Feminist cultural theory: Production and process.* Manchester: Manchester University Press), the concept of reflexivity has been involved in similar moves, whereby authority shifts from one of taking a position in order to make a political claim for a structural grouping, to one of owning that position as an individual, as a form of subjectivity (Skeggs, B. 2002. Techniques for telling the reflexive self. In T. May (Ed.), *Qualitative research in action.* London: Sage).

4. As Bogard notes, this is very close to Foucault's position of who affirms the connection of discourse and the sign but denies the sign's assimilation to representation and the signifier. Discourses do more than signs to designate things. It is the practical deployment of forces on bodies, in ways that harness their energies, hierarchise them, and make them functional.

5. The testimonial also demands a witness. Ahmed and Stacey (2001. Testimonial cultures: An introduction. *Cultural Values,* 5(1), 1–6) argue that recent testimonial moves (such as the South African "Truth and Reconciliation Commission" and the Stolen Generation testimony in Australia), enable the position of the witness and the victim to become aligned because both are presented as the site from which justice can be delivered (see Probyn, E. 2000. Shaming theory, thinking disconnections: Feminism and reconciliation. In S. Ahmed, J. Kilby, C. Lury, M. McNeil, & B. Skeggs (Eds.), *Transformations: Thinking through feminism.* London: Routledge). But, they argue, if testimony is bound up with truth and justice, then its coming into being also registers the crisis in both of these concepts; for one testifies when the truth is in doubt. Therefore, "truth" can be seen to be subject to appeal, the result of political claims, the result of political struggle between competing groups.

6. This is further complicated in the United States where a black middle-class does exist and it cannot be assumed that representations of blackness have a close association to working-classness. The term "white trash" highlights the

racialisation of the difference. This is not at all similar to the development of blackness in the United Kingdom in which it has always been produced through close discursive association with class (see Gilroy, P. 1987. *There ain't no black in the Union Jack.* London: Hutchinson; Gilman, S. L. 1992. Black Bodies, White bodies: Towards an iconography of female sexuality in late nineteenth century art, medicine and literature. In A. Rattansi (Ed.), *"Race," culture and difference.* London: Sage; Hall, S., Critcher, C., Jefferson, T., Clarke, J., & Roberts, B. 1978. *Policing the crisis: Mugging, the state and law and order.* London: Hutchinson.

7. Bob Powers and Alan Ellis, *A manager's guide to sexual orientation in the workplace.* Routledge: New York and London, 1995.

8. Hennessey (2000) is particularly critical of gay male mobilization of consumption and visibility to achieve political claims.

References

Abercrombie, N., Hill, S., & Turner, B. (1986). *Sovereign individuals of capitalism.* London: Allen and Unwin.

Adkins, L. (2000). Mobile desire: Aesthetics, sexuality and the "lesbian" at work. *Sexualities*, 3(2), 201–218.

Adkins, L., & Lury, C. (1999, November). The labour of identity: Performing identities, performing economies. *Economy and Society*, 28(4), 598–614.

Ahmed, S., & Stacey, J. (2001). Testimonial cultures: An introduction. *Cultural Values*, 5(1), 1–6.

Austin, J. (1962). *How to do things with words.* Oxford: Clarendon.

Berlant, L. (2001). Trauma and ineloquence. *Cultural Values*, 5(1), 41–58.

Berlant, L., & Warner, M. (1998, Winter). Sex in public. *Critical Inquiry*, 24, 547–566.

Bogord, W. (1998). Sense and segmentarity: Some markers of a Delevzian-Guattarian sociology; *Sociological theory*, 16(1), 52–74.

Bonnett, A. (1998). How the British working class become white: The symbolic (re)formation of racialised capitalism. *Journal of Historical Sociology*, 11, 316–340.

Bourdieu, P. (1992). *Language and symbolic power.* Cambridge: Polity Press.

Bower, L. (1997). Queer problems/straight solutions: The limit of the politics of "Official Recognition." In S. Phelan (Ed.), *Playing with fire: Queer politics, queer theories* (pp. 267–291). New York: Routledge.

Brown, W. (1995). *States of injury.* Princeton: Princeton University Press.

Brown, W. (2001). *Politics out of history*. Princeton: Princeton University Press.

Cohen, E. A. (1995). *Self-ownership, freedom and equality*. Cambridge: University Press.

Cosslett, T., Lury, C., & Summerfield, P. (Eds.). (2000). *Feminism and autobiography: Texts, theories, methods*. London: Routledge.

Cronin, A. (2000). *Advertising and consumer citizenship: Gender, images and rights*. London: Routledge.

Deleuze, G., & Guattari, F. (1977). *Anti-Oedipus: Capitalism and schizophrenia*. New York: The Viking Press.

Diawara, M. (1998, Winter). Homeboy cosmopolitan: Manthia Diawara interviewed by Silvia Kolbowski, *October*, 83, 51–70.

Engels, F. (1844/1958). *The condition of the working-class in England*. St. Albans, Herts: Panther.

Evans, M. (1999). *Missing persons: The impossibility of autobiography*. London: Routledge.

Foucault, M. (1979). *The history of sexuality: Volume one, an introduction*. London: Penguin.

Fraser, N. (1995). From redistribution to recognition? Dilemmas of justice in "post-socialist" age. *New Left Review*, 212, 68–94.

Fraser, M. (1999). Classing queer: Politics in competition. *Theory, Culture & Society*, 16(2), 107–131.

Gilman, S. L. (1992). Black bodies, white bodies: Towards an iconography of female sexuality in late nineteenth century art, medicine and literature. In A. Rattansi (ed.), *"Race", culture and difference* (pp. 171–198). London: Sage.

Gilroy, P. (1987). *There ain't no black in the union Jack*. London: Hutchinson.

Goody, J. (1983). *The development of family and marriage in Europe*. Cambridge: Cambridge University Press.

Hage, G. (1998). *White nation*. Melbourne, Australia: Pluto Press.

Hall, S., Critcher, C., Jefferson, T., Clarke, J., & Roberts, B. (1978). *Policing the crisis: Mugging, the state and law and order*. London: Hutchinson.

Haraway, D. (1997). Modest_witness@second_millenium. *Femalean c_meets_ Onco_Mouse tm: Feminism and technoscience*. London: Routledge.

Haylett, C. (2000). 'This is about us, this is our film!' Personal and popular discourses of "underclass." In S. Munt (ed.), *Cultural studies and the working class: Subject to change*. London: Routledge.

Haylett, C. (2001). Illegitimate subjects? Abject whites, neoliberal modernisation and middle class multiculturalism. *Environment and Planning D: Society and Space*, 19, 351–370.

Hennessy, R. (2000). *Profit and pleasure: Sexual identities in late capitalism*. London: Routledge.

Honneth, A. (1995). *The struggle for recognition: The moral grammar of social struggles*. Cambridge: Polity.

Huff, T. E. (Ed.). (1981). *On the roads to modernity, conscience, science and civilisations: Selected writings by Benjamin Nelson*. Totowa, NJ: Rowman and Littlefield.

Hunter, I. (1992). Aesthetics and cultural studies. In L. Grossberg, C. Nelson & P. Treichler (Eds.), *Cultural studies* (pp. 347–367). London: Routledge.

Kopytoff, I. (1986). The cultural biography of things: Commoditization as process. In A. Appadurai (Ed.). *The social life of things: Commodities in cultural perspective* (pp. 64–65). Cambridge: Cambridge University Press.

Lingis, A. (1994). The society of dismembered body parts. In C. Boundas & D. Olkowski (Eds.), *Gilles Deleuze and the theatre of philosophy* (pp. 289–303). New York: Routledge.

Lury, C. (1998). *Prosthetic culture: Photography, memory and identity*. London: Routledge.

Macpherson, C. B. (1962). *The political theory of possessive individualism*. Oxford: Oxford University Press.

Marcus, L. (1994). *Auto/biographical discourses*. Manchester: Manchester University Press.

Maynard, M. (1998). Feminists' knowledge and the knowledge of feminisms: Epistemology, theory, methodology and method. In T. May & M. Williams (Eds.), *Knowing the social world* (pp. 120–138). Buckingham: Open University.

McCarthy, C. (2000). Reading the American popular: Suburban resentment and the representation of the inner city in contemporary film and TV. In D. Fleming (Ed.), *Formations: A 21st-century media studies textbook* (pp. 271–297). Manchester: Manchester University Press.

Miller, T. (1993). *The well-tempered self: Citizenship, culture and the postmodern self*. Baltimore, MD: John Hopkins University Press.

Nietzsche, F. (1969). *Geneology of morals*. New York: Vintage.

Pateman, C. (1988). *The sexual contract*. Cambridge: Polity.

Phelan, P. (1993). *Unmarked: The politics of performance*. London: Routledge.

Pietz, W. (1985). The problem of the fetish. I. *Res*, 9, 5–17.

Pietz, W. (1987). The problem of the fetish. II. *Res*, 13, 23–45.

Povinelli, E. (2000). The state of shame: Australian multiculturalism and the crisis of indigenous citizenship. In L. Berlant (Ed.), *Intimacy* (pp. 253–289). Chicago: University of Chicago Press.

Probyn, E. (1993). True voices and real people: The "problem" of the autobiographical in cultural studies. In V. Blundell, J. Shepherd, & I. Taylor (Eds.), *Relocating cultural studies*. London: Routledge.

Probyn, E. (2000). Shaming theory, thinking disconnections: Feminism and reconciliation. In S. Ahmed, J. Kilby, C. Lury, M. McNeil, & B. Skeggs (Eds.), *Transformations: Thinking through feminism* (pp. 48–61). London: Routledge.

Pulp Fiction (1994). Directed by Quentin Tarantino. Miramax Films.

Rouse, R. (1991). Mexican migration and the social space of postmodernism. *Diaspora*, 1(1), 13–27.

Said, E. (1991). The politics of knowledge. *Raritan*, 11(1), 21–24.

Shrek. (2001). Directed by A. Adamson & V. Jensen. DreamWorks.

Skeggs, B. (Ed.). (1995a). *Feminist cultural theory: Process and production.* Manchester: Manchester University Press.

Skeggs, B. (1995b). Theorising, ethics and representation in feminist ethnography. In B. Skeggs (Ed.), *Feminist cultural theory: Production and process* (pp. 190–207). Manchester: Manchester University Press.

Skeggs, B. (1997). *Formations of class and gender: Becoming respectable.* London: Sage.

Skeggs. B. (2002). Techniques for telling the reflexive self. In T. May (Ed.), *Qualitative research in action* (pp. 349–375). London: Sage.

Skeggs, B. (2004). *Class, self, culture.* London: Routledge.

Smith, A. (1776/1970). *The wealth of nations.* Harmondsworth: Penguin.

Stallybrass, R. (1998). Marx's coat. In. P. Spyer (Ed.), *Border fetishisms: Material objects in unstable places.* London: Routledge.

Steedman, C. (2000). Enforced narratives: Stories of another self. In P. Summerfield (Ed.), *Feminism and autobiography: Texts, theories, methods.* London: Routledge.

Strathern, M. (1992a). *After nature: English kinship in the late twentieth century.* Cambridge: Cambridge University Press.

Strathern, M. (1992b). Qualified value: The perspective of gift exchange. In S. Hugh-Jones (Ed.), *Barter, exchange and value: An anthropological approach.* Cambridge: Cambridge University Press.

Svensson, B. (1997). In D. E. Reed-Danahay (Ed.), *Auto/ethnography: Rewriting the social self.* Oxford: Berg.

Taguieff, P.-A. (Ed.). (1991). *Face au Racism.* Vol. One. Les Moyens D'Agir. Paris: Editions La Decouverte/Essais.

Taylor, C. (1994). The politics of recognition. In D. T. Goldberg (Ed.), *Multiculturalism: A critical reader.* Oxford: Blackwell.

3

MAKING CLASS THROUGH FRAGMENTING CULTURE

Beverley Skeggs

Goldsmiths, University of London, United Kingdom

Introduction

This chapter draws on debates from France, Australia, the United States, and the United Kingdom that work on issues of class, feminism and gender, sexuality, and race. It assumes a knowledge of Bourdieu's use of capitals—economic, social, symbolic, and cultural—as they accrue in bodies over periods of time in volumes and compositions in different social spaces (see Bourdieu, 1987, 1989; Skeggs, 1997). It is a condensed version of the arguments presented in *Class, Self, Culture* (Skeggs, 2004).

My central concern is how bodies, people, and groups attain value through different systems of symbolic exchange, which enable, and limit, how they can move through social space. Part of this process involves how inscription sets limits on the *evaluation* of particular bodies and practices, making them the site for what Foucault (1979) identifies as the "dense transference point for power." The emphasis in this chapter is on the transference, the process by which value is transported into bodies and the mechanisms by which it is retained, accumulated, lost, or appropriated. In order to understand these processes, we need to know the different forms of exchange from which value emerges.

As a challenge to the classical political economy of Adam Smith and Ricardo, Marx (1967) argued that we have to move away from paying attention to generalised exchange and focus our attention on production. Here I call for a reversal of this analysis, arguing that we need to focus on the different forms of exchange that make up the symbolic economy (of which the monetary system is just one element). Part of the reason for this is the changing economic processes that have led to the *de-materialisation* of commercial production and therefore the predominance of symbolic exchange in postindustrialisation (the shift from manufacturing to services). Waters (1995) identifies these as hypercommodification and the industrialization of culture. Both imply the production of more mobile and easily tradable products; hence, globalisation will increase the extent that world production is devoted to these nonmatter commodities (the de-materialisation he identifies) precisely because they are so mobile (p. 75). Culture can be converted into a highly mobile commodity and is used effectively in the sign/symbolic economy of transnational advertising (e.g., the use of racial signifiers to generate a "multicultural appeal" for the Bennetton Clothing Company (see Back, 1996; Back & Quaade, 1993; Franklin, Lury, & Stacey, 2000; Lury, 2000).

The exchange-value of different forms of culture illuminates different transference points of power and differential values, showing how value is attributed and flows from subject to object, object to subject. But it is also, importantly, about how experience, dispositions, and affect become central to the evaluation process; how value is produced from the attachment and detachment of experience, dispositions, and affect in the resourcing of the self, and then how this is read back onto bodies so that people know what they are worth (morally, socially, and economically). This process is significant in terms of what makes the culture of some groups propertisable for others and makes us ask who is entitled to and can use the culture of others.

Yudice (2004), in his analysis of the expediency of culture in which culture becomes a resource to be managed, breaking down divisions between high and low, argues that culture has become something to be invested in, distributed in the most inclusive ways, used as an attraction for capital development and tourism, as the prime motor of the culture industries, as an inexhaustible kindling for new industries dependent upon intellectual property, and as a means of solving a range of social issues, from racism to the maintenance of community. Arguing that this neoliberal view of culture opens up possibilities for challenge, we also need to think about what the use of culture as a resource closes down. If culture is relativised as a commodity, an analysis of the systems of exchange in which value can be realised becomes essential. It is in this analysis (made here) that the dynamics of current class relations become not only apparent *but* absolutely central to the workings of exchange and new types of property and exploitation.

The unrelenting capitalist desire for new markets is now a different search than that produced through imperialism. Instead, the logic of late capitalism, which, as Deleuze and Guattari (1983) suggest was Marx's great innovation, understands capital as something, which, unlike all previous social systems, is founded on a continual overcoming of its limitations, contradictions, or "lines of flight," that which escapes its regimes. With the emergence of control, capital increasingly comes to operate directly *on* its lines of flight. That is, it seeks less to maintain fixed moulds, which are not always so quick to capture that which escapes, but operates through increasingly flexible and varying modulations of social activity (see Thoburn, 2001). There is, therefore, little beyond capital's commodification. The logic of late capitalism is also what Zizek (1997) shows to be perfectly attuned to the identity politics of multiculturalism, which offers capitalism new possibilities on a global scale. The move towards the immaterialisation of labour and culture signals both a shift from objects to affects but also from distanced others to proximate strangers (Bhabha, 1996). It is a way of capital capturing that can be commodified.

The search for new markets and new experiences exists within and beyond national frames. The contradictions between the capitalist desire for global markets, and the ways in which people are able to have personhood within the nation, exist simultaneously and often mark fracture lines in capital–state relations (e.g., the neoliberal contradictions in which, for example, capital searches for new markets whilst retaining punitive legislation such as Section 28 in the United Kingdom). But this also marks different ways in which political claims can be made and who can make them (e.g., through the territorialisation of commercial space—a symbolic economy, or through citizenship and discourses of rights and responsibilities). So whilst we have the demands of global capitalism looking to open out new markets via representations and the transference of affect, we also have state-defined sovereignty—often explicated through political rhetoric—which is still significant for deciding who can belong and what it means to belong to a particular nation. I want to explore how both these frames, markets, and national belonging set limits on who can be seen to exist with value.

For example, Hage (1998) provides an excellent analysis of what it means to be Australian. He analyses which groups and bodies (for capitals are embodied, see Bourdieu, 1986, 1987) can acquire the "right" type and amount of cultural capital seen as having worth, or more importantly, seen as not pathological and problematic to the safety and security of nation formation. To understand how certain bodies can or cannot belong, he argues, we need to identify the processes by which certain representations become attributed with moral value, thus being defined as good/bad (having worth/being worthless), so that boundaries can be drawn and value attributed. These representations of moral value are the mechanisms by which social positioning is *known*. We know who we are and how much value our culture and practices enable us to accrue through discourse, representations, and the dialogical interaction generated via these representations.

To understand this process fully, we need also to understand the changing formations of the middle-class self, variously identified as aesthetic, prosthetic, mobile, reflexive, individualised, omnivorous, or possessed (but that is another chapter; see Skeggs, 2005).

This chapter is organised by exemplars providing some examples of how the symbolic formations of class relations are presently constituted and showing how historical legacies become recombined and refigured through the present, in which the attribution of moral worthlessness (that has a very long history in the representation of the working class) is being reworked in new ways. That is, representations are constitutive, not just reproductive (Coward & Ellis, 1977) producing new forms of value, potential for exchange, and national belonging. This chapter is concerned with understanding how value is attributed to bodies and how good and bad subjects are framed through value-attribution.

Rhetoric and Representations

This is a massive area but some of the ways in which moral value is attached to and identified with the working-class, as I show in *Class, Self, Culture* (Skeggs, 2004), include excess, waste, entertainment, authenticating, lacking in taste, unmodern, backward, escapist, dangerous, unruly, and without shame,[1] and always spatialised. These moral attributions are attached to bodies in different compositions and volumes. Moreover, evaluation and positioning are completely apparent to those whose bodies are meant to carry the value. That is, the working-class know how they are being evaluated and read as previous research demonstrates (Charlesworth, 2000; Reay & Lucey, 2000; Skeggs, 1997). I'm now going to outline some of the processes. The first example shows how class is being increasingly defined as a moral-cultural property of the person, related to his or her attitudes and practices (not named and known directly as class). The second illustrates how class becomes a defining feature of the nation that is fixed to particular groups of people and specific bodies in a way that makes them constitutive outsiders. The third exemplar analyses how these social positions of class are intimately entwined with gender but also represent a fixed space. The fourth example details how this positioning is "euphemistically transferred" (Bromley, 2000) or spoken through debates on taste. The final example shows how race and class entwine and become a resource deployed by entitled others. My interest is in how that which is a valuable cultural practice for some groups becomes devalued when attached to others. I'm interested in how culture can be propertisable and here I refer to all the legal debates over property and propriety (see Davies, 1994; Moran, Skeggs, & Corteen, 2004). Each performs a different way of attributing, extracting, or denying value.

Exemplar One

On the February 9, 1997, the *Daily Mirror*, a national tabloid newspaper with a readership of 2.5 million, conducted a survey asking readers to classify themselves by completing a questionnaire that included 20 questions about cultural practice, with only three questions on economic issues (owning/renting a house, employed/unemployed, and pension plan). The cultural questions were about cultural activities and attitudes such as "I own a large dog!", "I have sex too much," "I regularly eat out in restaurants," and "I go to Tuscany for my holidays" (agree or disagree to be ticked). High-value scores were given to the most middle-class pursuits (holidaying in Tuscany—a venue associated with the British prime minister). The value attached to each practice was clearly based on *morality*: big dogs and excess sex produced the lowest value. Practices also relied on *the right knowledge* (knowing *how* to go to Tuscany, *how* to appreciate the theatre, and *how* to eat out correctly[2]). Morality and the right knowledge were also dependent upon economic resources; affording to holiday in Tuscany, theatre visits, and eating in restaurants depend on having disposable income. In this exemplar, the attribution of value (produced through morality, knowledge, and economy combined—or cultural, social, symbolic, and economic capital) to social positioning is made abundantly clear.

Exemplar Two

The next example also shows how value is *not* attributed to certain bodies and how this is spatialised: some bodies fixed in place whilst others are mobile. Gender here makes a class difference. Again drawing from popular culture, this time Hollywood films, Tasker (1998) shows how women's excessive attention to their appearance is used to denote low moral value and to condense and place lack of value onto certain bodies. This attribution of appearance = conduct has a long history, particularly in distinguishing between the redeemable and unredeemable of Victorian women (Nead, 1988), also having a long history in more general United States popular culture whereby "big hair" or "big bodies" connotes white trash (Ortner, 1991; Rowe, 1995). These are speedy signifiers. Tasker charts a range of transformation narratives in which the visually excessive white working-class woman is turned into the subtle and discreet middle-class woman, usually helped into the "right knowledge" by a powerful man (e.g., *Working Girl, Pretty Woman, Up Close and Personal*). In the British version (*Pygmalion/My Fair Lady*), attention is given to language as well as appearance. In the transformation, the audience learns of the change through the gradual loss of excessive style.

Tasker argues that the attraction of these films is the tension and pleasure generated by the risk of the women being exposed, caught out and discovered, and then ultimate redemption and escape. This encodes class not only as something that has to be left behind, that which is fixed in order for mobility to proceed, but also as that which has no value. These films also offer middle-class taste and positioning as the mechanism by which being working-class can be overcome and eradicated, but also as something worth having, to which to aspire, reproducing Bourdieu's (1986) definition of cultural capital as high capital. Class here becomes a matter of "getting it right" by learning middle-class cultural practices and knowledge in order to be able to transcend working-class signifiers. The process at work is the signification of appearance (a cultural practice, and here a very specific version of working-class femininity) as the shortcut to immoral worthlessness, as something that has to be eradicated in order for morality (and hence, value) to be established. Again, it is the combination of knowing *how, having the resources* and *escaping* class that enables worth to be known. This is a very particular way of establishing taste. Also, as Bourdieu (1986) has shown, women's bodies are often used as the carriers of taste cultures. By highlighting movement (or escape) from working-classness, a particular form of fixity is attached to certain cultural practices: those that need to be moved on from for social mobility to proceed. So, in this sense, the technique of value attribution is produced through the narrative structure, which positions working-classness as that which must be overcome.

In a reversal of this process, the Hollywood film, *Legally Blonde*, sets up this transformation narrative (from west coast excess to east coast tastefulness), but then offsets the transformation by giving credit to the power of feminine knowledge about appearance—it is the technology of perming hair—that leads to the challenge to the superiority of middle-class knowledge and disposition.

Exemplar Three

However, the wider discourse of tastelessness continually works to attribute immorality and lack of knowledge to the working-class in general. A good example can be seen in the promotion of and resistance to satellite dishes (see Brunsdon, 1997 for an extensive account). In the United Kingdom, a whole traunch of "alternative" comedy was devoted to making the association "tasteless = use of satellite dishes = working-class." Even recently, the same sentiments are being expressed by middle-class cultural intermediaries. In a supposed architectural review of the Lovell Telescope at Jodrell Bank (a 1,500-ton, 76.2-meter bowl, which looks like an enormous satellite dish) in the local Manchester listings magazine, *City Life*, Phil Griffin, notes: "It is particularly touching that so many people in Wythenshawe appreciate it so much, they display little scale models of it on the outside of their houses" (1999, p. 6).

The spatialisation of class present in the New Labour rhetoric of problem council estates is signified through reference to Wythenshawe (the largest council estate in Europe, in Manchester, North West United Kingdom). In this statement, Griffin manages to insult and insinuate that people from Wythenshawe clearly have no taste. He thus attributes taste to himself because he is the clever knowing one who can draw ironic distance and make distinctions. It is a subtle move but is one of the ways in which class is frequently played out. Here, lack of knowledge, the subtle association of immorality with watching trash TV (cultural practices and the spatialisation of class), is condensed onto one signifier, the satellite dish.

This is a general example of how taste can be attributed to some practices by those with access to the symbolic distribution and circulation circuits to establish value. Lack of knowledge of how to use and place artifacts appropriately is the central clue in the film, *The Talented Mr. Ripley*. It is the superior taste of the detective (a narrative device that is regularly repeated in the BBC TV programme, *Inspector Morse*) that enables the villains to be caught.

Whilst all the above examples from popular culture fix class with lack of moral value in particular ways, this example fixes it even more firmly, through association with space and cultural practice.

I now want to shift attention from that which is valued as morally worthless, generated through the wrong cultural practices, which cannot be turned into symbolic value, to how other aspects of working-class culture are continually reproduced as a resource for others to use.

Exemplar Four

This example, again drawn from contemporary popular culture, but with a long history (Diawara, 1998), shows how black (working-class) masculinity is a resource—a mobile cultural style that can be used by different characters in film, be they black or white (see also chapter 2 in this book). He shows how, in a tradition taken from Baxploitation films, black maleness, coded as cool, can be "transported through white bodies" (p. 52). Black characters become fixed into playing "blackness" (Eddie Murphy is probably the most obvious example, even as the donkey in *Shrek!*, and Samuel Jackson in everything he plays), whilst white characters who need to achieve "cool" can move between black and white. Race thereby becomes a resource: fixed and read onto some bodies as a limitation, culturally essentialised, whilst it appears as mobile and transtextual on others (e.g., John Travolta in *Pulp Fiction*). That is, the fixed black character appears to be not acting; they just *are* culturally essentialised and made authentic. This is the most obvious use of rebranding, whereby particular forms of whiteness become rebranded through dispositions initially associated with blackness.

However, this has a long and difficult history and it could be argued that the "blues," as a form of music appropriated by white musicians, was the site where "cool" as an attribute was formed. "Cool" sticks to black bodies in a way that it does not to white bodies is about the repetition of association between dispositions and bodies over a long period of time, in which it is not just about the power of those who can influence the dominant cultural symbolic economy, but also about those who have shaped the symbolic through oppositional struggle. So, Black Power becomes an important intervention in contesting black representation, which tries to fix and essentialise. Using race, class, or femininity as a resource exists for those who are NOT positioned by it, but this is open to contestation by those from whom the resource has been extracted.

This use of "ethnicity," however, has a more ambivalent function. The ambivalence of the discursive associations of glamour with danger and criminality with different categories of race and ethnicity is made apparent in the *Sopranos* (Series One, Video 4). In an argument with a black gangster (who is represented with every heavy sticking signifier possible), Tony Soprano claims ethnic authenticity "We were the first niggers in this country." Yet later, after a game of golf with his white middle-class neighbors, he states: "I never really understood what it was to be used for somebody else's amusement until I played golf with these guys." Here, dispositions are not taken off one body to be re-evaluated when attached to another. Rather, the whole body and culture are used as sources of not just authentic entertainment but also reflexivity.

Whilst this appears to be similar to the traditional colonial use of bodies, for labour, for entertainment, or for artifact, I'd argue that it is in fact different because the experience of product use (i.e., the fun associated in playing with other people's culture, of being a tourist who collects the attributes of others) is now read back onto the marketing of the product itself. So, danger as an emotion is read back into the experience of the appropriation of young white working-class men, and cool is similarly read back into the bodies of black working-class men. Rap music, for instance, embodies both of these affects and not surprisingly is used to open up new markets;

its biggest market is young white men between the ages of 13–19. Yet, those who live the lifestyle from which the affective dispositions are generated and appropriated, are increasingly criminalised, contained, and live in poverty (Skeggs, 1994). These readings back of experience-use fixes and locks certain attributes onto some bodies whilst others can deploy them as a mobile resource and even make careers out of them, consolidating cultural capital through the ability to *convert* the cultural capital of others and by aligning it with different forms and compositions of cultural and symbolic capital. The culture of others becomes a propertisable resource for those with power to use it in their own self-making, but not for those who generate the culture in the first place.

Payback

However, this is not a straightforward process and a significant class struggle is waged. In the *Sopranos* example, the white middle-class men display their own stupidity and naivety by their desire to discuss "the mob," and in the U.K., imitation cockneys are labeled "mockneys" as a term of derision, whereby Mr. Madonna (Guy Ritchie and others of similar upper middle-class positioning) becomes a laughing stock through attempts to be, try on, and play with the dispositions of working-class black and white others. *The Royale Family* and other Caroline Aherne TV products are devoted to swinging attacks on the pretentiousness and use of working-class culture. There is, as Vicinus (1974) demonstrates, a long and substantial history to laughing at the middle-class. In addition, the ambivalence of the middle-classes to identify as middle-class (as shown in the research by Savage, 2000; Sayer, 2002; Savage, Bagnall, & Longhurst, 1999, 2001; Savage, Barlow, Dickens, & Feilding, 1992) may be a result of this cultural struggle. For instance, the immortal lyrics by Pulp for the track "Common People" in which the use of the working-class as a *resource* for the entertainment of others, is ridiculed and despised:

> I want to live like common people, I want to do whatever common people do, I want to sleep with common people like you ...
>   and the riposte:

> You'll never live like common people, you'll never do what common people do, you'll never fail like common people, you'll never watch your life slide out of view, and dance and drink and screw 'cos there's nothing else to do. (Pulp, written by Cocker/Senior/Mackay/Banks/Doyle, "Common People," 1995, Island Records)

Here, the impossibility of being and becoming working-class is made explicit, as is the despisement and resentment of those who know they are being used. However, the ability to fight this symbolic struggle is constrained by access to circuits of distribution and circulation.

When the middle-class use working-class culture as a resource, a relationship of *entitlement* is established, which also includes possibilities for resistance; for it is not just high cultural capital that relies on the right knowledge. There are aspects to working-class culture that also need the "right" accumulated knowledge: the right to "know how."

Yet, I would argue it is how the middle-class resources itself that is crucial to contemporary class relations. When "new" debates in social theory reference new forms of subjectivity (e.g., Berlant, 2000; Hardt & Negri, 2000; Rouse, 1995), they are referencing forms of middle-class entitlement (Skeggs, 2004) by those who want new experiences without incurring any loss or danger to the social positions that they already inhabit (see Brooks, 2001).

To summarise, in these different processes of representation and discourse, class is broken down into cultural elements, dispositions, and affects (all generated through historical repetition), some of which are convertible and propertisable and others of which have to be firmly fixed as that from which escape is needed. This process of fragmentation and appropriation is racial and gendered. In this sense, class is a cultural resource, as a form of property for some but an abject social positioning for others. When Yudice (2004) talks of class becoming *the* neoliberal resource, he is specifically referring (if inadvertently) to particular class formation and reproduction. The white working-class in the United Kingdom is divided into pure white/dirty white racialised positions and respectable/abject moral positions. Yet, whilst attempts are made to fix the negative side of these positions and attributions of value by political discourse, the user-friendly, appropriable aspects are made propertisable in popular culture, with middle-class cultural intermediaries carving their (exchange-value self) careers out of them. The progressions and mobility of some relies on the fixing of others. Working-class culture is also represented as a fault in the nation, something that represents backwardness, a failure to modernise, and a blockage to the inevitability of global transnational futures.

Conclusion

I contend that the majority of ways we have of understanding class are no longer adequate if we take into account the constitutive nature of the symbolic economy. When the immateriality of affect is unhinged from the source of its production and becomes a valued global commodity, we need ways to understand what this means for class struggle. Many of our current understandings are not adequate. The two major ways of understanding class were firstly, Marxist, where emphasis was placed on the labour theory of value (that is the extraction of surplus value from the labour power of the exploited working-class), firmly located in the economic, especially the forces of production and the division of labour. Secondly, the emphasis was placed on occupational stratification, where in the tradition of quantification and "political arithmetic," counting groups was considered necessary in order to assess their potential for taxation, representation, governance, etc. What both of these approaches have in common, however, is the centrality of production and economy. This is without noticing the history of both of these forms of analysis, which rely on the historical culture of which they were a product. They are *en-cultured* forms of analysis. The word "economy" began as a very specific term to describe the management of a household, then shifted to the management of national resources, and then became a "neutral" system discursively contained, with its own rules and laws alongside the promotion of a "discipline" of the economic, as Fine (2001) and Fine and Lapavistas (2000) show. Moreover, recent attacks on the "cultural turn" have missed the point. The history of focusing on culture is as a material force, as matter, as value (Gramsci, 1971), not just as discourse.

To turn attention to culture does not mean to say that capitalism is not an important framing factor. The search for new markets and the ability of capitalism to marketise its own contradictions has enabled the opening of new markets for which new resources and new consumers need to be produced. It is in this opening out that that which was once abject, legitimated through biology and science, is now being accessed and re-legitimated in order to produce the new and exciting. Moral boundaries are being redrawn whereby that which was once projected onto an "other" is now being drawn back into the mainstream. Yet, this is not a wholesale incorporation of bodies that were once positioned at a distance. Rather, it is aspects of prior immoral abject cultural dispositions that are being brought back to open new markets. The expanse of sexuality and violence as mechanisms for selling goods is one obvious example. Another example is how the display of sexuality, pathologised when attached to working-class women's bodies, is being reworked in novel ways as *Sex and the City* shows most explicitly. Sex is recoded as glamorous when attached to those with enough volume of other forms of cultural capital to offset connotations of pathology and degradation. The safe and secure boundaries that were seen to be necessary for the formation of the new bourgeoisie are now not being drawn so closely. Although they are being maintained spatially, Davis (1990) has shown that defensible space is now a positional good that maintains class distinction. So all that was sexual, dangerous, immoral, and criminal and projected onto the black and white working-classes is now being slowly drawn back in. The contradictions of neoliberalism are being partly assuaged. However, this is a piecemeal operation and it is the detachment of certain bits from the backward bits that creates the remoralising and remaking of class relations. Class struggle becomes not just about the entitlement to the labour of others, but also the entitlement to their culture, feelings, affect, and dispositions. This is a very intimate form of exploitation.

We need to be able to reinvigorate class analysis to deal with the contemporary shifts in neoliberal governance and transnational flexible capitalism. We need to analyse what is beyond the economic in the making of property relations through the consequences of cultural struggle and how this is part of new marketisation and new attributions of value and new forms of appropriation and exploitation, in fact, a neoliberal "ethical turn." We need to be able to understand how certain bodies and practices are evaluated and re-evaluated and how this is part of a moral symbolic economy.

We also require a model that sees class struggle (partially) fought out through entitlement to the cultures, dispositions, and affects of others, whereby working-class culture becomes essentialised and fixed, but plundered for elements for others to use and authorise themselves through the symbolic economy. This means more attention needs to be paid to the symbolic economy in the reproduction of class and on the new relationships formed in the making of new markets. It is about new connections that are different from the old colonial ones, whereby it was artifacts or bodies rather than pieces of affect or dispositions that were used to display middle-class distance. Bhabha (1996) argues that we are now experiencing politics based on proximity rather than difference and, if this is the case, it is how dispositions can sustain and signal different values when attached to different bodies. We need to know how this process of evaluation occurs and how it is contextualised by the whole composition and volume of the capitals at stake.

How the middle-class is being reconstituted is central to this new understanding. The working-class does not just figure as a culture to be plundered for opening of new markets. Rather, the progression and progressiveness of the new middle-class self is predicated on holding in place—fixing—that which must signify stagnation and immobility: The working-class is fragmented as a resource that functions in a variety of ways to sustain the modernity of factions of the middle-class. Only those not read as fixed can establish entitlement (it is a one-way relationship) to those fixed by that positioning (but this crosscuts race, class, gender, and sexuality). We also need to be aware of the different ways the middle-class uses working-class culture and experience: to accumulate (as in the Bourdieu and cultural omnivore model) or to play (as in the Baudrillard, 1983 and Lury, 1998 model).

We thus need to be cognisant of the fragility and vulnerability of the middle-class self, which has to be continually asserted to enable it to operate as a form of powerful difference, a self that struggles to be taken seriously and to be seen as worthy of moral authority. Entitlements have to be institutionalised, perspectives authorised, and property legitimated; these can be challenged.

We therefore require an analysis that can understand processes across a range of sites such as popular culture, political rhetoric, academic theory, economic discourse, and analysis that shows how the rhetoric of social inclusion actually excludes. We need a way of understanding how, what, and why bodies accumulate culture and how this can or cannot be used as a resource (for wealth, for the nation). The class struggle is being waged at an intimate level, on a national scale, on a daily basis through culture as a form of symbolic violence, through relationships of entitlement that are legitimised and institutionalised, and it is these processes that set limits on who can and cannot belong, be, and have worth on a national and global stage. These experiences are painfully felt by those from whom they are extracted. The hidden injuries of class, identified by Sennett (1977), are still well and truly intact, but now they may also be converted into a cultural resource for use by others.

Endnotes

1. Perfectly encapsulated in the television series *Shameless.*

2. As Erickson (1991, 1996) has shown, eating out is a prerequisite for the display of middle-class cultural omnivorousness and essential to the maintenance of social networks in business practice.

References

Back, L. (1996). *New ethnicities and urban culture: Racism and multi-culture in young lives.* London: UCL Press.

Back, L., & Quaade, V. (1993). Dream utopias, nightmare realities: Imagining race and culture within the world of Bennetton advertising. *Third Text, 22,* 65–80.

Baudrillard, J. (1983). *Simulations.* New York: Semiotext(e).

Berlant, L. (2000). The subject of true feeling: Pain, privacy, politics. In S. Ahmed, J. Kilby, C. Lury, M. McNeil, & B. Skeggs (Eds.), *Transformations: Thinking through feminism* (pp. 33–48). London: Routledge.

Bhabha, H. (1996). Rethinking authority: Interview with Homi Bhabha. *Angelaki*, 2(2), 59–65.

Bourdieu, P. (1986). *Distinction: A social critique of the judgement of taste*. London: Routledge.

Bourdieu, P. (1987). What makes a social class? On the theoretical and practical existence of groups. *Berkeley Journal of Sociology*, 1–17.

Bourdieu, P. (1989). Social space and symbolic power. *Sociological Theory*, 7, 14–25.

Bromley, R. (2000). The theme that dare not speak its name: Class and recent British film. In S. Munt (Ed.), *Cultural studies and the working class: Subject to change* (pp. 51–69). London: Cassells.

Brooks, D. (2001). *Bobos in paradise: The new upper class and how they got there*. New York: Shuster and Simon.

Brunsdon, C. (1997). *Screen tastes: Soap opera to satellite dishes*. London: Routledge.

Charlesworth, S. (2000). *A phenomenology of working class experience*. Cambridge: Cambridge University Press.

Coward, R., & Ellis, J. (1977). *Language and materialism*. London: RKP.

Daily Mirror (1997). What class are you? February 9, p. 7.

Davies, M. (1994). Feminist appropriations: Law property and personality. *Social and Legal Studies*, 3, 365–391.

Davis, M. (1990). *City of quartz*. London: Verso.

Deleuze, G., & Guattari, F. (1983). *Anti-Oedipus: Capitalism and schizophrenia* (Vol. 1). New York: The Viking Press.

Diawara, M. (1998, Winter). Homeboy cosmopolitan: Manthia Diawara interviewed by Silvia Kolbowski. *October*, 83, 51–70.

Erickson, B. (1991). What is good taste for? *Canadian Review of Sociology and Anthropology*, 28, 255–278.

Erickson, B. (1996). Culture, class and connections. *American Journal of Sociology*, 102, 217–251.

Fine, B. (2001). *Social capital versus social theory: Political economy and social science at the turn of the millenium*. London: Routledge.

Fine, B., & Lapavistas, C. (2000). Markets and money in social theory: What role for economics? *Economy and Society*, 29(3), 357–382.

Foucault, M. (1979). *The history of sexuality: Volume one, an introduction*. London: Penguin.

Franklin, S., Lury, C., & Stacey, J. (2000). *Global nature, global culture*. London: Sage.

Gramsci, A. (1971). *Selections from prison notebooks of Antonio Gramsci*. London: Lawrence and Wishart.

Griffin, P. (1999). Satellites. *City Life*. p. 6.

Hage, G. (1998). *White nation*. Melbourne and London: Pluto Press.

Hardt, M., & Negri, A. (2000). *Empire*. Cambridge, MA: Harvard University Press.

Inspector Morse. (1987–2000). Produced by McBain. ITV.

Legally Blonde 1. (2001). Directed by R. Luketic. MGM.

Lury, C. (1998). *Prosthetic culture: Photography, memory and identity*. London: Routledge.

Lury, C. (2000). The united colours of diversity: Essential and inessential culture. In S. Franklin, C. Lury, & J. Stacey (Eds.), *Global nature, global culture*. London: Sage.

Marx, K. (1967). *Capital* (S. Moore & E. Aveling, Trans. Vol. 1). New York: International Publishers.

Moran, L., Skeggs, B., Corteen. K., & Tyrer, P. (2004). *Sexuality and the politics of violence and safety*. London: Routledge.

My Fair Lady Musical. (1956–2007). Lyrics by A. J. Lerner.

Nead, L. (1988). *Myths of sexuality: Representations of women in Victorian Britain*. Oxford: Blackwell.

Ortner, S. (1991). Reading America: Preliminary notes on class and culture. In G. R. Fox (Ed.), *Recapturing anthropology: Working in the present* (pp. 163–191). Santa Fe, NM: School of American Research Press.

Pretty Woman. (1990). Directed by G. Marshall. Touchstone Pictures.

Pulp Fiction. (1994). Directed by Q. Tarantino. Miramax Films.

Pygmalion. (1938). Directed by A. Asquith & L. Howard. Gabriel Pascal Productions.

Reay, D., & Lucey, H. (2000). I don't really like it here but I don't want to live anywhere else: Life on large estates. *Antipode*, 32(4), 4410–4428.

Ricardo, D. (1817). *Principles of a political economy and taxation*. London, Macmillan.

Rouse, R. (1995). Thinking through transnationalism: Notes on the cultural politics of class relations in the contemporary United States. *Public Culture*, 7(2), 353–402.

Rowe, K. (1995). *The unruly woman: Gender and the genres of laughter*. Austin: University of Texas Press.

Savage, M. (2000). *Class analysis and social transformation*. Buckingham: Open University Press.

Savage, M., Bagnall, G., & Longhurst, B. (1999). *The ambiguity of class identities in contemporary Britain.* Paper presented at the British Sociological Association Conference, Edinburgh.

Savage, M., Bagnall, G., & Longhurst, R. (2001). Ordinary, ambivalent and defensive: Class identities in the northwest of England. *Sociology,* 35(4), 875–892.

Savage, M., Barlow, J., Dickens, P., & Feilding, T. (1992). *Property, bureaucracy and culture: Middle-class formation in contemporary Britain.* London: Routledge.

Sayer, A. (2002). What are you worth? Why class is an embarrassing subject. *Sociological Research Online,* 7(3).

Sennett, R., & Cobb, J. (1977). *The hidden injuries of class.* Cambridge: Cambridge University Press.

Sex in the City. (1999–). Produced by J. Rabb, A. Ellis, J. Rottenberg & E. Zuritsky. HBO.

Shrek. (2001). Directed by A. Adamson & V. Jenson. DreamWorks.

Skeggs, B. (1994). Refusing to be civilized: "Race," sexuality and power. In H. Afshar & M. Maynard (Eds.), *The dynamics of race and gender* (pp. 106–127). London: Taylor & Francis.

Skeggs, B. (1997). *Formations of class and gender: Becoming respectable.* London: Sage.

Skeggs, B. (2004). *Class, self, culture.* London: Routledge.

Skeggs, B. (2005). Exchange value and affect: Bourdieu and the self. In L. Adkins & B. Skeggs (Eds.), *Bourdieu, feminism and after* (pp. 75–97). Oxford: Blackwell.

Smith, A. (1776). *Wealth of nations.* Harmondsworth: Penguin.

Tasker, Y. (1998). *Working girls: Gender and sexuality in popular culture.* London: Routledge.

The Sopranos. (1999–2007). Written and directed by D. Chase. HBO.

The Talented Mr. Ripley. (1999). Directed by A. Minghella. Paramount Pictures.

Thoburn, N. (2001). Autonomous production? On Negri's "New Synthesis." *Theory, Culture and Society,* 18(5), 75–96.

UpClose and Personal. (1996). Directed by J. Avnet. Touchstone Pictures.

Vicinus, M. (1974). *The industrial muse: A study of nineteenth century British working class literature.* London: Croom Helm.

Waters, M. (1995). *Globalisation.* London: Routledge.

Working Girl. (1988). Directed by M. Nichols. Twentieth-Century Fox.

Yudice, G. (2004). *The expediency of culture.* Durham, NC: Duke University Press.

Zizek, S. (1997). Multiculturalism, or the cultural logic of multinational capitalism. *New Left Review,* 225, 28–52.

4

TOWARDS A DISHARMONIOUS PLURALISM: DISCOURSE ANALYSIS OF OFFICIAL DISCOURSES ON SOCIAL DIVERSITY

Lena Martinsson
University of Gothenburg, Sweden

Eva Reimers
University of Linköping, Sweden

Introduction

This chapter focuses on the discourse about social diversity, a discourse in which pluralism and heterogeneity primarily are regarded—or at least that is the rhetoric—as assets that will lead to not only a more creative society, but also to economic growth. We argue that it makes a difference whether the inclusion of hitherto excluded categories is motivated by human rights, charity, or by economic reasons. Heterogeneity and pluralism are made meaningful through different discourses such as identity politics, politics of recognition, equality politics, and politics of difference (Taylor, 1994; Young, 1990). By analysing three Swedish official documents, we want to show that this discourse is not as innocent as it first might appear. First, it is based on a presupposition that individuals and social groups can be expected to possess specific qualities based on, for example, gender, ethnicity, or sexual orientation. A common expression in the discourse about diversity is that individuals should be granted the right to "be who they are," a statement based on a presumption of stable and essential identities. Furthermore, the discourse repeats an idea of consensus and unity. It hereby discloses inequality and executes power in the way it designates both content and hierarchy of different subject positions. Second, it is a discourse that is articulated in and together with an economic discourse. The value of economic growth is taken for granted and employed as a foundation for the whole discourse. It thereby strengthens the hegemony of capitalism and its numerous relations of subordination. In the article, we stress the importance of deconstructing the processes in which differences are produced in various contexts, how different subjects are made into stable positions—instead of positions under continuous construction, and positions that are experienced through different interpretative frameworks (Laclau & Mouffe, 1985).

In order to make way for alternative politics of difference, we believe in the necessity of deconstructing the notion of stable identities, the close links between different discourses, and the prevailing hegemony of capitalism. In order to subvert relations of power that subordinate people according to how they are categorised, new hegemonies need to be created. In this endeavour, it is necessary to engage in a never-ending confrontation, and questioning of boundaries, traits, and positions of different categories—a process that we have labelled a disharmonious pluralism. The way to achieve this is what we have called a deconstructive and self-reflective solidarity. It is a position that takes into account that identities and categories are social, relational, and contingent, and that each and every social category is made meaningful in relation to other categories. In order to subvert the domination, a deconstructive and self-reflective solidarity constantly questions how the position of the subject becomes constitutive for the subordination of other subject positions.

The Swedish Discourse on Diversity

Diversity is high on the official agenda in many countries (cf. Cox, 1993). The term appears in various contexts, from debates on how to increase profit and growth by diversity management, measures on how to counteract discrimination and intolerance, to proposals for migration quotas and increased border control. We employ the Swedish official and public discourse about diversity as a point of departure for a more general discussion about the almost omnipresent norm about the benefits of social diversity.

In Sweden, the management of diversity is enforced by a recommendation that every workplace with more than 10 employees should have plans for both gender equality and social diversity. This need to plan for social diversity in different sections of society, and the term "diversity manage-ment," frequent in business and enterprise contexts, indicate that diversity needs to be managed. The diversity discourse, regardless if it is expressed as a disturbing diversity that induces discrimination, or a positive diversity inducing creativity and growth, can thereby be seen as a response to a dis-course that constructs diversity as a problem. The dialogical character of all discourses (Bakhtin, 1981) suggests that unless there already existed a discourse that presented social diversity as a predicament, there would be no need to talk either for the good diversity or against discrimination.

The dialogical character is also obvious in another sense. The discourse on diversity is repeated in the organisation theories gathered under the name performance management (McKenzie, 2001). This model for organisation of working life is a response to Frederick Taylor's scientific management (Braverman, 1974). In Scientific Management, the goal was to control differ-ences and develop standardisation. The process of production should, at its best, be totally predictable. This stress on standardisation inevitably created a monocultural environment defined by a uniform set of values and ways of being and doing. The norm was sameness and the worker was preferably a heterosexual, protestant man. This homogeneity was, of course, never fully realised. This induced the importance of controlling differences in the work-force. Performance management criticised the monotonous organisation of work. Instead of controlling differences, performance management wanted to *manage* differences. Instead of standardisations, the goal became creativity. Managers are now increasingly promoting the positive dimensions of cultural diversity, including not only gender and ethnicity, but also sexuality, age, and physical ability. Among the benefits of this strategy, the theorists maintain, are improved organisational reputation vis-à-vis potential employees, greater worker morale, increased problem-solving capabilities, and greater competi-tive advantages in the global economy. A multicultural workforce leads to greater creativity and innovation. Instead of standardisation, the object is innovation, change, and transformation. A monoculture like Taylor's is per-ceived as an obstacle for development (McKenzie, 2001, pp. 56–69).

Scientific and performance management are two examples of how man-agement of diversity, or coping with heterogeneity, can be solved in different ways. This can also be illustrated by Swedish policies and rhetoric regarding migrants in which there has been a shift from assimilation to integration. The official ideology no longer declares that migrants or other deviating catego-ries of people should adapt and become like the imagined majority. The goal is instead integration where supposedly significant cultural identity mark-ers are perceived as assets. That is, the ideal has changed from homogeneity to heterogeneity. This transformation could be described as a hegemonic shift in the discourses regarding difference and deviance. However, despite this rhetoric, it is important to keep in mind that there are clear limits to the approved diversity, limits in the form of values, language competence, appearance, and performance.

Discourse and Identity

Social diversity is a concept that does not primarily describe or reflect social facts. It is rather a perspective on the world. In the words of Jeffrey Weeks: "Diversity is not just given. We find it because we seek it out; we seek it out because it has special value for us" (2000, pp. 22–23). Different discourses constitute contingent interpretative frames for how to perceive and make sense of existence. They induce specific perceptions and exclude others. What is to be constructed in a certain discourse is neither totally predictable nor completely open. Because traces of previous usages and definitions are articulated and reformulated together with other discourses, there are both limits and unexpected possibilities. Content, definitions, evaluations, and boundaries are continually modified (Laclau & Mouffe, 1985, p. 105; Smith, 1998, p. 87). This is also true for the discourse about diversity. It is a discourse that governs what is possible to say regarding cultural pluralism at a workplace or in society.

The discourse about diversity concerns identity and subjectivity. Discourses are performative in the sense that they always are prior to formations of identities and subjectivities (Butler, 1993). Both of these categories are constructed through discourses. No individual can choose to stand outside the discursive. The discursive process that enables identity and subjectivity is hierarchical and exercises power (Butler, 1993, p. 15; Derrida, 1981, p. 41; Smith, 1998, p. 57). To exemplify, categories such as woman or homosexual are created as different from the norm: the upper hand that is man and heterosexual. The categories are continually related to different subject positions that entail instructions of how to perform one self. These categories are the tools that languages provide in order to make individuals understandable and agency possible. There is no way to make sense of individuals outside language. A person has to have a sense of her own identity, or subject position, in order to act. However, it is not possible to predict how specific individuals will employ different identity categories or subject positions. They can be combined, fused, and mixed in innumerable ways. Every individual contains a multiplicity of subject positions, which correspond both to different social relations in which the individual is situated and to the discourses that constitute these positions. This means that subject positions, and the identity construction they entail, always are discursively constructed. Furthermore, subject positions are points of antagonism and forms of struggle (Laclau & Mouffe, 1985, p. 11).

At the same time that the discourse of diversity promotes difference, it delineates the boundaries both for what is to be considered as sameness and as difference. In defining diversity in terms of gender, ethnicity, age, disabilities, or sexual preferences, certain aspects are privileged as the essence of identity, as the element that makes the subject what it truly is (Smith, 1998, p. 44).

Three Different Ways to Talk About Diversity

In the following, we will present a discourse analysis of three official documents that employ and participate in the Swedish discourse of social diversity from different positions. The documents are a report from the Ministry of Industry, Employment and Communication on how to increase diversity at workplaces, an action program from the same ministry on how to counteract discrimination, and a constitutional text from the Swedish Missions Covenant Church. The three documents all base their argument on a liberal notion that individuals possess an essential identity, and on the value of the right to express and develop that true identity, that is to be "who she is." They differ in what foundation they employ for their argument. The first document refers to an economist discourse, the second to a discourse of social rights, and the third to a primordial essential diversity, rooted in creation.

In 1999, the Swedish Social Democratic government and the Ministry of Industry, Employment, and Communication launched a project with the object to:

> ... at the same time, and from a perspective of growth, survey and analyse the effects of gender, class, ethnicity, age, sexual disposition and functional disorder on the possibility for individuals in the labour market to start companies, and how social diversity in trade and industry can influence economic development. On the basis of this analysis, measures will be proposed in order to eliminate obstacles and induce increased growth. (Näringsdepartementet, 2000, p. 1) (Authors' translation)

The project was completed in December 2000 and was presented in a report entitled *Everyone Equally Different* (Närings departementet, 2000). In the report, the discussion about social diversity is articulated together with an economic discourse. One example of this articulation is that it presents people principally as the economic category "human resource." The question discussed is how to make use of the entire resource as efficiently as possible. A statement from the ministry says: "A crucial factor to obtain increasing and long-term growth and employment is to make use of the country's human resources" (Näringsdepartementet, 2000, p. 185).

Another example of the prevalence of the economic discourse is how economic growth is assigned fundamental importance. Simultaneously, as the report states that growth is indispensable for achieving job equality, it asserts that job equality induces growth. Job equality is henceforth not important in itself but is appreciated as a means to achieve and maintain growth.

A third example of the economic perspective in the report *Everyone Equally Different* is its assertion that manpower—a resource of which there is, or soon will be, a shortage—is a prerequisite for economic growth. However, the report maintains that Sweden has a hitherto unexploited resource of manpower. Immigrants, women working part-time, and the disabled need to become active participants in the workforce. In order to accomplish this, the report declares that it is important to re-examine prevailing conceptions of distinctive traits of what is to be considered a good workforce. It states that it is not homogeneity but heterogeneity that makes the workplace competitive and prosperous. Its main message is the importance of recognising the potentialities inherent in a heterogeneous group of employees. This indicates that the problem addressed by the project is not primarily that social categories are excluded, but that there is a lack of manpower.

A fundamental supposition in the report is that social diversity induces creativity and is good for both business and national growth. It hereby reiterates the theory of performance management. The presumption is that with different cultures, genders, and ages follow different perspectives or ideas. Social diversity will make industries more efficient and, henceforth, more prosperous. The document states that different perspectives will enrich both separate companies and Sweden as a nation. We argue that the right to be oneself here runs the risk of becoming a demand. If the individual in some sense can be categorised as deviating from normality, she has to behave differently. A woman is expected to act differently from a man, non-Swedes to behave differently than imagined genuine Swedes, and so forth. To "be yourself" becomes equivalent to acting according to one or several stereotypes. According to this argument, it is when these expected differences are mixed that social diversity develops into an asset for the employer.

The economic perspective, and its ensuing demand to be oneself, is also expressed from another, slightly psychological, perspective. The author discusses the problem with homosexuals not being open about "who they really are," and thereby keeping their sexual preference a secret. The report states that this is a serious problem for the company, because:

People who do not dare to be themselves at work hardly perform to the best of their ability. An enforced streamlined conduct does not promote the dynamic and creativity that is so important in large areas of the current labour market. (Näringsdepartementet, 2000, p. 72) (Authors' translation)

In this case, it is not the mix of different qualities that benefits the employer, but that each employee can take advantage of her full capacity. This is another example of how the economic discourse constructs the demands connected to production as the basis for advocating social diversity. The individual must adapt her "self" to the demands of the company, and or the nation Sweden. The report demonstrates the presence of an economic discourse on growth that asserts that growth is important not only for companies but for the whole nation. To achieve economic growth, to do what is best for the nation is also what the main author of the report, Marie Granlund, points out as paramount. In spring 2000, Granlund declared in a television programme that promoting social diversity has nothing to do with "feeling sorry" for people. People are simply needed. We agree that employment of people cannot be based solely on empathy, but question if measures for inclusion of hitherto excluded categories can be based on pure economics. Our position is that, in order to make way for a labour market without discrimination, political work ought to subvert categories and hierarchies, not simply redistribute access. In asserting that diversity and heterogeneity is good and profitable, the discourse only considers preconceived differences according to identity categories, not differences in opinions on management, division of labour, salary claims, or divergent opinions about the necessity of growth. Consensus and agreement in these issues are taken for granted. The norm about diversity hereby reiterates the dominant economic discourse that emphasises the importance of harmony between people with different interests. In stressing a harmonious diversity signified by consensus regarding significant values and goals, the diversity of the diversity discourse conceals inequality and processes of power.

In January 2001, the Ministry of Industry, Employment, and Communication presented a second report on similar issues. It was entitled *Action Program Against Racism, Xenophobia, and Discrimination*. Differing from the aforementioned, it did not combine social diversity with economic growth. The problem addressed in the report is not lack of manpower, but discrimination against various social categories. The fact that people are more or less excluded from the labour market is presented as a problem, but differing from the aforementioned document, it is written not on behalf of the economic market, but for those who are kept out. The argument is based on a liberal discourse about equity and citizenship. Due to this perspective, it is the negative term discrimination that is put to the forefront rather than the positive term social diversity. The action program focuses on citizenship, human rights, and justice. The central message is that everybody is entitled to be who she is and to be treated fairly and justly, and that every citizen is responsible for achieving a just society.

> We all have a responsibility to fight against racism, xenophobia, homophobia and discrimination. Each one, who lives in Sweden, has an individual responsibility to react, in our own everyday life and according to our own prerequisites, when people are affronted because they are who they are. (Näringsdepartementet, 2001, p. 70) (Authors' translation)

This document does not make differences between people into an economic category, but talks about and, thereby, constructs difference as a human right. Discrimination and exclusion are presented as unwanted, and as an exception from a common norm that is inclusive and nondiscriminating. The implicit idea seems to be that discrimination and exclusion can be solved through legislation; that is, that a law against discrimination is a way to remove this deviation from an inclusive nondiscriminatory norm. However, the document fails to present any discussion about how differences are created. On the contrary, categories of race, nationalism, and sexuality are taken for granted and thereby presented as grounded in themselves, not created in hierarchical and conflicting cultural processes. The responsibility for the citizen becomes limited to respecting differences, not to challenging them, and asking questions about how and why individuals are assigned different qualities based on stereotypes. We, therefore, put into question its construction of difference as a human right. It does not problematise how differences, in the sense of essential characteristic qualities connected to specific social groups and categories, are created.

The two reports from the Ministry of Industry, Employment, and Communication exhibit two different ways to talk about the problem of exclusions in the Swedish labour market. However, they also display similarities. One is that neither is reflexive. Both reports place themselves, as governmental authorities, outside the problem and refer to discrimination and exclusion as problems in workplaces, schools, and sexist and racist groups. Discrimination and exclusion are not presented as traits of Swedish society in general, but as unwanted exceptions; and the consensus that these tendencies ought to be counteracted is taken for granted. Another similarity is that they express and presuppose the liberal message about the significance of assuring everybody the right to be who they essentially are.

At the General Assembly 2000, the Swedish Mission Covenant Church decided on a new constitution. Attached to the constitution is a text that states the fundamental tenants of the faith of the church. Together, these documents are given the title *A Free and Open Church* (Svenska Missions-förbundet, 2001). When reading the document, it becomes clear that the word "open" encompasses a notion of a church signified by social diversity. The term "diversity" appears 11 times, and the document states that "God's church is meant for all human beings" (p. 219) and "the Mission Covenant Church of Sweden wants to ... be a meeting place for people from different cultures and social backgrounds. The fellowship is founded in everyone's equal value. Differences and diversity is an asset" (p. 220). It furthermore says, "Diversity mirrors the kingdom of God as a community without borders" (p. 217). Besides being founded in the notion of equal value, the argument for diversity is founded in a theological conception of the church as a mix of people where each one is endowed with unique gifts and faculties that will enrich the community. This notion is not far away from the theory of performance management that diversity will induce creativity and economic growth. The difference is that the true self in the context of the church is essential in another way—it is what God has intended the individual to be. It is a primordial identity founded in creation. Subsequent debates in the same and other churches regarding homosexuality reveal that it is this primordial diversity that from a Christian perspective justifies difference. The Church of Sweden, the Missions Covenant Church, and other churches are prepared to show some tolerance regarding gays and lesbians provided that their sexual preference is "genuine," that is, a true primordial self for which they are not responsible (Svenska Missionsförbundet, 2001; Svenska kyrkans teologiska kommitté, 2002). This notion of essential identities, with accompanying capacities, designates the boundaries for what the churches can accept as a tolerable diversity. There are certain predetermined ways to express human nature, the argument goes. Expressions or behaviour that fall outside these limits are designated as unnatural and, henceforth, repudiated. In March 2002, the Mission Covenant Church of Sweden clearly restricted the meaning of diversity when the board decided that people who lived in open same-sex relationships were excluded from being ordained to pastor or deacon. This evinces that the rhetoric and reasoning about, or organisation based on diversity does not necessarily challenge the hegemonic forces. The discourse about social diversity does not efface discrimination and exclusion.

The three documents discussed earlier can all be seen as measures to meet challenges to institutional and decision-making structures posed by categories that in some sense or another fall outside normality and thereby are included in different diversity measures. By launching an ideal of diversity based on the notion that individuals possess different qualities and capacities based on which category they belong to, critique and challenges against structures that favour the interests of a dominant social category, or group, can be silenced simply by redistribution of money, social positions, and work (Young, 1990, p. 3). More fundamental injustices, inherent in norms, processes, and notions, which are perceived as "natural," thereby escape re-evaluation.

Our most essential point of critique against the self-evident and unreflective positive evaluation of social diversity is that it obscures inequality. Social diversity is not a self-evident variation that needs acceptance and affirmation. The rhetoric tends to conceal relations of power and domination. We believe that a focus on how social groups are discursively constructed as subjects for social diversity is a means to develop alternative ways of thinking about politics of difference in which difference can be both recognised and challenged. In the following discussion, we want to point out some issues that we believe could promote such a process.

Disharmonious Pluralism

The implicit conception of economy as an indispensable foundation and shared interest for all citizens creates the notion that there are common collective interests with which everyone is supposed to agree. When the interest of the particular excluded individual, for example, the unemployed male migrant, is presented as the same as those of privileged social categories, the importance of the system into which the excluded is supposed to be included becomes fortified. Capitalism is never questioned but employed as a self-evident foundation for the whole discourse. To talk about social diversity is beneficial for everyone because it induces growth and, thereby, universalises capitalism as a common good (Zizek, 2000, p. 60). To state that society needs diversity is to simultaneously state that capitalism is in everybody's interest.

Both the economic approach to social diversity and the perspective on exclusion characterised by the idea of equal rights are problematic. These perspectives tend to found and justify ideas of difference that disregard the fact that individuals have different prerequisites and possibilities due to how they are socially categorised; and they both fail to focus on the subordinating creation of division. In order to problematise how divisions are created, we believe it is necessary to speak and act more radically about diversity and pluralism. A salient feature in our suggestion is an emphasis on the importance of a nonfoundational and anti-essentialist approach to discussions about social diversity. The radical democratic pluralist theory advanced by Laclau and Mouffe (1985) is a theoretical vantage point by which it is possible to demonstrate the difference between the prevailing politics of social diversity and a politics of difference. To put it differently, it elucidates why politics about social diversity fail to become politics of difference.

Instead of discussing social diversity as a question of the right to be who you are, in other words to understand identity as something stable and essential, we suggest a discussion about identity that focuses on the multiplicity of discourses and the categories they create. These discourses do not only constitute possibilities and limitations for identity constructions, they also make hierarchies, superiority, and subordination in multiple ways. No identity is unambiguous; identities are always produced in antagonistic discursive fields (cf. Derrida, 1981, p. 41; Mouffe, 1992, p. 372). To say that you have "the right to be who you are," without discussing relations of power and the conditions in which construction of subjectivity and identity take place, is cynical. These designations and identifications concerning gender, ethnicity, sexual preferences, and so forth are created, and in their reiteration repeatedly made important. The documents presented earlier presuppose essential identities and conceal the political dimension of how identities are designated and perceived.

The discourse about diversity as an asset fuses demands based on equal rights with discourse of economy and growth. This articulation not only strengthens the capitalistic discourses as a hegemonic force; it also conceals that the capitalist relation of production is a root of numerous relations of subordination. In line with Laclau and Mouffe (1985, p. 178), we argue that a project for a radical democracy should imply a socialist dimension, which maintains a critical perspective on capitalism but without perceiving relations of production as fundamental for social analysis. Deconstruction of notions about stable identities, and the close ties between different discourses can elucidate and thereby dissolve the way in which the discourse about diversity affirms the capitalistic discourse.

Deconstruction is not enough. In order to subvert and counteract subordinating categorisations, it is necessary to create new contingent hegemonies that challenge the prevailing (cf. Elam, 1994, p. 109). It is necessary to abandon the ontological individualism of the liberal tradition in order to grasp the collective character of the political struggles that pluralism facilitates. In order to transform present hegemonic discourses, it is essential to deal with alliances that take a critical stand toward normative notions and practices. Prevailing differentiating discourses that define boundaries between healthy and sick, normal and abnormal, us and the other cannot be subverted and dissolved without collective action. However, this subversion should not be unequivocal; that would only result in alternative stable and normative categories. A democracy has to promote a never-ending confrontation and questioning of the boundaries, traits, and positions of different social groups and categories; that is, a disharmonious pluralism.

In order to make this mobilisation of antagonistic social groups and discourses possible, it is important to challenge ideas about privileged categories. In Marxism, and in some feminism, categories of class and gender are given privileged positions. It is from their perspective that society and history is understood. Class and gender struggles are considered to be the most important force in historical change. A challenge of these privileged categories can make way for different social and political interlacings to hook on to each other into what Mouffe terms a hegemonic formation (Mouffe, 2000, p. 29). A feasible starting point for this endeavour could be to recognise that groups or identities continually are constructed as subordinated or superior and in relation to each other. No social group or identity escapes this process of domination and subordination. This recognition ought to induce a self-reflexive attitude regarding how different movements or groups continually create difference. Examples are how the feminist movement reiterates heteronormativity, how the gay movement has a history of subordinating women, and how different categories of disabled tend to affirm hierarchies between different disablements.

We believe it is necessary to launch a notion of a self-reflexive deconstructive solidarity that does not limit itself to fighting on behalf of the disadvantaged, but focuses on how identities and positions contribute to subordination of other identities and categories. To reflect on oneself is not the same as to stand outside the discourse (cf. Benhabib, 1992). In making sense of its own subjectivity and identity, a subject can contribute different meanings and importance to the same subject position. There are numerous possibilities of how to understand, perceive, and imagine oneself. The self-reflexivity in our notion of solidarity pertains to a deliberate ambition to deconstruct how one's own subject positions and identifications subordinate and depreciate other categories. The reflexive solidarity we propose is not primarily an individual endeavour. Subject positions are social constructions, and reflexive solidarity is always collective. Social movements, regardless of whether their aim is identity politics or if they are directed against other injustices, have to reflect on how they participate in subordination of others—what categories they are subordinating and how this process can be subverted. To exemplify, the queer movement has successfully demonstrated that feminism, to a large extent, has affirmed heteronormativity and, thereby, excluded and subordinated homosexuals. Likewise, the feminist movement has convincingly criticised the labour movement for its negligence of the situation of women.

A self-reflexive deconstructive solidarity differs significantly from the notion of "reflective solidarity" presented by Dean (1996). Dean proposes communication and "a responsible orientation to relationship" (p. 3) as a means to transform disagreements that accompany diversity. Her position is that it is possible to reach a communicative understanding of "we" in which differences can be respected as a necessary trait of solidarity and not as sources of conflict. Our main critique of Dean's conception of solidarity is that she disregards aspects of power in the construction of differences and, therefore, fails to acknowledge that differences are not innocent variations but means for subordination and oppression. Although she acknowledges that every conception of a "we" to which we act and feel in solidarity entails exclusion, her notion of reflective solidarity conceals oppression and subordination because the aim is to include every social category and subject position in a common "we." Although the concept of solidarity always implies some sort of collective, the "we" in our notion of a self-reflexive solidarity, is not, like in Deans' reflective solidarity, an all-inclusive "we," but a "we" consisting of "us" who strive for equality. By using the term "self" in "self-reflexive solidarity," we want to stress the need for a conscious and deliberate effort to subvert both the individual and the collective vantage point from which each individual and each social movement understands itself. Self-reflexive solidarity focuses on how all subject-positions entail inclusion and exclusion. It is a continuous endeavour to subvert and question the seemingly stable boundaries of groups and categories. One should also ask how differences are made into pertinent distinctions in different situations and relations. For example, in being identified and identifying herself as a white woman, an individual simultaneously has subordinated and superior positions. As a woman, she is subordinated in a society with patriarchal discourses and, as white, she is given a superior position through colonial discourses on race and ethnicity. In order to subvert categories that homogenise and exclude identities, it is important for her to question how she, in and due to her identity definitions, partakes in the suppression and homogenisation of others.

To conclude, we are convinced of the necessity of a never-ending discussion about the construction of categories and differences and about the conditions under which identity and subjectivity are created and understood. This means that we need a change of focus in identity politics from identity categories to identity discourses. Political movements that are now based on identity categories of class, gender, ethnicity and so forth, need to question and challenge their own preconditions and the assumptions that follow. Our proposal is to employ a self-reflexive deconstructive solidarity in order to achieve and maintain a disharmonious pluralism.

Author Note

This study is part of the research project "Diversity in Theory and Practice—Industry and Church as Societal Norm-Producers" supported by the Swedish Council for Working Life and Social Research (FAS).

References

Bakhtin, M. (1981). *The dialogical imagination*. Austin: University Press.

Benhabib, S. (1992). *Situating the self: Gender, community, and postmodernism in contemporary ethics*. New York: Routledge.

Braverman, H. (1974). *Labor and monopoly capital: The degradation of work in the twentieth century*. New York: Monthly Review Press.

Butler, J. (1993). *Bodies that matter*. New York: Routledge.

Cox, T. (1993). *Cultural diversity in organizations. Theory, research & practice*. San Francisco, CA: Berrett-Koehler.

Dean, J. (1996). *Solidarity of strangers: Feminism after identity politics*. Berkeley: University of California Press.

Den hemlösa sexualiteten [Homeless sexuality]. (2001). Örebro: Libris.

Derrida, J. (1981). *Positions*. London: Athlone.

Elam, D. (1994). *Feminism and deconstruction: Ms. en abyme*. London: Routledge.

Laclau, E., & Mouffe, C. (1985). *Hegemony & socialist strategy: Towards a radical democratic politics*. London: Verso.

McKenzie, J. (2001). *Perform or else: From discipline to performance*. London & New York: Routledge.

Mouffe, C. (1992). Feminism, citizenship, and radical democratic politics. In J. Butler & J. Scott (Eds.), *Feminists theorize the political* (pp. 369–384). New York: Routledge.

Mouffe, C. (2000). Hegemoni och nya politiska subjekt med sikte mot ett nytt demokratibegrepp [Hegemony and new political subjects: Towards a new concept of democracy]. *Fronesis, 3–4*, 27–43.

Näringsdepartementet [Ministry of Industry, Employment and Communication]. (2000). *Alla lika olika* [Everyone equally different] (Departementsserien No. 2000:69). Stockholm: Regeringskansliet.

Näringsdepartementet [Ministry of Industry, Employment and Communication]. (2001). *En nationell handlingsplan mot rasism, främlingsfientlighet, homofobi och diskriminering* [Action program against racism, xenophobia, and discrimination]. (Skrivelse. No. 2000/01:59). Stockholm: Regeringskansliet.

Smith, A.M. (1998). *Laclau and Mouffe and the radical democratic imaginary*. London: Routledge.

Svenska Missionsförbundet. (2001). *En fri och öppen kyrka: Konstitution för Svenska Missionsförbundet* [A free and open church: Constitution for the Swedish Mission covenant church]. Falköping: Svenska Missionsförbundet.

Svenska kyrkans teologiska kommitté. (2002). Homosexuella i kyrkan [Homosexuals in the church]. Retrieved June 2007, from http://www.svenskakyrkan. se/utredningar/samtalsdokumentet_homosexuella_i_kyrkan

Taylor, C. (1994). Multiculturalism. Examining the politics of recognition. Princeton, NJ: Princeton University Press.

Weeks, J. (2000). Making sexual history. Cambridge: Polity Press.

Young, I. M. (1990). Justice and the politics of difference. Princeton, NJ: Princeton University Press.

Zizek, S. (2000). Mångkulturalismen eller den multinationella kapitalismens kulturella logic [Multiculturalism, or the cultural logic of late capitalism]. Fronesis, 3–4, 60–84.

5

BEING ASIAN IN ENGLISH:
Gender, Ethnicity, and Class in the American Professoriate

Joseph S. Eng

California State University, Monterey Bay

Introduction

... I think that one of the unspoken discomforts surrounding the way a discourse of race and gender, class and sexual practice has disrupted the academy is the challenge to that mind/body split. Once we start talking in the classroom about the body and about how we live in our bodies, we're automatically challenging the way power has orchestrated itself in that particular institutionalized space. The person who is most powerful has the privilege of denying their body.... (bell hooks, 1994, pp. 136–137)

Similarly, as a white university teacher in his thirties, I am profoundly aware of my presence in the classroom as well, given the history of the male body, and of the male teacher. I need to be sensitive to and critical of my presence in the history that has led me here. Yet it is complicated by the fact that you and I are both sensitive to—and maybe even suspicious of—those who seem to be retreating away from a real, maybe radical consciousness of the body into a very conservative mind/body split. Some male colleagues are hiding behind this, repressing their bodies not out of deference but out of fear. (Ron Scapp, in hooks, 1994, pp. 135–136)

— Excerpted dialogue is between bell hooks and Ron Scapp, her colleague and friend, from Building a Teaching Community, in *Teaching to Transgress* (hooks, 1994).

Identity politics, hooks argues, "... emerges out of the struggles of oppressed or exploited groups to have a standpoint on which to critique dominant structures, a position that gives purpose and meaning to struggle" (p. 88). In her American university context, "... [c]ritical pedagogies of liberation respond to these concerns and necessarily embrace experience, confessions and testimony as relevant ways of knowing, as important, vital dimensions of any learning process" (p. 89). Responding to Diana Fuss's critique of essentializing experience, especially in the classroom as a potentially silencing agency, hooks posits that "the authority of experience" is a privileged standpoint already utilized, perhaps unknowingly, by traditionally dominant groups, only now reenacted by marginalized students. In her feminist theory classes, hooks observes students expressing rage against work that is not supported by concrete experience: "Frustration is directed against the inability of methodology, analysis, and abstract writing... to make the work connect to [students'] efforts to live more fully, to transform society, to live a politics of feminism" (p. 88). As a response, she "circumvent[s] [the] possible misuse of power [the authority of experience] by bringing to the classroom pedagogical strategies that affirm their presence, their right to speak, in multiple ways on diverse topics"; she adds, experiential knowledge will "enhance" learning experience (p. 84).

As a black woman professor, bell hooks is not unaware of her own body/mind split, and her own negotiation has led to what is now familiarly known as an "engaged pedagogy" through self-actualization. If hooks's students in her feminist theory class desperately needed to "live" a politics of feminism, might faculty of color develop, grow, or even prosper with a politics unique to their location, as an identity construct to be articulated by the faculty her/himself? If ostensibly, how might a professor's experiential knowledge enhance her or his teaching experience, especially, at the specific location/s? Deconstructing her pedagogy scenario further, I have to ask, based on my own search for "purpose and meaning" for almost two decades of teaching in American higher education, might "we," as *non-native-born* faculty of color, even *have* a politic of roles as location? This chapter will address a few of these questions central to the less-researched professor's identity as a construct shaped by the intertwined and interlocking entities of gender, ethnicity, and class.

The Question of Legitimacy

As a result of fast-changing demographics in United States institutions, departments of English and English Studies face an interesting reality as a workplace—the coexistence of mainstream faculty and the nonwhite professor as "other." Within composition studies, discussions of identity theory and location politics are not new, tracing back, perhaps, to Adrienne Rich's 1984 phrase "a politics of location" (2001). In addition to hooks and Fuss, feminist academics Gesa Kirsch, Joy Ritchie, and Gayatri Spivak have each problematized extensively the nature of and relationships among self-identity, audience, and textuality. More specifically on race and composition, United States composition scholarship has posed new questions based on the field's research interest in subject positions (Bizzell, 1986; Chiang, 1998; Harding, 1987; Romano, 1999), the practical interest in work conditions (Braine, 1999; Holbrook, 1991; Horner, 2000; Miller, 1991), and the pedagogical interest or possibility for effecting changes (Shor & Freire, 1987; Villaneuva, 1997). From the teacher-scholar perspective, some have argued that while nontraditional, nonwhite English faculty struggle to locate themselves, their colleagues and students remain skeptical of any values these new faculty might have (Chiang, 1993; Johnson, 1994; Prendergast, 1998; Sciachitano, 1993). Ironically, non-native English faculty's roles are, not unlike Sansei (grandchildren of Japanese immigrants) in America, unimagined (Mura, 1991). Such a phenomenon becomes interestingly complex in writing instruction.

Student text has been repeatedly characterized as marginal or marginalized discourse for its technical errors, inarticulate voices, and personal subject matters that are not affiliated with or sanctioned by the convention of academic discourse (Bartholomae, 1988; Rose, 1985, 1989; Shaughnessy, 1977; among many others). Further, since Shaughnessy's study on developmental or basic writers, many in the late 1990s still argued that one of the major teaching challenges was assisting beginning college students to make the shift from the personal to the academic. In addition, the National Council of Teachers of English (NCTE) has asked writing teachers to practice the art and craft of writing and to write alongside their students for personal and pedagogical purposes. In this perspective, nontraditional students might share similar challenges with their nontraditional professors, for both parties seem to have the need for defining (and redefining) their places within traditional academia.

At their reimagined locations, non-native English professors of color might occupy a rather crucial position that, at the same time they negotiate their nontraditional identities or unimagined roles as English faculty, their own reading and writing could in turn help students develop their voices and further engage their learning interest.

This chapter thus explores the increasingly significant relationship between teacher identity and pedagogy. Essentially, it discusses pedagogical issues politically by noting current research in identity politics, relating personal narratives, and proposing five location strategies within the academy and beyond.

Twenty Years as "Other"

I'll start with a personal experience. Returning to the United States from a trip abroad in 1999 (the pre-September 11, 2001 era), I proceeded with my wife through the customs at Los Angeles International Airport before connecting back to Spokane, Washington. Exhausted from the long flight, I did not think twice when answering the question from a customs officer: "What do you do for a living?" He, a well-built man in his forties, uniformed, sat rather casually on a stool while processing the line of "Permanent Resident/Citizen" at an average of five minutes per person. I, wearing a drab suede jacket on top of a white T-shirt, answered matter-of-factly, "I teach English." He seemed surprised, then continued, "How about this?" pointing at the NG, the original spelling of my last name, on the customs declaration form. Without waiting to hear what I had to respond, he said, "It's a joke. You have a nice day." I quickly proceeded forward for the connection. But, in my mind, the typical questions or questioning reappeared, almost expectedly, regarding my name and my profession.

Did my last name seem *unusual* compared to many other travelers the customs officer had processed? Was it *strange* compared to those declaring *English* as a profession? Was he looking for a vowel for pronunciation purpose? Still, couldn't he have waited so that I would pronounce it for him? (Should people even dally at the port of entry?) What seemed so *noteworthy* that deserved his extra attention? And, how about all the similar incidents for the past 20 years since I came to this country? Is my job or livelihood ever on the line? If not, why bother?

The following list of anecdotes will portray a pattern of experiences perhaps commonly shared by most nontraditional, nonwhite academics of English. I would underscore that as much as being a marginalized English professor is a personal issue, it is fundamentally a discipline-based one. Instead of addressing apparent victimization, this essay will visit marginalization within reimagined contexts of teaching, intellectual, and professional locations. First, the anecdotes, chronologically:

- As a beginning M.A. student in a large southern university in 1985, I ran into an English professor (with whom I had never taken a course) at the writing center. Hearing that I was there for an English degree, he casually suggested that perhaps I should change my major, preferably, for one in "something related to international relations." I would "benefit more," he said.
- When I began teaching college composition as a Ph.D. candidate in the midwest, most people on and off campus assumed that I taught, or rather tutored, writing to non-native students. Further, I must have been perfect in grammar and usage.

- In 1992, a small group of community-college students uttered, "There is your teaching Ching," glancing at me sideways as I walked past them around a building's corner on the campus where I started teaching full time. In an otherwise favorite class of mine, a seemingly well-intentioned student told me informally that he really thought that I should work in fields such as translation or international business.
- In most composition classes I have taught in the midwest, west, and northwest, it is not unusual for students to ask me, as they walk into the room on the first day, "Is this an English class?"

Would all these have been the same had I been native and white? Probably not. Within Composition Studies, nonetheless, it would be meaningful if I, as a teacher-scholar, could also theorize who I am, link who I am and what I am to pedagogy, and examine how effective it might become. Following are five location strategies within professional contexts; together they position the nontraditional professor as an agent for change.

First Location: The Ethnic Teacher as Writer

The portion of composition theory that focuses on textuality and social constructionism is particularly relevant. While textuality research fosters a manuscript culture and the play of text, social constructionism has led to a pedagogy of collaborative and cooperative learning. Both theoretical tenets, in general, present a pedagogy of community. Such an approach, when set parallel to composition's current interest in ideology, would seem to include equity as well.

Throughout the 1990s, the sites of college composition have been characterized as "Contact Zones" where people of unequal power may interact under conditions that allow for sharing and understanding (Pratt, 1991) or as "borderlands" (la frontera), places of cultural, geographical, and linguistic differences, where shifting and multiple identities exist in the face of discomfort and conflict (Anzaldua, 1987). Similar to doing composition, teaching composition in the postprocess classroom therefore necessitates an understanding of the interaction of ideas and voices represented in a diverse student body in terms of race, gender, and cultural backgrounds. Moreover, while computing technology plays central roles in instruction, compositionists could capitalize their knowledge of contact zones or borderlands in the Web-based environment by sharing with students their own online research, publishing, and communication experiences. This interest of polyvocality (Bakhtin, 1981) could further situate the nontraditional professor within a United States higher educational tradition that does not necessarily challenge the dominant culture public institutions help produce.

Confronting the history (especially its distorted version) involving non-native born English faculty of color, we might consider a significant argument about needed connection between tradition and change. "Hegemony exploits traditions," Villaneuva (1997) reminds us:

> The American Freireista can at least provide a way for students to discover those traditions that are in need of change. We can have students discover the traditions that form the foundations of the academy while simultaneously promoting and instigating change in the ideologies that shape the academy. Tradition and change for changes in tradition. (p. 633)

His design, after observing how one Freire-inspired instructor's political message only reached already predisposed students in limited fashion, calls for a writing space in the traditional classroom for the "dialectic between hegemony and counterhegemony, between tradition and change" to take place (George, 2001, p. 100). Villaneuva's course would have students read one canonical and one noncanonical text, discuss any relevance to their lived experiences, and then write about it. As a result, students would write in a sequenced assignment about conflicts they had had to confront and to examine the sources of those conflicts. He argues that, "... the dialectic might have students know the tradition critically, not only to acquire the literate, academic culture but to recognize their often antagonistic relationships to it" (p. 635). Ultimately, his belief is that "[a] dialectic between tradition and change would provide the means for access, acknowledge the political, the while avoiding propaganda" (p. 635). In quite the same vein, the postprocess composition classroom since the 1990s has solicited texts of various stages and shapes, highlighting the relationship among existing and emerging ones. Teacher-modeling, particularly approached as writing with students, further reinforces the communal text as one consisting of both student text and teacher text.

As an Asian male teaching English, my writerly role seems to position me most effectively at a location where, I envision, all ethnicities actively participate in the class discourse. When I share my manuscript experience as both a personal and social process, both a genred and politicized process, my students begin to view me as an authentic writer who manages several worlds at once. Like his students, this Asian-American writer transacts between tradition and change and among parties, going through stages of revision from author-based, to peer-based, to finally editor-based, as the result of a blind-review process. Gradually, the ethnic appearance or demeanor comes across to students as a fellow writer who pursues a common process shared by all, which involves many decision-making stages that have to be sustainingly negotiative.

Second Location: The Ethnic Teacher as Cultural Agent

Theorizing her literature class dynamics, Johnson (1994) asserts that the instructor is actually "the third party" that provides "another voice and text to be deciphered" in the reader-text dynamics. This teacherly role, contends Johnson, "... becomes interestingly complicated when the author and the major characters of a text share with the teacher the marked identity of blackness or femaleness, or both" (p. 410). In her case as "both," Johnson ponders on the complexity that might affect her white students' experiences. She perceives the involuntary, complex role as a constant "struggle," a negotiation between empowering her black students and silencing others (p. 412). This intricate dynamic, I argue, also suggests an opportunity for further student engagement. Since imaginative literature by nature invites participation, an already racialized instructor must negotiate on an identity spectrum—between the authoritarian or the literary-expert role on one end and the nonauthoritarian or the emphatic/interested reader on the other. Importantly, nontraditional faculty could indeed extend on Johnson's reading involving self-identity by devising teaching strategies that demand *participatory* roles.

While the traditional literary canon continues to expand and, in some cases, change, most noticeably in the popularly adopted anthologies among large survey courses, the Asian-American image seems to shift as characters vary, including, sometimes, previously diminished male roles. In *China Men*, Maxine Hong Kingston depicts an unusual side of a railroad man, Ah Goong, "who, while dangling from a basket one beautiful day, was overcome with sexual desire and ejaculated high above the earth" (Okihiro, 2002, p. 152). "I am f—king the world," Ah Goong said. His "masculine thrust through the most resistant of mountain," Okihiro maintains, "was an exercise in futility, especially when set against the world's 'big as the sky' vagina, and his seed fell on barren ground" (p. 152). The seemingly defiant and sexual act, I would add, also manifests itself as a Chinese laborer's desolate solitude, an alien to the vast land to which he was attached for his existence in 19th century America. In terms of Johnson's critical class dynamics, the "shared" racial role between Ah Goong and the instructor might embarrass me as an Asian male instructor; such an unusual portrayal, however, befits the western tradition of antihero, an important literary construct for the class itself. In addition to literary terminology, I bring to the class a needed Asian-American historical context about the Sierra Nevada, sometimes from family narratives (primarily involving two great uncles serving in World War II as American soldiers). In other words, the "constant struggle" that Johnson confronts is also a frequent teachable moment for the racialized instructor playing necessary and timely cultural roles.

Cultural studies and critical pedagogies offer much to untangle social plots via instructors' conscious choosing of text and strategies linked to students' direct life experience, values, and methods of analysis (Freire, 1998). Preparing the class for historic feminist voices in the making, for example, students and I first brainstorm individually for current issues that contemporary women faced, and then reconstitute or reimagine them within contexts of such pioneers as Charles Brockden Brown, Margaret Fuller, Elizabeth Barstow Stoddard, Rose Terry Cooke, and Louisa May Alcott in the 19th century. Likewise, the class would problematize social, cultural, political metaphors, and the civil rights movements before we approach passages from Booker T. Washington and William E. B. DuBois in the early 20th century. (How can I, as a non-native–born Asian male, eschew such an exciting opportunity for a contact zone? I cannot, instead I must participate fully with my students in responding to feminist or African-American texts.)

In other words, in an attempt to situate historic texts here and now, class members seek critical understandings by developing individual gendered, racial identities as cultural roles. In my class, as students did their assignments, I read and wrote side-by-side, telling my reading and writing experiences, my understanding of American culture and history—my own negotiation with text. These classes are true discourse communities because both teacher and student read, speak, and write frequently in order to forge and reforge their public identities and voices in this full-contact environment where all members, *including the instructor*, are participants in the language process.

Beyond a visual marker, then, instructor identity could operate as a literary construct in the literature classroom. As in composition instruction, where we find value in personal essays exploring individuals' relevance (thus helping students develop authorial voices) (Brannon & Knoblauch, 1982; Danielewicz, 1997), in literature instruction, I can take the same risk I desire students to take, by making a voice and by reading the self. As a foreign-born Asian-American instructor, teacher-modeling enhances my visibility from multiple and concrete standpoints. From day one, my ethnicity has been my pedagogy. While my Asian identity was only "unimagined" and "inevitable" in the "world of English tradition" (Chiang, 1993, p. 23), it is now an agency, arguably, within a larger social plot constituted by the many cultural texts and roles.

Third Location: The Ethnic Teacher as Feminist Faculty

Yuet-Sim D. Chiang (1993) of the University of California, Berkeley, argues that one should not treat the comment, "How can a Chinese teach you

English?" lightly, because it reminds her, a woman of color, of other examples of marginalization. She is curious about her perceived identity as an English as a Second Language (ESL) teacher, although her specialty and current employment are in rhetoric and composition. At a faculty meeting in another university, her friend's colleague once argued that non-native speakers should not be awarded English degrees because they would become English teachers (Chiang, 1993, p. 27). Chiang views these phenomena collectively as a manifestation of "entrenched Eurocentricity." In Composition Studies, one might argue that, based on the field's "feminization" (as interpretative lens, according to Holbrook, 1991, to understand the profession's reliance on and association with female faculty), or its "counterhegemony" (as political practices, according to Miller, 1991, to address gender inequalities), Eurocentricity appears in composition as "androcentricity" (Schell, 1996, p. 100). This entrenchment, Schell observes, could be directly addressed by Susan Jarratt and bell hooks who "represent feminism as an oppositional pedagogy designed to boldly and unapologetically confront—rather than avoid—issues of gender, race, class, and sexuality" (p. 99).

Throughout my professional transformations, I remember critical, but helpful, remarks made about writing program administration and composition studies beginning from the satirical "I want a writing director," by Bloom (1992), to the narratives of Welch (1993) or of Bishop and Crossley (1996), and to the recent growth of feministic scholarship within composition studies. Mentored by Gail Hawisher and a few other leading United States female professors, I realize that I must be shaped by their theoretical perspectives, professional roles, and work. Might faculty of color learn from their female colleagues, especially in terms of identity negotiation within department politics and then in composition studies as a broader intellectual field? I turned to bell hooks.

Foss, Foss, and Trapp (2002) have argued that, different from traditional rhetoricians, hooks's theory of marginalization and marginality points to how the location of the rhetorical theorist or rhetor informs the kinds of knowledge generated about rhetoric and the types of rhetoric that are produced. In other words, her theory explicitly takes into account race, gender, and class. For hooks, marginality becomes a "site of radical possibility, a space of resistance ... a central location for the production of a counter-hegemonic discourse" (quoted in Foss et al., 2002, p. 272). hooks legitimizes the personal experience by asserting that in "certain circumstances, experience affords us a privileged critical location from which to speak," and rhetors, accordingly, with particular identities employ a "passion of experience" that "cannot be acquired through books or even distanced observation and study of a particular reality" (p. 273). To hooks, direct experience, sometimes, can be "the most relevant way to apprehend reality" (p. 273). Understanding hooks's subjectification of the black female's experience as a vantage point, one might argue for a parallel regarding the feminist faculty. As a construct, then, the feminist teacher as rhetor operates from a vantage point enabling a double vision of both her own knowledge and the knowledge of the dominant culture. More importantly, the feminist teacher, like the black female in hooks's theorizing, offers an experience that demands a rich presentation and re-presentation, as an active rather than passive agent, in the mainstream academic culture. According to hooks, the feminist professor has joined in a movement functioning as a constructive, proactive force. This force seeks to transform relationships and the larger culture so that "the alienation, competition, and dehumanization that characterize human interaction can be replaced with feelings of intimacy, mutuality, and camaraderie" (p. 274).

Schell (1996) defines feminism, in practice, as a broad label for a certain pedagogy, a research methodology, a rhetoric, and a social critique related to other movements for social change and transformation (p. 97). Particularly related to this chapter would be feminist pedagogical methods, which Schell summarizes as an emphasis on personal voice, shared pedagogical authority, and collaboration. Influenced as a graduate student in the mid-1980s, I could see nothing but articulation among the social-theoretic model of writing, the feminist initiatives, and classroom strategies when I began teaching full time in 1992. Among other teaching theories, I subscribed to the concept of writing community as a pedagogy of equity almost immediately and continue to do so.

Fourth Location: The Postmodern Instructor in the Modern University

Despite the belief that most English Ph.D. programs aim at producing vigorous academics, the better graduate transitioning into the job market must be an excellent teacher-scholar, who needs to continue his or her research interest both in theory and in practice. The candidate, I would argue, should be prepared in negotiating his or her "postmodern" self that underscores dialogues and differences, while facing recruiting committees in the "modern" institution that concerns itself more with curriculum uniformity, measurable objectives, and accountable budgets, than empowering students. This perspective necessitates an ideology of location and the reflection of it, placing the candidate (or new faculty) along the spectrum of roles ranging from the intertextual, dialogic, or even antifoundational position on one extreme end, and the budget-driven, outcome-assessment-based, and uniformity-minded position on the other. Understanding "our evolving field, our priorities, and the changes in writing instruction and administration," as Bishop and Crossley (1996) remind us, is most important so that it would be possible for us to avoid "our own misunderstanding" that could perpetuate the story of victimization (p. 78).

While composition studies as a field has been critically informed by postmodern theory, the full strength and benefits of postmodern pedagogy that desires and supports emerging student voices, especially in lower-division classes, are yet to be realized. At the heart of the challenge lies the irony of encouraging student autonomy on the one hand, while reinforcing formal academic discourse (writing programs normally endorse) on the other. As a newer director of English Composition, I have been asked to review the program, implement the curriculum, and assume a central role in preparing new teaching assistants for their teaching assignments. One significant challenge I face, while balancing national recommendations and local needs, is to transform and transition the previously prescriptive program into a desirably democratic one. And yet, as a more recent graduate in rhetoric and composition, I had experienced difficulties in understanding the old program (which called for absolute uniformity down to the common daily agenda, an argumentative exit exam, and weekly program assignments). As a result, I needed to reposition myself by acquiring a renewed and necessary understanding of the transition by probing the heart of the challenge—which is a gradual realization or repositioning of the postmodern faculty identity in a modern university. I realized that if I made all the desirable changes, I would have a completely different theoretical overview and rationale; I also knew that my new overview would seem to align more with things postmodern—less emphasis on assessment and more room for the dialogic or personal—even if ideas might come from graduate teaching assistants themselves. Perhaps not as a surprise, the first project I took on was to replace the single-essay exit exam calling for an in-class argument, assessed analytically, with an exit writing portfolio soliciting multiple genres (including a student-chosen piece and a reflective essay), assessed holistically. While periodic instructor and student surveys have indicated high satisfaction regarding the change, I also encourage open communication especially via a composition program listserv.

As a teacher-model encouraging dialogues, the writing program administrator needs to reflect on his or her daily multiagenda, which invites constructive feedback from students and instructors. Such an attempt often fosters transformation and equity in discourse in composition classes. From the postmodern perspective, this position statement remains tentative—awaiting responses from the community as an ongoing conversation.

The Fifth Location: The Reflexive Self

Now I Get It: A Comp Tale

In the fall of 1992, I taught English full-time at a community college of 4,000 in the suburb of St. Paul, Minnesota. Still shocked by the heavy teaching load and the less-than-motivated students at mid quarter, I decided to tell one of my freshman composition classes a classic Chinese story on the relationship between knowledge and perspectives. "Long, long time ago, there were two teenage monks engaging in a heated debate in front of a flag post. While speculating on the movement of the flag flying in the wind, one of them says, 'The flag is moving.' The other responds, 'No, the wind is moving, and that is the only truth.' They continue for a while until the Grand Master appears. Hearing what they have said, he quickly gives the monks knocks on their heads, and says, 'Nothing is really moving except your busy minds!'" My class responded with a minute of silence, and then slowly expressed their surprises about the philosophical overtone of the story. I chipped in a thought about epistemic perspectives. Two interesting incidents followed that telling.

At a student-teacher conference, Katie, a fair-complexioned, young lady in her usual sweatshirt and khakis, expressed her concern about my telling the story. "You know, Dr. Eng, some of us were not very comfortable hearing the story. ..." she hesitated to continue. "Why, Katie?" I asked. She then uttered, without looking directly at me, "You know people don't use the word 'monk' because it is a bad word." "Oh, really?" I was genuinely surprised. "You know monks are *stupid* people?" she added, "You can get into trouble just by saying that...." "Well, I never thought about it that way—I thought I meant the priests in the Buddhist context," I professed nothing but ignorance. (Even if I later found out that she might have confused "monk" with "Hmong," the refugee population settling in St. Paul since the early 1980s, the hint of racism remains.)

At another conference, Jennifer, in her typically gothic makeup and Oakland Raiders attire, seemed curious as to why I questioned part of the information she included in her invention process, which was a mapping exercise aiming for discovering ideas to include in her essay on interracial dating. In one of her circles of ideas, she had two issues phrased as "dealing with kids," and "planning on having more kids." Reading it again, I simply asked if they belonged to the paper. I said, "Are you expanding on the topic now, Jennifer? Is it interracial *dating* or interracial *marriages*?" "No, I don't want to talk about marriages," she seemed certain about it. "But," I continued, "people who date don't plan on having kids unless they are getting married, right?"

"No, some people do." I paused and thought about it for a minute, then said "Got you!" as soon as I could utter the phrase. For her, not me, it did belong to the essay.

Of the many events that happened in my first year of teaching in a community college, these three incidents seem to stand out in my memory, and I can't tell if they were really separate cases or all in the same boat. In retrospect, I remain amazed at how the worlds are different and how apparently it is so especially between the teacher and the student. Or, how it is even more so along socioeconomic lines, between national and linguistic origins, and indeed between the nontraditional English professor and the traditional composition student. When it comes to communicating with students and understanding student text, it truly demands our reading with an open mind.

Beyond the empathetic standpoint, I have found co-inquiry to be central to a pedagogy that underscores the discourse community, knowledge construction, and voice. Not unlike hooks (1994) who is "willing to be critical" of her own pedagogy by attaching herself to her writer identity (instead of the professor's) (p. 134), I can teach with more investment in all of my classes by locating myself as a co-inquirer with my students. We, as a class, read, think, and write together both in spirit and in practice. In undergraduate composition classes, we frequently use personal experiences as springboards, approach topics situated in their socioeconomic and sociopolitical contexts researched collaboratively, and share works in progress and its experience. In graduate rhetoric classes, we debate about contemporary rhetoricians' relevance to classical rhetoric, our favorite rhetorician and its justification, and develop and share our own concept papers. In research methodology classes, we bring to the seminar table interests, questions, and challenges existing in current projects, data collection and analysis, and even human subject review protocols.

As a co-inquirer, I am more than willing to consider different viewpoints and philosophical differences; I don't speak, according to course evaluation in the form of anonymous student surveys, in authoritative terms. Further, there have been numerous opportunities for which I could articulate connections among teaching, research, and university service. Students in the co-inquiring classroom, I hope, continue to benefit from the professor's investment both physically and intellectually. While I am aware of my privileged location as a male university professor compared to many of my students' as first-generation college attendees, co-inquiry as a pedagogy can exist ethically when one is vigilant against research appropriation, selfishness, and abuse. The best classroom then functions as a learning forum co-owned by students and their professor, therefore expanding opportunities for critical discourse involving all class members.

Envoi

While the five locations developed in this chapter might sound arbitrary, they are in fact interrelated, evident in links between I and II, III and IV, IV and V, and, from the critical teaching standpoint, among all. The challenge, it seems, is to keep positioning oneself from a pedagogically vantaged point so that, other than dispelling myths, the nontraditional professor is teaching effectively *and* meaningfully because of a needed incorporation of the reflective, interactive, and cultural roles. Such a role requests conversation and underscores participation among colleagues, students, and audience inside and outside academia.

The feeling of double-consciousness is particularly significant among nontraditional English faculty. To many, having the experience of domination and exclusion simultaneously while teaching within a postprocess decade suggests both complexity and opportunities. In the end, we cannot deny that, while critiquing systems of domination, lines between native and non-native–born faculty, and those between privileged and nonprivileged locations have to be blurred and that the critiquing act itself has to be understood with complexity as a reflexive activity.

In reflection, Villaneuva (1997) captures a major slice of the faculty of color's growth, similar to my own as a person born in the colonized Hong Kong but having my graduate education and professional growth entirely grounded in the United States:

> ...He [American mainland-born, of Puerto Rican ancestry] has gained access but not much power. He abides by rules his coworkers don't even recognize as rules, rules of a system created by, peopled by, serviced by, and changed by, members of cultures and classes and histories much different from his own; systems created and maintained by those whose memories do not include having been colonized. He is often taken aback by how his co-workers think in worldviews radically different from his own. Yet he struggles to join in the conversation with the privileged whose senses of decency compel them to seek equity for those who have been traditionally excluded from the mainstream of society and from the academic tributary. Sometimes he thinks he's heard. (p. 623)

As postprocess pedagogy exposes inequality and powers (Tobin, 2001), I believe that this pedagogy, being a mix of efforts somehow mobilized in effecting changes, also fosters equality and integration within classroom discourse and beyond. As Prendergast argues, in a rather timely and constructive way, for a critical awareness of *all* racialized selves within composition studies:

> ... if we are to understand the mechanisms (like racism) that prevent some students from being heard, we need to recognize that our rhetoric is one which continually inscribes our students as foreigners. We might observe, for example that Asian-American students don't exist in composition studies—they are either ESL students or unnamed (white). The discrimination that Asian-Americans face (in some cases through their positioning as "model minority") is culturally unintelligible within composition's discursive space. Meanwhile our white students are not portrayed as "having race" at all. The present challenge for compositionists is to develop theorizations of race that do not reinscribe people of color as either foreign or invisible, nor leave whiteness uninvestigated; only through such work can composition begin to counteract the denial or racism that is part of the classroom, the courts, and a shared colonial inheritance.... (1998, p. 51)

Times have indeed changed. Decades ago, the customs officer would probably never admit to his condescending humor. Likewise, as student or faculty, I would not have pursued this research on the connection between pedagogy and identity politics, had it not been for the growing scholarship in composition studies, feminism, and beyond, role models as professors of color, and even the existence of this forum on symbolic struggles. As a fellow language-user in the classroom, the proposed locations and the concept of co-inquiry have helped me situate identity politics within the practical teaching contexts. In cycles, I *learn from* my students as I *teach them* English. Within complex educational systems of ideological production and reproduction, students and their instructors need to learn and grow together in active discourse environments that underscore voice and identity.

At the year 2000 Conference of College Composition and Communication, Wendy Bishop, convention chair that year, asked me rather personally if she did pronounce my name correctly as a travel grant recipient, and I said, "Really close." Other memorable events happened that year, together with a family loss of my great uncle, Yee Gee, who had served in WWII as an American soldier and lived in this country since the early 1910s. Claiming a passionate and reflexive role in composition instruction, I now seize the opportunity of transforming the pedagogy by admitting that I am, after all, marginal and marginalized, but meaningfully so.

References

Anzaldua, G. (1987). *Borderlands/la frontera*. San Francisco: Aunt Lute Books.

Bakhtin, M. (1981). *The dialogic imagination* (M. Holquist, Ed.), (C. Emerson, Trans.). Austin: University of Texas Press.

Bartholomae, D. (1988). Inventing the university. In E. R. Kintgen, B. M. Knoll, & M. Rose (Eds.), *Perspectives on literacy* (pp. 273–285). Carbondale: Southern Illinois University Press.

Bishop, W., & Crossley, G. L. (1996). How to tell a story of stopping: The complexities of narrating a WPA's experience. *The Journal of the Council of Writing Program Administration, 19*(3), 70–79.

Bizzell, P. (1986). Foundationalism and antifoundationalism in composition studies. *Pre/Text, 7,* 37–56.

Bloom, L. Z. (1992). I want a writing director. *College Composition and Communication, 43,* 176–178.

Braine, G. (Ed.). (1999). *Non-native educators in English languge teaching*. Mahwah, NJ: Lawrence Erlbaum Associates.

Brannon, L., & Knoblauch, C. H. (1982). On students' right to their own texts: A model of teacher response. *College Composition and Communication, 33,* 159–166.

Chiang, Y. D. (1993). In the world of English tradition, I was unimagined. *Illinois English Bulletin, 80*(4), 22–27.

Chiang, Y. D. (1998). Insider/outsider/other? Confronting the centeredness of race, class, color and ethnicity in composition research. In C. Farris & C. M. Anson (Eds.), *Under construction: Working at the intersections of composition theory, research, and practice* (pp. 282–291). Logan: Utah State Press.

Danielewicz, J. (1997). Developing voice in the writing classroom. *Dialogue: A Journal for Writing Specialists, 3,* 23–40.

Foss S. K., Foss K. A., & Trapp R. (2002). *Contemporary perspectives on rhetoric* (3rd ed.). Prospect Heights, IL: Waveland Press.

Freire, P. (1998). *Teachers as cultural workers: Letters to those who dare teach*. Boulder, CO: Westview.

Fuss, D. (1989). *Essentially speaking: Feminism, nature, and difference*. New York: Routledge.

George, A. (2001). Critical pedagogy: Dreaming of democracy. In G. Tate, A. Rupiper, & K. Schick (Eds.), *A guide to composition pedagogies* (pp. 92–112). New York: Oxford University Press.

Harding, S. (Ed.). (1987). *Feminism and methodology: Social science issues* Bloomington: Indiana University Press.

Holbrook, S. E. (1991). Women's work: The feminizing of composition. *Rhetoric Review, 9*, 201–229.

hooks, b. (1994). *Teaching to transgress: Education as the practice of freedom.* New York, NY: Routledge.

Horner, B. (2000). Traditions and professionalization: Reconceiving work in composition. *College Composition and Communication, 51*, 366–398.

Johnson, C. L. (1994). Participatory rhetoric and the teacher as racial/gendered subject. *College English, 56*, 409–419.

Kingston, M. H. (1989). *China men.* New York: Vintage Books.

Kirsch, G. E. (1993). *Women writing the academy: Audience, authority, and transformation.* Carbondale: Southern Illinois University Press.

Kirsch, G. E., & Ritchie, J. S. (1995). Beyond the personal: Theorizing a politics of location in composition research. *College Composition and Communication, 46*, 7–29.

Miller, S. (1991). The feminization of composition. In R. Bullock & J. Trimbur (Eds.), *The politics of writing instruction: Postsecondary* (pp. 39–54). Portsmouth, NH: Boynton/Cook.

Mura, D. (1991). *Turning Japanese: Memoirs of a Sansei.* New York: Atlantic Press.

Okihiro, G. Y. (2002). *Margins and mainstreams: Asians in American history and culture.* Seattle: University of Washington Press.

Pratt, M. L. (1991). Arts of the contact zone. *Profession, 91*, 33–40.

Prendergast, C. (1998). Race: The absence presence in composition studies. *College Composition and Communication, 50*, 36–53.

Rich, A. (2001). Notes toward a politics of location. *Arts of the possible: Essays and conversations* (pp. 62–82). New York: W.W. Norton & Company.

Romano, S. (1999). On becoming a woman: Pedagogies of the self. In G. E. Hawisher & C. L. Selfe (Eds.), *Passions, pedagogy, and 21st century technologies* (pp. 249–267). Logan: Utah State Press.

Rose, M. (1985). The language of exclusion: Writing instruction at the university. *College English, 47*, 341–359.

Rose, M. (1989). *Lives on the boundary.* New York: Penguin Press.

Schell, E. (1996). Feminism. In P. Heilker & P. Vandenberg (Eds.), *Keywords in composition studies* (pp. 97–101). Portsmouth, NH: Boynton/Cook.

Sciachitano, M. M. (1993). Reclaiming spaces for our voices, our histories, our writings, ourselves: Women of color in the writing classroom. *Illinois English Bulletin, 80*(4), 28–34.

Shaughnessy, M. (1977). *Errors and expectation: A guide for the teachers of basic writing.* New York: Oxford University Press.

Shor, I., & Freire P. (1987). *A pedagogy for liberation: Dialogues on transformative education.* Westport, CT: Greenwood, Bergin-Garvey.

Spivak, G. (1987). *In other worlds: Essays in cultural politics.* New York: Methuen.

Tobin, L. (2001). Process pedagogy. In G. Tate, A. Rupiper, & K. Schick (Eds.), *A guide to composition pedagogy* (pp. 1–18). New York: Oxford University Press.

Villaneuva, V., Jr. (1997). Considerations for American Freireistas. In. V. Villaneuva, Jr. (Ed.), *Cross-talk in comp theory: A reader* (pp. 621–637). Urbana, IL: NCTE Press.

Welch, N. (1993). Resisting the faith: Conversion, resistance, and the training of teachers. *College English, 55,* 387–401.

6

WHITE WOMEN TEACHERS IN INDIGENOUS CLASSROOMS:
Ruptures and Discords of Self

Jan Connelly

School of Education, University of New England, Australia

Introduction

This chapter focuses only on the experience of being a white woman teacher in a school serving an indigenous semi-urban community. These experiences challenged the teacher's notion of identity and its inherit subject/subjectivities and revealed her complicity inside whiteness processes. What became apparent, in the educational scholarship and pedagogies surrounding white teachers' concepts about how best to "be" teacher, was that critical dimensions remain unquestioned inside fields of indigenous education in Australian schools.

A chapter such as this cannot do justice to the historical legacy of indigenous people of Australia. Many indigenous people work hard to overcome the daily trauma that issues of racism, poverty, and health effect their communities. In light of this, the commentary here may seem too subjective in respect to broader indigenous educational issues. Although I make no mention of the enormous efforts many educators and community members make towards alleviating the educational disenfranchisement indigenous students experience, I hope that I convey a story that offers an archive strongly supporting a shift of focus away from sole solution remedies of resource allocation (human and material) towards the problematising of white teachers' concepts of their pedagogies, particularly the implicitness of their subjectivities and the performance of these inside their pedagogical practices.

As a white female academic with a strong sense of social justice, I aim to offer an extract from an inquiry recently undertaken in a field of difference—an indigenous educational context. The inquiry focus sought an answer to the question, "How do white women teachers respond to localised indigenous educational settings?" I believe that by answering this question I can create some archival data to add to a body of new knowledge and thus contribute to the broader understanding about pedagogical discourses surrounding indigenous education.

Here is just one white women's narrative drawn from a set of such data collated in a poststructural inquiry during the processes of doctoral research.

A White Woman Teacher

Jenny is a vibrant woman in her late 40s. She holds a strong commitment to the education of all children and an enduring concern for equality of opportunity and learning. With the 1970s hippy mantra of "peace, love, and happiness" still echoing in her psychic, Jenny commenced teaching 26 years ago in a small country town with a highly visible indigenous community.

Focus on Identity

Having experienced the performance of teacher as subject in similar contexts, I have come to understand that one's identity/ies and their embedded subject positions predetermine the responses a person makes to various contexts. It might be accepted that as a person forms an identity, he/she "lives it out" but it is by no means fixed, as over time there are shifts due in part to social, political, economic, and educational influences—rendering a performativity of multiple identities. Identity shifts can be painful; tensions such as value incongruence create distortions and external influences press for change. When expressions such as "loss of identity," "not knowing who I am," "losing one's way" are voiced, they exemplify such tension. This inquiry is premised on the notion that teachers' identity tensions emanate from the conforming, "normalising" pressures of white identity constructs of what it means to be a woman and what it means to be a professional teacher. Such tensions and identity shifts do in turn impact enacted pedagogy particularly when the pedagogy is manifested at cultural borders of difference.

A Story from and with Jenny

Jenny:

It takes a certain type of person to move into a school like Ridgeville and be effective with the Aboriginal kids. The average Anglo-Saxon white person from the middle class would find it extremely difficult to see where the Aboriginal kids are coming from, be able to relate to them, empathise with them and teach them.

What constitutes *a certain type of person* for Jenny is somebody who has a background that predisposes them to be able to "relate." Within minutes of the interview commencing, Jenny had created just such a subject position for herself. She explained:

Jenny:

I think the big difference between me and other teachers was being able to empathise with the Aboriginal kids, but the white community resented me for it. I was called a "black lover" by one parent. I remember once when I was walking down the street and one of the mothers, who was drunk was sitting in the gutter of the bottom pub at Ridgeville. She could hardly walk and was really sick; she sang out, "Miss Green, Miss Green", I went over and said "Martha I will help you home". And here I was walking up the street, the local schoolteacher with this drunken Aboriginal woman. I helped her up to the school, which was near the mission. A white person called me a black lover. That happened to me a number of times. We had a number of school functions and all the Aboriginal kids would be milling around me and I would be talking to these drunken parents and the white community couldn't relate to that at all and didn't like it very much.

Jenny's responses to the indigenous students and the community, represent as nonconformity to the white community's imposed normalizing discursive practice of the subject position of "white woman teacher." Throughout the narrative, Jenny articulates her values and practices. Her performance of the white teacher rests on these, and delineates her identity at any one time. However, they are in contrast to the white community's construct of the subject position of the white woman teacher. According to the white community, a white woman teacher wouldn't condone behaviour such as public drunkenness. The white teacher would instead, be detached, thus showing distain for such behaviour and conveying the message that acting in this way is unacceptable. To help, as Jenny did, is a failure to perform that white woman-teacher-subject position that calls for detachment and noncondoning of the behaviour.

Jenny:

I think that the big difference with me was that I had an alcoholic father. I look back at that and hated it at the time but we cared for him, loved and looked after him and I think it taught me a lot of compassion. I think that it was the best thing that ever happened to me, for in later years I was able to understand where his alcoholism came from, With the wisdom of hindsight I can see why these Aboriginal women were alcoholics too. They were deprived, they weren't allowed to speak their language; they were dispossessed of their land and their language and were just so traumatised. These were all women mainly by themselves, the men just came and went and they [the women] were all raising the families. I was able to empathise with them and I still do today.

When you've been teaching there a long time you do either one of two things;

1. You turn off and become so straight and won't change for anyone; that is, you can't empathise with the Aboriginal kids or the white kids in crisis. When teachers respond this way they haven't got a hope of getting through to the kids. They have discipline problems in their classes all the time, and they kick the kids out all the time, or
2. You are flexible and empathise with the students and keep trying.

The first type of teacher cannot relate to all that they experience here; they find it really alien. They don't even try to understand where people are coming from. They expect everybody to react the same and behave the same as they would or their children would. They find it hard to cope if they don't.

The absenteeism/truancy issue is really big here, even when kids turn up at school there can be partial absences too as a result of a lot of the kids deciding they don't want to do something, so they go and hide under a building and some of the teachers are really stressed. They find it hard to cope. If one of the Aboriginal kids leaves the classroom, the teachers don't even try to bring him back. They just don't want that extra pressure.

What Jenny infers is this: That when indigenous students don't reflect normalizing practices, that is, those expected behaviours and responses that the dominant white culture endorses, then teachers are "thrown"; they don't know how to cope/how to respond. They either reject the student's responses and detach themselves from the task of educating the indigenous student, or they are empathic. Although it is not mentioned in Jenny's narrative, this later response can be unproductive too, if it is one that also compromises the curriculum because of sympathy for the socioeconomic or emotional plight of the students.

In the process of identity construction, Jenny names her own "otherness." Counter to the identity of a professional teacher, Jenny's identity reflects characteristics of *compassion, understanding,* and respect for *traditions,* awareness of *dispossession* and *traumatisation* and acknowledgement of the strains of *raising families* alone. Jenny's subjectivity can be described as one of *empathy* and *humanitarianism*. These inscribe her default identity (in the e-sense). Deviations/alternatives to this default occur. Circumstances bring forth different responses when the acting out of the default identity creates a dilemma; for example, when it fails to be congruent with a professional teacher-subject position. It is at these times that Jenny's shifts of subjectivity emerge. What was of concern for Jenny was that such fluidity was emotionally and professionally unsettling.

It could be claimed that the humanitarian identity Jenny claims for herself is her inscribed identity, and is an always already "becoming" subject. It is fluid and is shaped by the unfolding years of experience and influenced by social, political, and educational changes. Jenny uses the metaphor of a journey to convey the influences and changes that bring them about. Her construct of a humanitarian identity is a rational response born out of the era of free spiritedness of the 1970s, the influence of a very loving and compassionate mother role model, and also her own experiences of poverty. Closely linked to the humanitarian/missionary identity is the Christian notion of a martyr; Jenny demonstrates that she can take hardships personally inflicted on her.

> It has been a journey. I have definitely had a journey working with Aboriginal people. When I first got to Ridgeville I was very green, keen, very naïve and bent over backwards to cater to the needs of the Aboriginal kids and the community. I really loved it and learned heaps. Now when things get really tough, I experience a level of physical exhaustion that I have never experienced before; there are just so many things happening I just can't cope with. I think, I just have to tough this out, and I get really tight and really stressed in the shoulders. I just feel like setting my forehead against the flint stone or holding onto that plough like in the scripture in the Bible and just doing it.
>
> At the end of last term I had been physically assaulted and I was physically and emotionally exhausted. I was on playground duty and everyone was collecting marbles and stealing marbles. There was so much theft going on and one little boy accused a little girl of stealing his sister's marbles. He is a really violent boy and he is on ADHD (Attention Deficit Hyperactive Disorder medication). He is actually quite psychotic and he thinks people are looking at him. He came up to this little girl and he said, "you stole my sister's marbles," and he was really threatening. I said to him, "You need to go out of this playground" and I said to Samantha "you stay with me because I don't trust him." As I went to walk away with Samantha he had this big bag of marbles and with two hands he just hit her over the head with it. I thought her head was going to fall apart. He punched her three times really hard. I stepped in between them because I thought he was going to kill her. He just attacked me

with the bag of marbles and hit me across the arms and punched me so
hard in my right kidney that I nearly fell down.

Then he realised what he had done and there were all these other kids
around and he just took off. The kids would have lynched him if they had
got hold of him for hurting me. I don't hold anything against him for that
because he has emotional problems. I said to his parents, "It is all right;
I know that he has problems" and I made them feel a bit better about it
because the mother was feeling so bad. I don't hold grudges.

In the mid 1980s, economic circumstances in Ridgeville saw the closure
of the timber mill and the turn down in production at the small goods meat
works. This had an impact on school practices and policy as Jenny explains.
It also presented a challenge to her humanitarian identity positioning.

Jenny:
    I got to a point in my career where I felt really frightened about how
I was thinking. I felt I was becoming racist. I had been working there in
the school with many indigenous students, and also in what was a very
poor white community with very depressed dairy farmers and men working at the mill for less than the basic wage. And the white kids were really
poor, they were in a poverty cycle. These poor white kids could never go
on school excursions and it is still the same today. Yet the Aboriginal kids
always had so much tangible support. They get Abstudy[1] and there is the
ASSPA[2] (Aboriginal Student Support and Parents Association) funding for
indigenous students which was used by this association for taking the kids
away for a week. We would spend thousands of dollars on experiences that
not only Aboriginal kids would never have had before but the poor white
kids would never have had either. You'd see the poor white people in the
community and then you'd see some drunken Aboriginal people throwing
bricks through people's car windows and shop windows in town, and you
would just think; where is the equity in that?

    I thought I was becoming really racist; I was going to the other end of
the spectrum from starting off so keen and being all for Aboriginal rights;
then I found myself going in exactly the opposite way. Now I think there
is more of a balance; I speak of "mutual responsibility", where there has to
be a two-way street.

    But even having said that, I see a contradiction because at the same time
I can see that the Aboriginal people in Ridgeville historically lost their land,
lost their language, and almost lost their culture. At the same time I understand that a lot of Aboriginal parents didn't have a very good school experience; they didn't learn and found it hard to fit into the school situation; most
of them left school early and school for them was just an alien thing. Add
to this the fact that we struggle to know how to cater to the needs of our
Aboriginal students. Still today a lot of them aren't learning as well as they

should. So I have gone from the one extreme of being very keen and really pro-Aboriginal, to feeling quite racist and quite negative about what is happening; but I am more in the centre now. I still get really frustrated that the parents can't be bothered to feed their children properly and that they don't take any interest in the education of their kids and it is almost impossible to get them up to the school.

Jenny's language reveals identity shifts conveyed through incidents of emotional exhaustion, resulting from the encounters with a community in crisis: impoverished circumstances involving various degrees of drug abuse, violence, and sexual abuse. Occasionally, the identity shifts are framed inside self-posed questions: "How can I get through and maintain my integrity?," "Who am I?," and "Who can I be for them?"

A Poststructural Analysis

In the following, I draw out the philosophical concepts of identity and subject/subjectivities, that is, the condition of being subject *to*, or a subject *of*. For Jenny, these were essentially the "teacher" subject, the "woman" subject, and the "white" subject. The notion of subjectivity is constituted of direct and indirect experience and mediated by the discourses that lend conceptual order to our perceptions, points of view, investments, and desires. Subjectivity is both our conceptual ordering of things and the deep investments summoned by such orderings. It organises an individual's ideas about what it means to recognize oneself as a person and a teacher and arranges strategies for the realisation of these multiple identities (Britzman, 1995, p. 57).

The use of subjectivity as a focus for deconstruction exemplifies what I have come to label a poststructuralist analysis of narrative data. This was achieved by overlaying the tools of Critical Discourse Analysis (CDA) on narrative episodes in order to deconstruct subjectivities. Luke (1997) and Van Dijk (1993) explain that CDA is a repertoire of political, epistemic stances: principled reading positions and practices for the critical analysis of the place and force of language, discourse, text, and image in changing contemporary social, economic, and cultural conditions.

The analysis was alert to significant words, statements, inferences and innuendo, and philosophical concepts:

1. That demonstrated the frames of reference out of which a white woman operated her teaching life.
2. That revealed relationships of power and resistance between the teacher, students, and community.

3. That recognized discourses of truth/knowledge that conveyed what the participant held as "truths," that in turn formed the "knowledges" from which she operated.
4. That demonstrated the subject position of subjectivities that the teacher projected.

There have been a number of methods proposed as analytic categories/taxonomies (Fairclough, 1989, 1992; Van Dijk, 1997; Wodak, 1996). Although they vary, they do share a common strategy that involves a principled and transparent shunting back and forth between the microanalysis of texts using varied tools of linguistic, semiotic, and literary analysis and the macroanalysis of social formations, institutions, and power relations that these texts index and construct (Luke, 2002).

The following extract attempts to draw out how a white woman teacher was being positioned by and was positioning herself through her linguistic choices and appropriation of particular discourses, representations, identities, and intertextuality cues. In order to carry out the work of critical discourse analysis, I used a taxonomy of deconstruction tools ("unpickers") taken from the writing on CDA.

Through the use of these tools, tensions were identified in the narratives; these were the entry points for analysis. CDA theorists would say that the approach enables a close and responsible reading of the data. At the same time that I utilised these analytical tools by zooming in on data samples, for the purposes of microanalysis, I also recognized the need to zoom out and pan the horizons and contours, and perform what I will call macroanalysis. This is where social and cultural formations are foregrounded. These include historical processes, institutions, and power relations that further inform the meanings that were constructed and indexed through microanalysis.

CDA Microanalysis

What follows is a visual representation of the adaptation of CDA based on Van Dijk's approach discussed in "Critical Discourse Analysis" (2001). The first two categories are drawn from the linguistic influenced models of CDA (Halliday, 1985). The third traces the discourses of social formations, power relations, and subjectivities more aligned with the work of Foucault.

Table 6.1 Critical Discourse Analysis Taxonomy

---

(1) **Linguistic signs: lexical and surface structure**

- – Generalisations
- – Nominalising phrases
- – Lexical pairs
- – The use of persuasive and biased vocabulary

(2) **Pragmatic signs**

- – Use of metaphor
- – Questions
- – Answers, evasions, contradictions
- – Implications and presuppositions
- – Use of pronouns such as "I" and "we" and their implied group references
- – Inclusions, exclusions and allegiances

(3) **Discourses flows**

- – The dimensions of the relationship between discourse and power across the social domains of inequality, gender, and race
- – "We" discourse, justifications, blaming the victim/deficits/trivialisations, denials, constructing the other as enemy, patronization, and colonialisation
- – Other discourses, where cultural differences in terms of sociopolitical differences, deviations from the norms and values, pathologies, violence, and threat are enhanced and magnified and similarities ignored or mitigated

---

Adaptation of CDA (Van Dijk, 2001)

The manner in which the category of tools (Table 6.1) was applied is demonstrated below in an extract of Jenny's narrative drawn from *The Ridgeville Meeting*. The words and phrases highlighted align with the CDA categories and are explained below each data section, thus demonstrating the employment of the criteria used in the processes of microanalysis.

The Ridgeville Meeting

> *We started a food program through ASSPA (Aboriginal Student Support & Parents Awareness Program) funding, it is pretty ironical though, the white kids can't get any benefit, even though we have a lot of poor white kids at school. So this fruit is laid on for the Aboriginal kids—but most of the Aboriginal population seems to be very prosperous. So they might get three or four pieces of fruit but they have got five or ten dollars to spend and they will go down to the canteen and will buy Twisties and those horrible flavoured shapes and just eat so much junk.*

Discourses

Contradiction

'*pretty ironical*'—a threat to values and beliefs—the abuse of tenets of welfare and equity—Aboriginal kids get free fruit yet have plenty of money.

Linguistic signs

Generalisation

'most Aboriginals seem prosperous'

Equity/Disadvantaged

Equity concept shaken—contradiction binary of fair/unfair apparent on the one hand '*but*' on the other

Bias

'horrible flavoured shapes – eat so much junk'.

It actually spun out of control last year, none of them brought any food to school; they are doing more so now. We were spending thousands of dollars out of ASSPA funding just in food. I remember one day, I got so cranky about these secondary girls never bringing their lunch that I said to the Principal,' I am going to go to the next ASSPA meeting and talk to the parents about this', as it was just more of this 'handout mentality'.

Pragmatic Signs

Metaphor

'*spun out of control*' signals a deviation from the 'norm' and Othering process in evidence

Discourses

A pathology deficit

'*handout mentality*' a discourse prevalent among whites to explain the perceived dependency Indigenous people have in respect to welfare assistance.

'*Othering*' *Comparisons*

'*like our kids have got to*' equating white kids—her own—with Indigenous teenagers.

These kids are old enough to pack their own lunches, they have got plenty of money to spend at school, they can go and buy it and learn a bit of responsibility, like our kids have got to, and pack their own lunches. The word must have got around the Aboriginal community, so I go to this ASSPA meeting and it was loaded [many Aboriginal parents present], there were a couple of people that were really militant and they were there.

Discourses

Re-inscription/normalization

Jenny takes a stance, Her adherence to the subjectivity of humanitarianism of equity has propelled her 'into action'... she does not want to go against the tenets of this subjectivity and thus compromise her values, which she feels has been happening until now when she decides to take this stance. Co-dependency has been occurring, *'it is much easier to just keep feeding the kids...'* in terms of one's values and beliefs thus an 'absorbing' of what one doesn't really want to do. There is a saturation point; Jenny has reached it, a point when this symbolic violence—of 'deviational responses' from her norm—will not be continued. Wanting to maintain normalcy propels Jenny to act.

I thought, I'm putting my head on the chopping board here. It was really fiery to start with but I felt really strongly about it, and I said. "I wouldn't do this if I didn't care, if I didn't care about you people, I wouldn't be here saying this, I would say, "Well, it is much easier to just keep feeding these kids". I said I care and I hate seeing these kids that are just as capable as my own kids, who can't even pack their own lunch. This is survival stuff here I am talking about.

Pragmatic Signs

Imagery

Use of sacrificial imagery 'putting my head on the chopping block', 'I do it because I care and in order to':

- keep the school structures looking normal, i.e., kids being fed and alert to learn,
- maintain the professionalism of the role as teachers.

Discourses

Patronization/Colonialism & Othering

I wouldn't do this if I didn't care about you people.

The Ridgeville Meeting: Its Analysis via Microanalysis CDA

The "handout mentality" prevailing in the discourse of the teachers was due to a perceived abuse of a welfare strategy: poor white students did not have the benefit of free lunches, thus issues of equity were called into question. Jenny wanted to "do something." Calling a meeting was a brave move. Jenny realized that when it came to indigenous issues in the school, most teachers would take the easy option, that is, just keep providing the lunches. The purpose of the meeting was to bring to the attention of the parents and community members the abuse of the free lunch welfare strategy because there were students who had money, and yet took a free lunch and also purchased food at the canteen. These were older students who were capable of making their own lunches at home, but it seemed they were increasingly relying on the free lunch.

Given that tensions existed and were growing as equity discourses were being challenged, the question to be asked is: Did the meeting resolve tensions? It was determined that free lunches would continue to be provided—ASSAP funding is primarily targeted towards the needs of indigenous students and finances are set aside for that specifically, so the school had "no leg to stand on" in challenging the provision of the lunches. The meeting outcomes were that the lunches would be given out under the following conditions:

1. In order to receive a free lunch, the senior students must bring in a note from a parent that says there is no food in the house (perhaps it is one or two days before the next pension/benefit pay).
2. It is also determined that a note from home can cover those times when parents are "on a binge" (an extended period of intense drinking).

There are complexities and ironies here: If the meeting was called because it was believed that high school students were capable of making their own lunch, couldn't they also write the note as if they were the parent? Even if there was food in the house, were students taking advantage of a free lunch to save themselves the trouble of preparing it at home? And, why shouldn't they take the free lunch? It was ASSAP who determined the money be earmarked for lunches after all. Another aspect of the note writing is that the onus is placed on parents to prove that they are needy. This could appear to be a colonising act, in that, indigenous people have to justify their need and yet again appear to be beholding to the "whitefella." What presumption can be drawn from this? That alcohol binges are seen as the norm and thus a legitimate reason why the students wouldn't have lunch? Or, is it a reality that both the school personnel and Ridgeville residents accept? Given this reality, in practical terms, how can parents on a drinking binge write a note?

Did the meeting provide a solution, or just a number of strategies that appear as a form of a resolution? When I asked Jenny if the situation changed after the contestation occurred from there being too many inappropriate free lunches given out (when students appeared to have money to purchase their lunch), her answer was, "only slightly." What then did this attempt to normalise achieve? In reflecting on the meeting, it can be asked, did it, or did it not, placate Jenny's sense of justice and fairness in terms of equity for all students (both indigenous and non-indigenous) in the school who come from low socioeconomic circumstances? As nothing changed, Jenny was left to absorb the contradiction to her values by not preventing inequitable practices, and seemingly fostering a lack of responsibility and denying the older students practice in life skills.

Revealing Subjectivities

The processes depicted within this data extract demonstrate how the taking of a stretch of significant text and "reading" it through these given CDA categories can demonstrate how one teacher was being positioned through her appropriation of particular discourses and material practices. Via the above microanalysis, the teacher's linguistic choices and discourses represent her representations of enacted subjectivities and power structures and can be summarised in this way:

> When Jenny equates indigenous teenagers' practices with those of white teenagers, she is constructed as a teacher who appropriates racist categorisations, shows evidence of a "them" and "us" binary, and has "forgotten" or has "overlooked" the chasm of historical and social experience of being Othered, that indigenous people inherit as their legacy. There is discursive employment of "biased" phases and connotations of a "blame the victim" discourse, evidenced through patronising, and colonising expressions. I will argue here that a multilevelled analysis, as opposed to a microanalysis alone, provides a different "reading" and can be explained in this way:

When a teacher attempts to fulfil different subject roles and is faced with splintered and fractured ways of performing these (that is, the professional teacher, humanitarian woman, nurturing mother, with an overlay of white processes), what gets produced are responses to single incidents, that, on the surface, emerge as discourses that "look" racist and unsupportive of indigenous students and their communities. However, a broader lens—a macroanalysis—projects a more complex view.

Macroanalysis of the Extract

At a macrolevel, different interpretations are evident. These come about by considering the analysis of the microlevel against the backdrop of broader contextual elements and knowledge. This is where the internalised microanalysis meshes with, and is considered inside, broader structures of the research context. I refer here to sociopolitical and historical factors.

A Two-Level Analysis

When the two-level analysis was "performed," a (re)writing was then constructed that focused on how Jenny responded to her indigenous teaching context.

Jenny was a woman who had caring and nurturing at the core of her being. She had been a very strong person throughout her life. She ploughed on through life tackling all her school challenges as lessons to be learned and experiences to be endured. She did this with love and humour. She was the rudder upon which her school relied in aspects of indigenous education and negotiations with the community. Her years at the school had resulted in her knowing almost every one of the indigenous families; and she had some close friends amongst the women. She would be the first to admit that there was still much for her to learn and understand about the difficulties the indigenous people endure in their negotiations with a racially biased white world.

Jenny's dominant constructed subject positions were those of (a) nurturer and (b) professional woman teacher. These two subjectivities were not enacted without contradictions. In the school context, they were juggled and she found that due to this, fractures appeared in her identity construct. The incongruence between these subject positions was apparent when Jenny had to determine boundaries inside issues of fairness and equity. Jenny found that she could position herself inside the nurture-carer subject position only up to a point. It was not that she stopped performing out of this subject position, but that it carried a burden that got too heavy and she turned to the subjectivity of professional teacher to find solace in educational matters somewhat detached from the circumstances of the context the students were living in.

This is best exemplified in her response to the following probe:

> Jan (researcher):
> When you hear sad stories and experiences of abuse and neglect and poverty deprivations, how do you accommodate them? Do you take them on-board as a woman and a white person and pull yourself together and go back to school the next day and walk into the classroom as if these things didn't and aren't happening? How do you continue to be the best teacher that you possibly can? Do you think it affects you?

> Jenny:
> Yes I think it does and I think it can. I am trying to become less emotionally involved—more professional, I guess? One of the best things for me is being involved in professional development activities; these inspire me.

Values and Practices

Jenny's personal values and practices emanate from the Christian principles: "love thy neighbour," which could be set square in the camp of humanism; for example, the true will always be the same as the good and the right. Jenny's Christian ethics lead her to be alerted to injustices and inequalities. However, she finds these are too simplistic at times for they don't provide answers in her struggle to understand and respond to the complexities reflected in the lives of indigenous community members. Jenny also acknowledges other realities such as the fact that historical circumstances have brought about and sustained the disadvantages her students endure.

Whilst indigenous people have suffered the "wounds" of a colonised minority, whose historic treatment at the hands of a white majority was (and still is) framed in negative notions of the "Other," present circumstances of indigenous people's lives are becoming more complex with different traumatic circumstances occurring (e.g., the added cocktail of hard drugs and stimulants and alcohol). Although she understands this impact, at the same time she hopes for change in the future and works on new programs and plans new interventions that can help. However, she accepts that educationally, things have not gotten better in respect to successful student outcomes since she began teaching 25 years ago.

Concluding Comments

Schick's (2000) claims that women teachers hope that by performing the category of "teacher" they will find a place of comfort and security where their desires to make a difference to students' lives will be fulfilled and not thwarted. However, inside social, emotional, physical, and economic constraints of "the mission" where Jenny taught, there was much thwarting of this desire. Incredible ruptures to her white woman teacher identity construct were revealed. These were dislocations that presented as incongruence between Jenny's values and beliefs and notions of justice, and the values and beliefs of the indigenous community's members, due in large part to community people's lives being plagued by the legacies of colonialism and racism and by-products of poverty, unemployment, substance abuse, domestic violence, and sexual abuse of children.

Through the snippet of data and narrative analysis I have shared here, it is possible to "see" a white teacher juggling tensions between identity and subject positions. These, in turn, impact on her teacher enacted pedagogy.

Mindful of the knowledge created through this narrative analysis, an educational implication is to ask what now must be done, and how can this knowledge about performance tensions inside subjectivities generate different pedagogical understandings and possibilities for the education of Australian indigenous students? "What now must be thought and thought otherwise" (Derrida, 1994, p. 59).

Endnotes

1. A government financial support scheme to encourage indigenous students to stay on at school in high school.
2. ASSAP—Aboriginal Student Support & Parents Awareness Program. It is funded by the government, but is administered by the parents.

References

Britzman, D. P. (1995). The question of belief: Writing poststructural ethnography. *Qualitative Studies in Education, 8*(3), 229–238.

Clough, P. T. (1998). The end(s) of ethnographic authority. *Representations, 1*(2), 118–146.

Derrida, J. (1994). *Specters of Marx* (P. Kamuf, Trans.). New York: Routledge.

Fairclough, N. (1989). *Language and power.* London: Longman.

Fairclough, N. (1995). *Critical discourse analysis.* London: Longman.

Foucault, M. (1988). Technologies of the self. In Martin, L. H., H. Gutman, & P. Hutton (Eds.), *Technologies of the self: A seminar with Michael Foucault* (pp. 16–49). Amherst: University of Massachusetts Press.

Halliday, M. A. K. (1985). *An introduction to functional grammar.* London: Edward Arnold.

Luke, A. (1997). Material effects of the world: Apologies, "stolen children" and public discourse. *Discourse, 18,* 343–368.

Luke, A. (2002) Beyond science and ideology critique: Developments in critical discourse analysis. *Annual Review of Applied Linguistics, 22,* 96–110.

Schick, C. (2000). White women teachers accessing dominance. *Discourse: Studies in the Cultural Politics of Education. 21*(3), 299–309.

Van Dijk, T. A. (1993). Principles of critical discourse analysis. *Discourse & Society, 4*(3).

Van Dijk, T. A. (1997). *Discourse as social interaction. Discourse studies: A multidisciplinary introduction* (Vol. 2). London: Sage.

Van Dijk, T. A. (2001). Critical discourse analysis. In D. Tannen, D. Schiffrin, & H. Hamilton (Eds.), *Handbook of discourse analysis.* Malden, MA: Blackwell.

Wodak, R. (1996). *Disorders of discourse.* London: Longman.

7

DISCOURSES OF SCHOOLING, CONSTRUCTIONS OF MASCULINITY, AND BOYS' NONCOMPLETION OF SECONDARY SCHOOL IN NORTH QUEENSLAND, AUSTRALIA

Ingrid Harrington

School of Education, University of New England, Australia

Introduction

The educational experiences of rural young people are those of less success than their urban counterparts on a number of counts. Their participation in education at age 16, their school retention to year 12, and their participation in higher education are all lower than for urban youth; their achievement outcomes are also lower (Higher Education Council, 1999; Human Rights and Equal Opportunity Commission, 2000; Kenyon, Sercombe, Black, & Lhuede, 2001). Since educational participation and achievement contribute to employment and income prospects, and minimize the frequency and duration of unemployment, these lower rates for rural young people are a matter of concern (Ainley & McKenzie, 1999; Spierings, 1999). More generally, this imbalance has implications for Australia's National Goals for Schooling, the "intellectual, physical, social, moral, spiritual and aesthetic development" of rural young people (Ministerial Council on Education, Employment, Training and Youth Affairs [MCEETYA], 1999), especially in the context of contemporary economic, social, and cultural change (Youth Pathways Action Plan Taskforce, 2001).

The Higher Education Council (1999) points out that "local social and cultural networks and values" are important in this context, as "aspirations for higher education ... are influenced by a subtle web of interwoven characteristics" including "the collective values of the local community culture" (p. i–ii). The Council noted that there had been little research into "attitudinal factors influencing student choice among population subgroups" (p. 13). In fact, the use of single categories of rurality or isolation in large-scale studies has meant an almost complete dearth of studies that might capture any local community variations in these cultural influences.

This chapter will investigate the links between masculinity and early school-leaving within a rural cultural setting. This chapter concerns a perceived (and for some individuals, a real) risk attributed by society to those boys who do not finish their secondary schooling. The risk directly centres on the long-term ramifications for those boys who leave school early, and concerns itself that not all noncompleters have the resources to cope in the workforce without completing their year 12 qualification.

Background

A plethora of research has been conducted into the area of boys' school retention and associated factors (Ball & Lamb, 2001; Collins, Kenway, & McLeod, 2000; Dwyer, 1996; Epstein, Elwood, & Maw, 1998; Fensham, 1986; Gilbert & Gilbert, 1998; Jones, 1998; Poole, 1986; Teese, Davies, Charlton, & Polesel, 1995). In particular, the retention of boys to year 12 has been problematic (Collins et al., 2000; Commonwealth of Australia, 1994). The apparent retention rate (ARR)[1] to year 12 indicates that in 1999, 21.5% of females and 33.6% of males left before completing year 12 in Australian schools (Collins et al., 2000). It is this gender disparity that has focussed attention on the retention of boys. There is no suggestion here that increasing the retention of girls is not also an important issue. Indeed, evidence about postschool experience suggests that year 12 completion is more important for girls than for boys in its effects on employment and income (Alloway & Gilbert, 2001). However, it is still the case that boys' education is being curtailed to an extent that is a justifiable cause for concern. Ball and Lamb (2001) found that boys who are most at risk of school noncompletion experience low school achievement, attend government schools, live in rural or remote areas with a low socioeconomic status, are of indigenous origin, and/or have parents who were born in Australia or another English-speaking country, and who did not complete school.

Lamb, Dwyer, and Wyn (2000) suggest that boys and girls who decide to leave school early form an "exposed" category of young people, and they argue that noncompleters are likely to become the most vulnerable to economic and social change. They add that due to social and economic changes over the past 20 years, students have been forced to rethink the value of pursuing an education as there are likely to be future disadvantages for students who do not maximise their individual educational opportunities. A recent study by King (1999) discusses more specifically the individual costs associated with students who leave school early, and conservatively estimated the cost to the nation of early school-leaving alone to be in the vicinity of $2.6 billion a year, if costs to the government and the rest of society (as well as individual costs) are included in the estimates.

Studies into the differences among students' educational pathways have typically used large-scale statistical surveys of participation and retention, or questionnaire or interview attitudinal surveys. These studies have identified a range of contributing factors, including the interaction between rural location and socioeconomic status, gender, the quality of the school experience, and the cost of overcoming the tyranny of distance (Higher Education Council, 1999). However, Marks, Fleming, Long, and McMillan (2000) estimated that the variation in year 12 participation accounted for by measures of achievement, gender, occupational background, region, school type, and father's birthplace at only 14%. They show that the role of attitudes, motivations, and aspirations is just as significant. This focuses attention on personal and cultural factors.

Understanding gender and its role in the construction of masculine identities and available discourses to these boys in their geographical location, I concur with West (1993) who defined gender as the "local management of conduct in relation to normative conceptions of attitudes and activities that are appropriate for particular sex categories." She concluded that "... reconceptualising gender as an accomplishment that is ongoing in interaction means that we must locate its emergence in specific social situations, rather than in the individual or some loosely-defined set of role explanations" (p. 64).

Hence, the construction of gender must vary according to the specific local assumptions and social practices in a particular context (Connell, 1995a; Evans, 2000). The construction of masculinity, therefore, will also depend on the specific local assumptions of a geographical location (Kenway, 1997; Long, Carpenter, & Hayden, 1999). When this conception of gender is taken with Connell's definition of masculinity as "a configuration of practices around the position of men in the structure of gender relations" (Connell, 1994, p. 3), we can see how constructions of masculinity can be differently played out. The "configuration of practices" emphasizes what people do, not what is necessarily expected. What people do is embedded and constructed through large-scale organizations and the political system. Their actions have a rationale (although they may not be rational) and an historical meaning. The "position of men" is with respect to their male bodies and social relations, and the "structure of gender relations" refers to the fact that gender is more than the face-to-face interaction between men and women but also involves large-scale structures embracing the economy, state, family, and sexuality. Because these structures impinge on forms of masculinity in powerful ways, it follows then that while different masculinities are produced in the same social context, there is likely to be a dominant, or hegemonic form with other subordinate forms (Connell, 1995a). Any particular form of masculinity is complex and contradictory as masculinity does not equate gender with a category of persons, due to the fact it is not a sole characteristic of men (Connell, 1994).

Connell (1995a) claimed that male hegemonic masculinity is typically heterosexual and viewed as the epitome of what it means to be a "real" male in today's society. Subordinate masculinity is seen as the polar opposite of hegemonic masculinity as it recognises feminine traits and attributes men may exhibit; homosexual masculinities, and the more gentle, "soft" male are included in this form. Complicitous and marginalised masculinities occur when men, despite having a link to hegemonic masculinity, negotiate societal and cultural practices such as marriage, fatherhood, and aspects of community life in a more subordinate, covert manner. Connell refers to this as the "relations between the masculinities of dominant and subordinated classes or ethnic groups" (Connell, 1995a, p. 80). He argues that just as hegemony, subordination, and complicity are relations internal to the gender order, the interplay of other factors such as class and race also play central roles in the construction, maintenance, and deconstruction of this social masculine hierarchy.

Connell (1989) reminds us that school provides the opportunity for different male groups to partake in the construction, deconstruction, and maintenance of hegemonic masculine identities. This constant making and remaking of the boys' masculine identities is part of a much larger process of successfully negotiating multiple masculine identities required to navigate a way through the many different social contexts that constitute their daily existence, that is, son, older/younger brother, student, peer, and team player. This chapter will suggest that different hegemonic forms of masculine identities exist for boys; some are constructed through the discursive practices of schooling, and others exist outside school. It appears from the noncompleter transcripts that when boys effectively position school as the constitutive "other" (Davies, 1993; Soendergaard, 2000), they concurrently construct their masculine identity by considering the subordinate, complicitous, and marginalised forms of masculinity as the "other." A factor influencing the noncompleting boys' decision to leave school early appears to be their desire to be recognized as having membership of a nonschool-based discourse as they negotiate their masculine identity.

Analysis of the storyline to follow, "No one told me school was going to be like *this*" found in the noncompleting boys' narratives revealed that they had two significant agendas. One was a dislike of schooling per se typically characterized by the taking up of nonparticipatory discourses. Another agenda was an apparent constant jostling by the boys whilst at school to achieve their desired status within the masculine hierarchy in a "contest of hegemony" (Connell, 1994), organized around social power between different groups of males. Essentially, these boys were actively negotiating their masculine identity within this "contest of hegemony" set at school. The act of leaving school and being out in the workforce provided an opportunity for these noncompleting boys to re-create a masculine identity, one that they felt at ease with, and one they claimed was not achievable at school.

Despite the existing knowledge and research into boys' school performance, participation and retention, the role of masculinities in the decision-making process(es) of school noncompleters has received little attention. Acknowledging this gap in research relevant to masculinities, this chapter will examine the ways in which some noncompleting boys constructed their masculine identity through negotiating their positioning of the constitutive "other" whilst at school. It will further examine which aspects of educational discourse they took up in order to "make sense" of their school-leaving decision.

Method

This current research was set within a larger project co-managed between Education Queensland and James Cook University, Townsville. The research partnership between the ARC/SPIRT[2] and James Cook University was a three-year longitudinal study entitled *Factors Affecting Boys' Engagement with Schooling at the Secondary Level*. Relevant to this current research, questions were addressed through a single semistructured interview to a total sample of seven male noncompleters from Mitcham[3] and Listerfield in North Queensland. The noncompleting boys were chosen at random by the schools and each boy was contacted for an interview. The researcher was interested to make links between their school experiences and the masculine discourses they took up to "make sense" of their decision to leave school.

Mitcham is a small coastal town situated in far North Queensland of approximately 10,500[4] residents from diverse socioeconomic, ethnic, and cultural backgrounds. Mitcham offers the services of a Technical and Further

Education college (TAFE), and other community-based education learning centres to cater for its community's learning needs. It is well resourced for sporting and recreational activities. Mitcham's local economy is driven by a combination of tourism, sugar cane harvesting, and banana-growing interests. The town regularly experiences a seasonal influx of transient workers, taking up the opportunity of well-paid, casual employment, either harvesting sugar cane or bananas.

Listerfield is set inland and comprises a community of approximately 21,000 people from wide socioeconomic, ethnic, and racial backgrounds that gives the city a distinctly multicultural character. Despite its remote location, it is well serviced offering a range of sporting, recreational, cultural, and social opportunities. This is confirmed by strong support links with the community and welfare agencies providing necessary structures for the highly transient nature of its population. The city is dominated by a mine, which serves as the major employer in the city, and different forms of mine management such as strategic planning, restructuring, and resizing impact greatly on the community, small business, employment, and school enrollment. It is estimated that the mine employs directly and indirectly 80% of the town's local population.

The school leavers that were interviewed comprised three noncompleters from Listerfield and four from Mitcham. Of the Listerfield group, two boys left prior to completing year 10 (early school leavers) and one left with his year 10 certificate, and all three at the time of interview had locally based, full-time employment. The four boys from Mitcham did not return to school after successfully completing year 10, and three of them had locally based full-time employment, whilst one was trying to secure employment. The interview questions invited the boys to share their general experiences of school. Specific points of interest included the influence that peers, teachers, and parents had on their academic performance, participation in activities, subject choice, and postschool pathway plans.

This chapter will discuss the storylines (Bruner, 1990) found within the total sample of noncompleting boys' "generative themes" (Friere, 1972) relevant to their school experience, employment, and sense of masculine identity. Bruner's concept of "story" and "storylines" is a useful tool in understanding the ways in which the boys position themselves in their narratives and "make sense" of their experiences within their school cultural context. Additionally, using feminist poststructuralist discourse analysis, data were analysed through the use of positioning (the constitutive "other") and common binary sets found in the boy's storylines (Davies, 1993; Weedon, 1987). The notion of binaries is a conceptual framework that has been developed in order to understand how discourse operates. The basis for the binary analysis is the general pattern of the "first" (ideal construction) being offset by an "other," which, through a form of negative differentiation, helps to constitute the first position (Davies, 1993; Weedon, 1987). This process of positioning enables a clearer understanding of how boys' identities are continuously constituted and negated as a set of social and cultural premises within a particular geographical location. One set of cultural premises of gender of particular interest to this research are constructions of masculinity and femininity.

Initial thematic analyses of the transcripts indicate that common generative themes were evident in the narratives of the noncompleters. A significant view expressed by these boys was their dislike of school and each boy employed a range of different storyline discourses to explain this dislike. Other dominant themes that emerged from the boys' narratives, apart from their dislike or hatred for school, were boys' feelings of powerlessness and helplessness within the wider schooling system (Gilbert & Gilbert, 1998; Smyth, Hattam, Cannon, Edwards, Wilson, & Wurst 2001; Trent & Slade, 2001). Furthermore, most boys claimed their decision to leave school early was part of a larger process. They indicated their bitterness to the (mis)use of power and authority vested in teachers and commented on a feeling that teachers subscribed to a "put up or shut up" attitude when working with students. Some boys interviewed claimed they were happy with their decision to leave school, but others voiced regret for leaving school when they did. It is through the boys' positioning of school and certain masculine identities as the constitutive "other," that we are able to gain a good insight into the factors affecting their decision to leave school. We are able to understand what factors are deemed to be important to these boys when considering the discursive resources they privilege as they construct their masculine identities. I will now explore the first of the generative themes focussing on their general dislike for school.

"No-One Told Me School Was Going to be Like *This*"

Accompanying the boys' dislike of school, they expressed elements of surprise and disbelief when describing some of their school experiences. In explaining this aspect of the storyline, "No-one told me school was going to be like *this*," some boys discussed how surprised they were to discover how irrelevant some subjects were to their future; others talked about the mis(use) of the teacher's power and school authority, and the restrictive nature of activities; and for others, their discussion centered around their experience that school for them was simply "too boring." These elements are shared by the research of Trent and Slade (2001). In the main, the noncompleter's expectations about certain aspects of schooling such as teachers, homework, and subject content appear to have clashed unexpectedly with the reality that was school. Different boys illustrated this incompatible relationship by drawing from their school experiences what will be explored next.

At the interviews, most noncompleting boys appear to have aligned their masculine identity with what they understood to represent a particular hegemonic construct of masculinity found only in the workforce, and discussed in positive ways how this distinguished them from those boys who chose to remain at school. Analysis of the boys' narratives revealed that the noncompleting boys also positioned education and further schooling as the constitutive "other" (Davies, 1993), essentially negative and antithetical to being employed in the workforce. Recalling the significance of their school experiences, a number of boys linked these usually negative experiences, some as early as grade 6, to their understanding that they would not complete year 12. For instance, when some boys were asked whether they always knew they would leave school early, some responses were

Student:	Yeah.
Interviewer:	When did you decide you would not finish school?
Student:	Grade 6 or 7.
Interviewer:	What happened in those years?
Student:	I just got bored of school.
Interviewer:	How did you get bored of school at grade 6 or 7?
Student:	Well it's just you learn your basic English in Primary school, and after that it's not worth learning it again. Why go over it again? (Josh, Mitcham)
Student:	Yep.
Interviewer:	When did you know that you wouldn't finish year 12?
Student:	Grade 6.
Interviewer:	What happened in grade 6?
Student:	I just hated school. ... It's not the learning, it's just everything else. ... It's just really boring being locked in with other kids. (Brendan, Mitcham)
Student:	Oh yeah, I knew I'd get expelled from school before year 12. It was only a matter of time. ... I'd prefer to say 'I'll leave' before [the school] expelled me. ... It's like quitting before getting fired. (Max, Listerfield)
Student:	Yeah, I knew way back school's not for me 'cause there's no lifestyle at School. ... You just go there to learn a couple of things, but you actually learn more here out working, so that's what I'm doing. (Peter, Listerfield)

For these boys, their dislike of school and ultimate decision to leave school appeared to be part of a process of "making sense" of the negotiations of their gendered identity. When they discussed their school experiences, school was represented in the negative as not fulfilling their needs or expectations in some way. It seems that for Josh and Peter, the relevance of certain curriculum offerings was too vague and they considered it an unnecessary waste of time. For Max and Brendan, school appeared to represent a place from which escape was highly valued. It is apparent that for these boys, school in some ways did not provide what they deemed to be important for them. Each boy seemingly found aspects of school irrelevant or an impediment to their process to "become somebody" (Wexler, 1992), that is,

> ... the product of this process [being] identity, selfhood ... which the students work to attain through their interactions in school. The process is the organized shaping of a distribution of images of identity. These images ... make a difference for how the student defines herself and is reciprocally defined by and designing of friends, teachers and parents. (pp. 8–9)

At the time of the interview, Josh, Brendan, Max, and Peter were employed in full-time jobs, and it is from this perspective they discuss their school-based masculine identity. Justifying their decision to leave mainstream education, the boys recall questioning aspects of schooling. By constructing school as the constitutive "other," they effectively construct life outside of school (such as being employed) as easy, fun, exciting, and certainly not boring, and concurrently construct the "other" masculine forms (subordinate and marginalised) (Connell, 1994) associated with boys in school.

For these boys, they may have incurred difficulty in "becoming somebody" (Wexler, 1992) at school. Considering the "othered" forms of masculine identity as undesirable components of their ideal masculine identity, these boys left school to gain membership by becoming legitimate members of out-of-school discourses, in their case, out in the workforce. The act of taking up educational discourses of nonparticipation whilst at school was effectively a manner in which they flagged their disaffiliation and dissatisfaction with the masculine discourses at school. For those boys who are unable or unwilling to construct and maintain masculine identities that conform to the requirements of educational discourses of school, school appears to become a site for conflict and dissatisfaction. This may lead to the taking up of anti-authority schooling discourses usually resulting in inappropriate behaviour, poor participation, noncompliance, and a claim that school is both "irrelevant" and "boring." Ultimately, it appears to be these boys who opt to leave school early.

It is interesting to note the ubiquity and ease with which the notion of "boredom" is used by most boys interviewed as an explanatory tool for their dislike of school. To illustrate my reading of the context in which the boys use the term "boredom," I suggest the boys take up an aspect of a school-based popular culture discourse, and effectively engage the two binaries of relevance/irrelevance and significant/insignificant. This aspect of school-based popular culture discourse epitomises an expectation of instant gratification of school-based work with minimal effort by the student. It is easily recognisable through inappropriate attitudes and behaviour and participation at school from students. I suggest that constitutive of an aspect of this popular culture discourse is the storyline of school-based boredom, and it is this storyline that, in turn, is constituted by the two binaries of relevance/irrelevance and significant/insignificant. The noncompleting boys appeared to take up this aspect of popular culture when they deem one or more aspects of schooling as "boring." My reading of the context in which the noncompleters use the binary of relevance/irrelevance links directly to their perception of how relevant they feel learnt skills will be to their specific career application as illustrated by Josh and Peter. In explaining the boys' use of the significant/ insignificant binary to their school experience, I borrow from Polkinghorne's (1988, p. 25) definition of significance where he correlates the significance of an event to "meaningfulness and importance" to one's life. The noncompleting boys draw from the significant/insignificant binary when referring to the usefulness of learning to broader applications in their life.

Trent and Slade (2001, p. 33) found in their research that when boys talk about both schoolwork and teachers being boring, they do so through inseparable aspects of the one process they simply call "school." This included the school organization and culture, the length of the lessons, the day, the school week, the term, the homework, uniforms, attendance, and behaviour expectations from the teachers.

Another theme that emerged from the boys' narratives involved the role of the teacher in their overall educational experiences. Most boys had negative issues with teachers and when the noncompleting boys were asked what constituted a "good" teacher, the general consensus was one Instead of 'one' write 'the same'?

Student: … if they catch you doing something bad they won't just immediately get you in trouble, they'd talk to you, tell you not to do it again and understand. They'd reason with you instead of consequences brought straight up and you're in trouble, and try to talk you out of doing it again … It would just feel that she's not on your back the whole time. (Peter, Listerfield)

Student: … someone you can have a laugh with and that one who treats you more like an equal. (Mark, Mitcham)

It seems the noncompleters' ideal construction of teachers was one in which the teacher could be part of more informal friendly relations such as "having a laugh with," and were flexible enough to accommodate student behaviour within the confines of a classroom without taking behaviour personally, or be seen to be narrow-minded or old-fashioned. Unfortunately, most noncompleter's ideal construction of teachers appears to be antithetical to their school experiences. When the boys were asked to describe their feelings regarding teachers and their school experiences, they effectively positioned teachers as "bad" through their construction of the constitutive "other" as follows.

Student: They are just bad, bad, bad, bad, bad, I don't know, just arseholes like most of them are.

Interviewer: How were they bad?

Student: Oh, just their attitude towards you, they keep on starting with you, their language would be worse. … I've been called a dickhead and all that by teachers at school. (Brendan, Mitcham)

Student: If all the teachers aren't nice, you don't want to go to school, let alone learn … they can be really grumpy. … One day something good would happen and they would be really happy at school and you want to do work. … I don't know, you can just tell by their attitude when they walk in the door pretty well first thing what sort of day it's going to be. (Scott, Mitcham)

Student: If there's a pissed off teacher there and he's sitting down writing something and all that, you're not going to go up and ask for help and talk to him about this and that. You can tell, even if you want to go up and talk to him you can tell that he's pissed off … 'cause of his breathing; he'd be sitting there and sighing, and you just ask 'what's the point? There is no use sitting there and talking to him.' … and I've said that once, I said 'you get paid by the hour to help kids out and look at what you do, you just sit there,' and that was to the Maths teacher.

Interviewer: What did he say about that?

Student: He just laughed. (Brendan, Mitcham)

Student: Well, there was heaps to learn but they wouldn't continually help you out to make you learn it, they would just give you the work and say learn it, and that was it, just do it. … Once

	I got stuck, I just pretty well just packed the work up and sat around and did whatever I wanted to do. (Jim, Listerfield)
Interviewer:	Do you know why your marks were low? Why were you struggling?
Student:	Oh, the teachers mainly and a bit of keeping up, and then I just gave up. ... I don't know, when you get so far behind you can't understand what they're doing so you're even more behind and they expect you to keep up, so they don't understand and help you catch up, so what do you do? I just gave up. (Andrew, Mitcham)

It is evident by the boys' construction of "bad" teachers as the constitutive "other," that we see how in the spirit of a contemporary popular culture discourse, they appear to construct their ideal of teachers and learning as fun, easy, and being entertained. It is also evident by their positioning of "bad" teachers, that the boys link their poor academic performance, and lack of interest and participation in subjects to the teacher in some manner. Positioned as the "other," teachers and schooling generally ceased to be relevant and significant to these boys and school. Most boys left with no space to enunciate their displeasure of school partook in discourses of antiauthority embodying disruptive behaviour and oppositional resistance. As mentioned, this inappropriate behaviour, so often cited in research on boys' school behaviour (Archer, Pratt, & Phillips, 2001; Gilbert & Gilbert, 1998; Smyth et al., 2001; Trent & Slade, 2001), appears to serve two purposes: namely to forge and advertise their masculine identity at school to their peers, and to overtly show their feelings of frustration and disappointment of not having their expectations and ideal constructions of schooling met. Hence, as the noncompleting boys claim they found learning more significant and relevant outside the classroom, the choice to leave school must have appeared as quite an attractive alternative to school.

Another aspect of the noncompleters' interviews that will not be discussed in this chapter is that most noncompleters reported a barrage of other negativities linking the role of the teacher to the quality of their educational experiences. This concurs with existing research by Trent and Slade (2001) that reported boys' claims of poor academic performance, low self-esteem, a loss of motivation to learn, poor class attendance, and the decision to leave school early (resulting in what they claim to be limited career options), somehow linked to the influence of teachers. It could be interpreted that through their discursive actions, the boys positioned themselves in ways that fundamentally shifted responsibility for their own learning, by attributing blame to someone or something (not the "self") for an assortment of negativities at school.

Conclusion

There are commonalities that exist in the transcripts of the rural non-completers. The complexity of the constructions of schooling and their constitutive structures of power and gender are evident from the narratives of the noncompleting boys. I have illustrated the disparity that exists between the boys' ideal schooling constructions and their experienced schooling reality, emphasising how antithetical their relationship is to each other. I have shown that evident through the interview transcripts of noncompleters was a common theme of disaffiliation with school and the negative impact most boys perceived teachers had on their school experiences in general.

Some boys often remarked on an unwillingness to accept some strictures, constraints, and disciplines of school, and a number discussed how school failed to provide relevance and meaning in their schooling context. A shared sentiment about the boys' school experience is echoed by research that asserts that most noncompleters feel misunderstood and "let down" by the institution of school as a whole (Archer et al., 2001; Trent & Slade, 2001). In the absence of an enunciated "space" at school, the noncompleting boys take up a variety of discursive practices underpinned by common binary sets of relevance and significance to express their dissatisfaction with schooling.

This chapter has shown the existence of links between forms of masculinities and early school-leaving, also that there are distinctive schooling discourses and processes of positioning that illustrate the ways in which noncompleting boys continuously construct their masculine identities. This constant construction of boys' masculine identities is part of a much larger process of successfully negotiating multiple masculine identities required to navigate a way through the many different social contexts that constitute their daily lives. The boys draw upon these discourses and constructions as they attempt to "make sense" of their employment and schooling, that has implications for the cultural context in which they are living. These are important considerations for future schooling and education policy.

Taking the ongoing process of boys' construction of their masculine identities into consideration, recent initiatives by Education Queensland to address this aspect include a five-year trial of its *New Basics* framework to be delivered in 59 schools throughout Queensland. The project aims to have a strong curriculum delivery focus on four clusters of practices that are essential for survival in the worlds that students, especially boys, have to deal with. These four areas of transdisciplinary learning include Life Pathways and Social Futures, Communications Media, Active Citizenship, and Environments and Technologies. These new approaches have the potential to offer a much wider range of learning experiences in both primary and secondary schooling than has traditionally been the case. The curriculum now becomes more appealing and "in touch" with real world issues; hence, more realistic and relevant learning and assessment tasks are possible. Boys are now able to draw positively from discourses of school and relevant learning and maintain an association with their preferred masculine identity whilst still at school.

Other initiatives to address the education of boys have included the trailing of single sex classes, and the addition of ongoing professional development training for teachers specifically in the areas of pedagogy and curriculum assessment for boys. Literacy and numerical competence at the early childhood and primary levels has been shown to be central to boys' positive engagement and performance at school. Literacy and numerical support, early diagnosis and intervention for those deemed "at risk" of literacy underachievement, and the addition of remedial programs have been a strong focus in an attempt to ensure all boys' schooling experiences are positive.

Some considerations for the future schooling of boys are wide reaching and complex in nature. This chapter has highlighted a range of cultures that impact the learning and interpersonal styles associated with boys in school. The successful and enjoyable education of boys in the future depends upon flexibility, initiative, and meaningful links between the school, employers, and wider society. It is hoped that these initiatives will encourage more boys to stay at school and further their education and employment potential.

Endnotes

1. The Apparent Retention Rate is a crude index of retention in that it shows the number of students who remain in year 12 as a percentage of the number, in that cohort, who started secondary school the relevant number of years previously (Collins et al., 2000). It does not include intersector, interstate, or repeating students.

2. Australian Research Council and the Strategic Partnerships with Industry—Research and Training Scheme.

3. All locations and names used in this chapter are pseudonyms.

4. All population figures cited were provided by the Australian Bureau of Statistics, 2001 Annual Census data.

References

Ainley, J., & McKenzie, P. (1999). The influence of school factors. In Dusseldorp Skills Forum (Ed.), *Australia's young adults: The deepening divide.* Sydney: Dusseldorp Skills Forum.

Alloway, N., & Gilbert, P. (2001). *Factors associated with participation of male students in higher education studies at James Cook University.* Unpublished report, School of Education, James Cook University.

Archer, L., Pratt, S., & Phillips, D. (2001). Working-class men's constructions of masculinity and negotiations of (non) participation in higher education. *Gender and Education, 13*(4), 431–449.

Ball, K., & Lamb, S. (2001). *Participation and achievement in VET on non-completers of school* (LSAY Research Report Number 20). Melbourne: ACER.

Bruner, J. (1990). *Acts of meaning.* London: Harvard University Press.

Collins, C., Kenway, J., & McLeod, J. (2000). *The factors influencing the educational performance of males and females in school and their initial destinations after leaving school.* Canberra: Department of Education, Training, and Youth Affairs, Commonwealth of Australia.

Commonwealth of Australia. (1994). *Working nation: Policies and programs.* Canberra: Australian Government Printing Service.

Connell, R. (1989). Cool guys, swots and wimps: The interplay of masculinity and education. *Oxford Review of Education, 15,* 291–303.

Connell, R. (1994, September 27–28). The making and remaking of masculinities in contemporary societies. Address given at *Reproduktion und Wandel von Mannlichkeit Conference*, Munich, Germany.

Connell, R. (1995a). *Masculinities: Knowledge, power and social change.* Los Angeles: University of California Press.

Connell, R. (1995b). Theorising gender. *Sociology, 19*(2), 260–272.

Davies, B. (1993). *Shards of glass: Children reading & writing beyond gendered identities.* NSW, Australia: Allen & Unwin.

Dwyer, P. (1996). *Opting out: Early school leavers and the degeneration of youth policy.* Hobart: National Clearing House for Youth Studies.

Epstein, D., Elwood, V., & Maw, J. (Eds.). (1998). *Failing boys? Issues in gender and achievement.* Buckingham: Open University Press.

Evans, R. (2000). *You questioning my manhood, boy? Masculine identity, work performance and performativity in a rural staples economy* (Research Paper, Number 4). The Arkleton Centre for Rural Development Research, Arkleton. Scotland: University of Aberdeen.

Fensham, P. (1986). *Alienation from schooling.* London: Routledge & Kegan.

Freire, P. (1972). *Pedagogy of the oppressed.* London: Penguin.

Gilbert, R., & Gilbert, P. (1998). *Masculinity goes to school.* London: Routledge.

Higher Education Council. (1999). *Rural and isolated school students and their higher education choices: A re-examination of student location, socioeconomic background, and educational advantage and disadvantage.* Canberra: National Board of Employment, Education and Training.

Human Rights and Equal Opportunity Commission (HREOC). (2000). *Emerging themes: National inquiry into rural and remote education.* Sydney: Human Rights and Equal Opportunity Commission.

Jones, J. (1998). *An exploration study into selected health protective behaviours of rural and urban men in north and north west Queensland.* PhD thesis, Department of Education, James Cook University of North Queensland.

Kenway, J. (1997). *Will boys be boys? Boys' education in the context of gender reform.* ACT: Australian Curriculum Studies Association.

Kenyon, P., Sercombe, H., Black, A., & Lhuede, D. (2001). *Creating better educational and employment opportunities for rural young people.* Hobart: Australian Clearinghouse for Youth Studies.

King, A. (1999). *The cost to Australia of early school-leaving* (Tech. Paper). Dusseldorp Skills Forum, National Centre for Social and Economic Modelling, University of Canberra, Canberra.

Lamb, S., Dwyer, P., & Wyn, J. (2000). *Non-completion of school in Australia: The changing patterns of participation and outcomes* (LSAY Research Report Number 16). Melbourne: ACER.

Long, M., Carpenter, P., & Hayden, M. (1999). *Participation in education and training 1980–1994* (LSAY Research Report No. 13). Melbourne: ACER, September.

Marks, G., Fleming, N., Long, & McMillan, M. (2000). *Patterns of participation in year 12 and higher education in Australia: Trends and issues* (LSAY Research Report No. 17). Camberwell, Vic.: Australian Council for Educational Research.

Ministerial Council on Education, Employment, Training and Youth Affairs (MCEETYA). (1999). *The Adelaide declaration on national goals for schooling in the twenty-first century.* Melbourne: MCEETYA.

Polkinghorne, D. (1988). *Narrative knowing and the human sciences,* Albany: New York Press.

Poole, M. (1986). *Idols-ideas-identities: Women in society.* Melbourne: AE Press.

Smyth, J., Hattam, R., Cannon, J., Edwards, J., Wilson, N., & Wurst, S. (2001). *Listen to me, I'm leaving: Early school leaving in South Australian secondary schools in the late 1990s.* Adelaide: Flinders Institute for the Study of Teaching.

Spierings, J. (1999). A crucial point in life: Learning, work and young adults. In Dusseldorp Skills Forum (Ed.), *Australia's young adults: The deepening divide.* Sydney: Dusseldorp Skills Forum.

Soendergaard, D. M. (2000). Destabilising discourse analysis, Approaches to poststructuralist empirical research, In I. Henningsen (Ed.), *Gender in the academic organisation,* (Working Paper No. 7), Copenhagen: University of Copenhagen.

Teese, R., Davies, M., Charlton, M., & Polesel, J. (1995). *Who wins at school? Boys and girls in Australian secondary education.* Melbourne: Department of Education Policy and Management, The University of Melbourne.

Trent, F., & Slade, M. (2001). *Declining rates of achievement and retention. The perception of adolescent males.* Evaluations and Investigations Programme, Higher Education Division, Department of Education, Training and Youth Affairs, The Flinders University of South Australia.

Weedon, C. (1987). *Feminist practice and poststructuralist theory,* Basil Blackwell: London.

West, C. (1993). Theoretical achievements and challenges in European gender studies. *Rural society, 3*(4), 2–8.

Wexler, P. (1992). *Becoming somebody: Toward a social psychology of school.* London: Falmer Press.

Youth Pathways Action Plan Taskforce. (2001). *Footprints to the future: Report from the Prime Minister's youth pathways action plan taskforce 2001.* Canberra: Commonwealth of Australia.

8

LANGUAGE AND IDENTITY IN TRANSGENDER:
Gender Wars, Anatomania, and the Thai *Kathoey*[1]

Sam Winter

University of Hong Kong, Hong Kong

Introduction

We are all familiar with the war between the sexes. Less well known is another struggle playing across the world, involving transgendered people (TGs) ranged against elements in their respective mainstream societies. In some places (e.g., Hong Kong), the struggle is quite polite, even muted. In others (e.g., the United States and United Kingdom), it is loud and energetic. It is fought in newspapers, magazines, committees, tribunals, and courts. In the United Kingdom, it has been fought on television screens, where viewers have for some time been able to follow the fortunes of Hayley, a male-to-female transgender (MtF TG) on their favourite soap, *Coronation Street*. A similar drama has been played out in the United States on the set of *Ally McBeale*.

The conflict is all about what makes us male or female; do we give primacy to the physical reality (to be more specific, the external anatomy) with which a person has been born (his or her sex)? Or do we give primacy to the mental reality in which he or she lives and which he or she expresses to the world (his or her gender identity and gender presentation)?

As we will see in this chapter, language plays a key role in all of this, expressing and perhaps even helping to form opposing ideas, framing our answers to fundamental questions. Do we refer to MtF TGs as "he," "she," or by some other pronoun? Can we call them "transgendered males" or "transgendered females"? Are they perhaps neither, being better described as a third sex?

Do we label them as different or disordered? Are those MtF TGs who are attracted to males displaying a homosexual or heterosexual attraction?

At the root of the conflict is one between natal anatomy and social psychology. At the risk of oversimplification, the two sides line up as follows:

A Natal Anatomic Perspective on Gender

(1) We are born male or female, and remain so all our lives. The determination of our sex category is almost always (except in the most complicated intersex conditions) on the basis of our external anatomy. *A baby is male if it is born with a penis, and female if it isn't.*

(2) It is important that each of us grows up with a gender that matches what is considered appropriate for our sex category. *Those born male should grow up to be men, feeling that they are men and presenting to the world as such. Those born female should grow up to be women, identifying and presenting as such.*

(3) Those who fail to grow up gendered in accordance with their sex (feeling inside and presenting outside as the other gender, or even as some alternative gender) are morally depraved (the traditional Judaeo-Christian view, expressed in Deuteronomy 22:14), mentally disordered (the current psychiatric orthodoxy), or sexually deviant (a more informal popular view of TGs as closet gays, occasionally finding echoes in some of the literature (i.e., Bailey, 2003). *They are depraved, disordered, or deviant; bad, mad, or just sad.*

(4) Whether depraved, disordered, or deviant, the TG's identity continues to be as a member of the sex category into which he or she was placed at birth. *A MtF TG is first and foremost a male. A FtM TG is first and foremost a female.*

(5) An attraction to a person of the same birth sex is therefore homosexual. A MtF TG who is attracted to a male, and a FtM TG attracted to a female, are each displaying a homosexual attraction. So, too, are their sexual partners, at least if they know that the people they are with are TG.

The natal anatomic view of gender has been pretty much the mainstream view in some parts of the developed (particularly English-speaking) West, where the Judaeo-Christian and psychiatric schools of thought have taken deepest root. As will be evident in this chapter, this overconcern with anatomy is arguably irrational as well as damaging to large numbers of TGs. For that reason, I am inclined to dub it "anatomanic."

A Social Psychological Perspective on Gender

(1) The sex category into which we are placed at birth is simply a first guess as to what identity we will later assume. A child may be born male (at least in terms of his external anatomy), but that does not mean he will grow up to be a man. A child may be born female, but that doesn't mean she will become a woman. He or she will become a man or woman only in so far as he or she feels male or female inside, and presents as such to the world.

(2) Some of us will grow up with a gender that does not match the sex category into which we were placed at birth. A child born male may grow up feeling female, or at least nonmale. A child born female may grow up feeling male, or at least nonfemale.

(3) Those who do so are exhibiting a difference rather than any depravity, disorder, or deviance. TGs are an aspect of human diversity. *If there is any disorder connected with transgender, it is in the inability of society to accept their diversity. If there is any sin, it is in people's unwillingness to do so.*

(4) We should respect that diversity by viewing the TG's identity as being of the gender that he or she has chosen. *A MtF TG is first and foremost a female. A FtM TG is first and foremost a male.*

(5) An attraction to a person of the same birth sex is therefore heterosexual. A MtF TG who is attracted to a male, and a FtM TG attracted to a female, are each displaying a heterosexual attraction. Their partners, where they know they are with TGs, are also heterosexual.

This view, that a person's identity arises out of his/her sense of who he/she is and how he/she presents to the world, though unorthodox in much of the world, is quite deeply rooted in some Eastern cultures. Arguably, these ideas have survived best in some of the societies that have been least influenced by Judaeo-Christian or psychiatric thinking. Among them is Thailand, which is overwhelmingly Buddhist and only recently influenced by Western psychiatry in matters of sexual and gender diversity (Romjampa, 2003).

In this chapter, I will examine the conflict between the natal anatomic and social psychological views of gender in terms of three of the key issues outlined above.

(1) Whether we should view MtFs as male (or female), FtMs as female (or male), or indeed view them as further categories.

(2) How we should view the sexuality of TG people.

(3) Whether we should view TG people as different or disordered and, if
the latter, whether as people with "wrong minds" or "wrong bodies."

To the TG community, the course of this conflict, wherever they live, is a
matter of great concern; the outcome has consequences for the documents
they carry in their pockets (or purses), the passports upon which they travel
abroad, their social welfare rights when they grow old, their marrying and
parenting rights, their opportunities for getting a job and advancing within
it, and even their sense of security when they walk down the street.

Throughout this chapter, I will use MtF TGs (those who were ascribed
a male sex at birth but now choose to live a broadly female gender role) to
illustrate key general points about this conflict. In doing so, I do not mean
to ignore FtM TGs, or suggest that this gender war does not involve them.
Indeed, in some societies (e.g., my own Hong Kong) there may be more of
them than MtFs, and their struggles are just as real.

For each issue, I will outline the natal anatomic orthodoxy, then go on to
describe the thinking one often comes across in Thailand, a society unusual
(if not unique) both in terms of the number of people living as TGs (our
observations indicate that as many as one male in every 170 may be living as
a transgender), as well as in terms of the ways in which TGs are able to lead
their lives (Winter, 2002; Winter, 2005; Winter, 2006a).

The Thai view appears to share something of the social psychological perspective on gender. Buddhism teaches that each of us is composed of five
aggregates of elements—broadly associated with our physical state, our
sensations, our perceptions, our thoughts, and our consciousness—none
of which has any supremacy over the others. Note that only one of the five
aggregates is physical, and this, like all the others, is characterized by imper-
manence (Rahula, 1959). To the extent that we can talk about "self" (a centre
that coordinates and reflects, an individuality that sets us apart from others),
then that self is characterised by our mental reality as much as, if not more
than, our physical reality.

Most importantly, the Thai language fails to distinguish between "sex"
and "gender." One word *"phet"* says it all. The word is so versatile it can even
be used for "sexuality." All this lends great flexibility to the notion of sex and
gender. As we will see, Thai culture even allows for the possibility that there
may be more than two sexes and genders, for one of the common terms for a
TG person is *"phet tee sam"*—the third sex/gender.

Notwithstanding this and other terms used in Thailand, in this chapter I
shall refer to MtF TGs by one of the most widely used terms, *kathoey*. In using
this term, I am conscious of the fact that many Thai MtFs would prefer other
terms available in their language. There will be more about all of this later.

Male, Female, or a Third Category

The natal anatomic view (indeed "anatomania") is evident wherever, as so commonly is the case in the English-speaking world, MtFs are called "transgendered males" "transsexual males," "male transgenders," or "male transsexuals"; all of this regardless of how many years the MtF has experienced a female identity or presented to the world as a woman, or indeed how long ago (for some) the penis was removed and a neovagina was constructed.

See, by way of example only, the following research reports spanning several authors and several decades: Money and Primrose (1968), Skrapec and MacKenzie (1981), Doorn, Poortinga, and Vershoor (1994), and Green (2000), all of which refer to MtF TGs in these ways. The most telling of all, anatomanic thinking extends to a widely used reference such as the *Diagnostic and Statistical Manual of Mental Disorders* (DSM-IV; American Psychiatric Association, 1994), which refers to MtFs as males with gender identity disorder (and FtMs as girls).

The practical consequences of this view of transgender are enormous. Depending on the society in which she lives, a MtF who is attracted to a male may not be able to marry him, since the law may regard this as a same-sex marriage, and same-sex marriages may be proscribed. Where the TG manages to keep her birth sex a secret and then marries, she runs the risk of later having the marriage declared invalid. So living together may be the only viable option. However, if the couple is living together without legal union, they may have difficulty arranging an adoption.

Let's now turn to employment. A TG may find it difficult to get a job simply because her identity, appearance, and/or papers fail to match. Potential employers may point to likely objections by coworkers and customers when having to deal with a transgendered person. Almost inevitably, employers will point out the difficulty that staff toilets represent or point to duties that (the argument goes) the TG could not effectively perform.

The difficulty in getting a job is exacerbated where one "doesn't look the part," a risk greatest where the TG, as is so often the case in some Western countries, has failed early enough in her life to get a doctor to prescribe the hormones that can change her appearance. The sad truth is that failure to get or keep a job may in turn jeopardize the success of the "real-life test" (one to two years living successfully in the transgendered role) that Western psychiatry often requires a TG to pass before sex-reassignment surgery (SRS) is granted. In short, failure to get or keep a job may mean failure to get the SRS. There will be more discussion about psychiatry and SRS later.

Problems can dog the TG even towards the end of her working life. Where males and females have different retirement ages, a MtF may have to wait until the male age of retirement, rather than the female age, to receive a pension. As the supposed age of retirement approaches, the MtF may feel obliged to leave her work early to avoid letters that a government department might write to employers as retirement approaches, and which might signal her birth sex.[2]

Not surprisingly, the natal anatomic view often conflicts with TGs' views of themselves. Let us take the English-speaking world first of all. Tellingly, many MtFs refer to themselves as transgendered *females* (not males). Many FtMs label themselves and others as transgendered *males* (not females). Note that the emphasis here is on what they have moved towards rather than what they have moved away from. We have plenty of examples of this sort of thing in English of course—terms in which a past participle is used to indicate a change of status, with a noun referring to the status after the change. For example, we speak of an ordained priest or a qualified psychologist. Indeed, it would be a little queer to speak of an ordained novice or a qualified student. Yet, arguably, this is the logic of what we do whenever, as we so often do in the West, we refer to an MtF as a transgendered male.

Interestingly, I have noticed recently that some TGs are adopting an even more radical labeling approach. An MtF may say that she was "born transgendered" but is "now female." This poses a real challenge to our established way of thinking; the mainstream view is that there are two sexes and two genders, certainly at birth. The radical TG raises the possibility of at least three. All of this is very confusing to the man or woman in the Western street, who has little familiarity with any term except the ones with which this section opened.

The most common word, in Thailand, for MtFs is *kathoey*, a word that was historically used for any nongender-normative male, and was therefore extended to gays as well as TGs (less so now that the word *gei* is commonly used to refer to gays).

Historically, the collapsing together of these two categories seemed to rest on the notion that maleness is defined in terms not of what anatomy you have, but *what you do with it*. This is a view that contrasts sharply with the common Western (natal anatomic) view; that however often a man engages in same-sex activities, even as a passive partner, he remains a man. For the Thai, the MtF TG and sexually passive gay both lose much of their claim to maleness simply by allowing themselves to be penetrated. Both become in some important sense "nonmale." Remember, all of this happens in the context of a language that fails to distinguish between "gender," "sex," and "sexuality," employing the word "*phet*" for all three.

Other Thai terms for MtF TGs suggest that they go beyond being simply "nonmale," and are instead (a) a merger of the two sexes (e.g., *pumia/*

pumae—"male-female"), as well as the English loan word "ladyboy," (b) a subset of female (e.g., *sao praphet song*—"second kind of girl," and *phuying praphet song*—"second kind of woman") or, as we have seen (c) a third gender/sex category (e.g., *phet tee sam*—"third gender/sex"). A final term, *nang fa jam leng* ("transformed angel"), echoes the use of the term "transgendered female" that seems increasingly to be used in the West by MtFs—an adjective that describes a transformation, linked to the noun that describes the status after the transformation.

In short then, the Thai language offers a range of labels for transgender that enable the user to describe gender positions of almost any kind—a gender mix, a subset of female, or even a third gender. As we have seen, English does not presently allow for such terms, at least as would be understood outside the TG community. For more information on Thai terminology, see Jackson (1995).[3]

Together with Kulthida Maneerat and Nonguch Rojanalert (of Chulalongkorn and Silpakorn Universities, respectively), I recently examined the attitudes of 215 ordinary (i.e., nontransgendered) university students towards MtF TGs. We found them pretty evenly split on this issue, with 51% seeing them as males "who have something wrong with their minds," but the other half seeing them as either women born into the wrong body (12%) or as a third sex/gender (41%). Thanks to Pornthip Chalangsooth at the University of Arkansas, we have some comparison data for the United States. The corresponding figures were 63%, 14%, and 6%. Thai students are clearly less likely than their American counterparts to think of the MtF TG as a man, and much more likely (by a factor of seven!) to think of them as a third gender. For more figures, see Winter et al. (2005).

In summary, the names that Thais use for MtF TGs suggest a range of gender spaces, extending from nonmale through a blend of male and female, to a subset of female or even a third sex/gender. The range of names echoes a divergence of views as to what the nature of transgender is, with around half taking the natal anatomic view (that they are a subset of male) but the other half placing much less importance upon birth sex, and consequently viewing them as either female or a third gender.

How then do *kathoey* see themselves? A first answer is to be found in how they speak. One of the interesting linguistic features of Thai is that certain vocabulary items are gender-linked. A person uses different word forms according to whether he/she is a male/female—or sees him/herself as either of those things. The first person pronoun provides a nice example. Males will generally use just one word, *phom*, whereas a female can choose between *chan*, *dichan*, *noo* (literally "little mouse"), and even her own name as a pronoun. Each of these can be used to mean "I," "me," "my," or "mine." Another example of gender markers is provided by the polite particles that Thais attach to the end of a phrase or a sentence: *khrap* for males and *kha* for females.

What word-forms do the *kathoey* use? Invariably, they use the female pronouns and particles. Suppose she cannot find a book and says "Excuse me. I wonder if you have seen my book, because I can't see it now at all." In Thai, she will say it just like a female: *"Khor tod kha. Mei sap wa khun hen nang seu khong chan mai. Phroh thon nee di chan mong mei hen nang seu khong di chan loei kha"* (gender-markers underlined). The Thai male would say *"Khor tod khrap. Mei sap wa khun hen nang seu khong phom mai. Phroh thon nee phom mong mei hen nang seu khong phom loei khrap."*

In using female forms, the *kathoey* is taking advantage of a feature of the Thai language that simply does not exist in English (or many other languages for that matter), using it to express in the most direct way her sense of who she is. Such speech patterns develop at an early age. In a recent study of 190 *kathoey*, we found that some respondents started using the female pronouns (*chan, dichan,* etc.) almost as soon as they could talk, with 50% using it by age 14 (Winter, 2006a). The polite particle (*ka*) came soon after, with some reporting having used it from age 5, and half having used it by age 15. Given that half of our respondents were 16 before they started taking hormones, 17 before they started growing their hair long, and 18 before they were living full time in female clothes, it is clear that female word-forms were one of the earliest expressions of cross-gender behaviour for our sample; a harbinger of a fuller cross-gendered presentation to come.

Arguably, the language one uses may not be a good indicator of ones' identity. A more direct one might be to ask people what they think they are. We asked our 190 MtFs to say whether they thought of themselves as men, women, *sao praphet song, kathoey,* or "other." None thought of themselves as male, and only 11% saw themselves as *kathoey* (i.e., "nonmale"). By contrast, 45% thought of themselves as women, with another 36% as *sao praphet song* (i.e., as a subset of female) (Winter, 2006b). Unfortunately, we did not include the category *phet tee sam* ("third sex/gender"). Conceivably, if we had done so, there may have been many respondents who would have chosen to describe themselves using that term.

To summarise, there is a common perception that MtFs are female, or indeed a third sex. Furthermore, it is not only the *kathoey* who perceive their condition in this way. Many ordinary (non-TG) Thais believe this, too. Importantly, in all of this, the Thai language provides universally understood terms by which this perception can be expressed.

The view of MtF TGs as female or a third sex reflects, and perhaps in turn cultivates, a more liberal and accepting attitude towards transgender than is found in most Western societies. To the Western observer, the extent of this acceptance can be mind-boggling. When asked how their parents first reacted to their transgender, our sample of 190 *kathoey* revealed that 36% of fathers and 50% of mothers had accepted or even encouraged it! Indeed, 37% of our sample said that Thai society generally accepts or encourages transgender (Winter, 2006b).

These figures are high, even allowing for some bravado, and almost certainly higher than one would get from a similar study in the West. It's no wonder then that TGs can be relaxed about their own status, and can lead relatively unproblematic lives. Only 5% described themselves as lacking confidence or low in self-esteem, 7% as depressed, and 28% as anxious. Indeed, while the vast majority expressed a desire to be a woman in their next life, a substantial number (12%) actually said that they wanted to be transgendered again! Contrast all this with the patterns of isolation, depression, and suicide that are a feature of TG lives in the West, and which seem to stem directly from an inability to admit their transgender to themselves, or present to the world as TG and be accepted as such (Nuttbrock, Rosenblum, & Blumenstein, 2002).

I would note that the conflict between the two views of transgender (natal anatomic versus social psychological) is nowhere more evident as in the names given to the surgical operations in which a person's genitals are altered to match the person's gender identity. In English, the mainstream name for this procedure is "sex reassignment surgery," or (a more colloquial name) "sex change." The connotation is one of moving away from the sex that one more properly belongs to. In contrast, many transgenders talk about "sex *confirmation* surgery," the connotation being of moving towards the sex one always should have been. As for the Thais, they too talk about *plaeng phet* (in this sense "change sex"). However, the connotation here is exchange, rather than alteration.

In passing, we should note that, in almost all legal jurisdictions in which change of legal status is permitted, it is this surgical procedure that makes such change of status possible—not breast surgery, nor any nonsurgical procedure such as ingestion of hormones. There is a very special form of anatomanic thinking here—genitomania.

Homosexual or Heterosexual

If one's view of the MtF is natal anatomic, that she is male, then any attraction she has towards males must be viewed as homosexual. Indeed, this is the mainstream view. One sees it in academic papers, sometimes even those of a psychological nature (Blanchard, Clemmensen, & Steiner, 1987; Daskalos, 1998).

So endemic is the natal anatomic view that, at least in the West, the less-informed public finds it difficult to distinguish between gays and transgenders at all; a difficulty that rests in part on the fact that these two groups have so long lived in close physical association, socialising together at the margins of society. "Drag" has been seen as a part of gay culture, and the effeminate male has been seen as a gay stereotype. Never mind that the "drag queen" and effeminate male may be entirely comfortable with their identity as male, but the MtF TG is certainly not.

In a conceptual confusion that makes TGs no more than a subset of gays, as well as drawing on classic homophobic paranoia, one occasionally hears the view that MtFs are sexual perverts of some sort, living cross-gendered lives just so that they can catch men more successfully. It is a view often rejected by young Thais (52% in our recent international study of (non-TG) university students), and much less commonly rejected in many Western communities (only 35% of our American sample did so). A related view is that MtFs are gays who are scared to admit it to themselves (see Bailey, 2003). This is often also the view about the men who are attracted to MtFs.

Here is a word on effeminate men. Many TGs argue that what is often called homophobia is actually transphobia. They point out that when (as happens all too commonly on the streets of cities in the West) a gay is beaten up, it is not because of whom he has slept with (none of his assailants will even bother asking him). Rather it is because of the way he looks, and the way in which he walks and speaks. A masculine-appearing male is far less likely to be set upon.

Now it's time to turn to the TG's own view of his or her sexuality. Let us consider the case of an MtF who is attracted to men. She feels female, and may have felt thus as long as she can remember and, in all likelihood, back to a time predating any feelings of sexual attraction. Conscious that her attraction towards men is consistent with her feelings of identity, she sees herself as heterosexual. She probably sees her partner's attraction to her in the same light, as indeed he might.

How is sexuality of TGs viewed in Thailand? With so many people (TGs as well as onlookers) apparently viewing *kathoey* as female or third sex, is an attraction to men seen as homosexual or heterosexual? Here we run up against a problem: these two latter terms are recent imports to Thailand and seem to have no close Thai equivalents. Indeed, as we have seen, there seems to be no distinct Thai word for sexuality ("*phet*," the term also used for "sex" and "gender," is often used here, too).

Notwithstanding these difficulties, we found in our study of 190 *kathoey* that around one in three saw an attraction to men as heterosexual. Interestingly, about 10% saw an attraction to women as heterosexual, too.

What then, for a *kathoey*, constituted homosexual behaviour? Well, for some of our respondents, it was an attraction to another *kathoey*! This finding interests me greatly. It implies that, while Thai TGs (like most of us in the West) define homosexuality as a sexual attraction within the same sex/gender category, some of them (unlike most of us in the West) are thinking in terms of three sex/gender categories, not two.

Different or Disordered, the Wrong Mind or the Wrong Body

As we have already seen, the natal anatomic view so common in the West holds that MtFs are in essence male, and that they therefore have something wrong with their minds. Enter psychiatry, taking centre stage and giving the disorder a name, "Gender Identity Disorder" (GID), described in great detail in the fourth edition of *DSM-IV* (American Psychiatric Association, 1994), as well as in the tenth edition of the *International Classification of Diseases* (ICD-10) (United States Educational, Scientific and Cultural Organization, 1992).

Western psychiatry bolsters its case that transgender is a psychiatric disorder by pointing out (a) that it is rare (which of course makes it a de facto abnormality, and (b) that it involves an identity that is at variance with reality; one that is associated with emotional difficulties linked to frustration, anxiety, depression, helplessness, and hopelessness (all of which suggest that these people need treatment). What is ignored here is that those who would like to live TG lives may be more numerous than is commonly believed (see Conway, 2003), and that what often stops them is the fear of social opprobrium so great it can overwhelm one's mental health, leading to the emotional difficulties so often observed (Nuttbrock et al., 2002).

The irony is that the only treatments that seem to work for TGs are the ones that help them live their transgendered lives—things like surgery and hormone therapy, as well as voice therapy and social skills training designed to help them pass more effectively in their chosen gender role. One might observe, perhaps wryly, that it is a strange mental disorder indeed for which the best shot at treatment is to change the patient's reality to match his/her supposedly fevered mind!

How do TG people view themselves? Different or disordered? In the developed West, I detect a fair amount of ambivalence here. On one hand, TGs see themselves as part of human diversity. On the other hand, they realize that their access to state- or insurance-subsidised medical services, as well as much of their legal protection against discrimination, comes from being regarded as disabled.

However, if they are disabled, then what is the nature of their disablement? They will commonly argue that their minds are quite fine, thank you, but that they have been born into the wrong bodies, and that it is, therefore, their *bodies* that are wrong. Whatever mental problems they suffer come, they say, from their experience of (or anticipation of) reactions from family, friends, and society to their transgender. They may add, pointedly, that much additional frustration and depression comes from the way in which they are treated by psychiatrists and doctors! Nuttbrock et al. (2002) support their position here, suggesting that TGs function as well as the rest of us when they allow themselves to admit to and express their chosen gender status, and are accepted by those around them in that new role.

Incidentally, if TGs are disordered, then what of those who are physically attracted to them? One of the most interesting pieces of transgender research I have ever come across was titled, "Men with a Sexual Interest in Transvestites, Transsexuals and She-males" (Blanchard & Collins, 1993). The article itself was mundane enough. More interesting was that it appeared in the *Journal of Nervous and Mental Disease*. So Western academia apparently considers even the sexual partners of TGs to be disordered. So far, there is no suitable category for them in DSM-IV or ICD-10. Perhaps one day there will!

What of the Thais? What sort of pathology, if any, do they ascribe to transgender? Interestingly, in our recent study of (non-TG) university students in Thailand, we found that only 13% believed them to be mentally disordered (compared with 49% of American students). Only 28% seem to think MtFs need psychological help (compared with 66% of American students). By contrast, a striking 53% of Thai students thought them "normal, just different from the rest of us." The corresponding figure for American students was much lower at 38%. In short, then, the majority of Thais seem to feel, contrary to Western psychiatric orthodoxy, that *kathoey* are ordinary people like you and me; they are but one aspect of human diversity.[4]

In summary, then, Thai society broadly operates on the basis that transgender is a difference rather than a disorder. It stands by as the *kathoey* around them make cross-gendered transitions in large numbers in ways that bypass psychiatric services (and thinking) entirely. True, such services would be expensive, but the point is that no one seems to think them necessary, or even helpful. When young boys begin to act in a feminine way, use female language forms, grow their hair long and dress as female, neither parents nor school appear to feel the need to refer them to professionals. When *kathoey* decide to change their bodies, they do not feel the need to visit a psychiatrist (or even a doctor). Instead, they just go to their local pharmacy and buy some hormones (a major chain keeps 23 different brands in stock at some of its urban branches) or else borrow some from older *kathoey* (every school, every street seems to have at least one). Some *kathoey* take hormones from the age of 10 years. When they dress in female university uniform, few, if any, teachers will complain. They are unlikely to be referred to specialists. In addition, if they decide that they want surgery, they just save up or borrow the money and then approach a surgeon. There are cases of *kathoey* who have had sex-reassignment surgery at age 15 (Winter, 2006a).

Concluding Comments

In writing this chapter, I may be accused of presenting a somewhat simplified view on all sides. Even within Western academia, law, and clinical psychiatry, one hears arguments that MtFs should be viewed as essentially female (with all that means for classification of sexual attraction), that transgenders are different rather than disordered, that Gender Identity Disorder (GID) should accordingly be removed from the psychiatric manuals (see Bartlett, Vasey, & Bukowski, 2000 for a powerful examination of the issue in regard to childhood GID), and that TGs should be able to obtain changes to their legal status based solely on personal identity and social presentation (see the United Kingdom Gender Recognition Act).

However, there are still many forces that, consciously or not, resist these developments. Bailey's (2003) text (portraying many transgenders as closet gays) is one. In addition, there are worrying turns in the discourse. As "apotemnophilia" (a desire to be an amputee) reveals itself as a new, apparently fast growing, disorder (Elliott, 2000), parallels are being drawn between it and GID. For if a desire to be an amputee is a disorder then surely, the argument goes, the desire for SRS is one, too. To the extent that all this is happening, we can continue to talk in terms of a battle fought between two opposing views of transgender; a gender war indeed.

Turning to Thailand, I may be guilty of oversimplification in what I have written about the circumstances in which *kathoey* live. They do not live unproblematic lives. Even in Thailand, some parents do not react well to their son's transgender. MtFs are forever marked as male in their documents, even after "sex reassignment surgery." Even those who pass as female may therefore encounter difficulties getting a job where their potential employer is in any way prejudiced, or fears prejudice among his other employees or his customers. The *kathoey* travelling abroad may encounter problems at immigration points. This is all the more likely if she passes successfully as a female, for her passport will show her to be male.

In short, Western perspectives on transgender may not be as uniformly "anatomanic" as I have suggested. Indeed, the mainstream view may be moving gently towards a more social psychological view, more in tune with that of most TGs themselves. It is also apparent that the accepting views of transgender evident in informal Thai society are seldom evident in the bureaucratic and legal spheres, which have been infected with natal anatomic thinking. Nevertheless, it remains true that the informal social environment in which *kathoey* grow up and live is commonly more accepting than the one in which TGs suffer so harshly in the West.

This difference may have massive consequences for the development of young TGs. Consider the young Thai boy, growing up displaying gentleness, mildness, sentimentality and weakness, excitability and emotionality. He is told that he has these characteristics and is treated accordingly. He is aware that these traits are stereotypically female (as they indeed are in Thai culture; Winter & Udomsak, 2002). Perhaps this boy has some female stereotyped interests, too: a love of playing with dolls, a liking for dressing up in girls' clothes, and a preference for the company of girls. He and everyone around him, rather than being inclined to shrug all this off as evidence that here is a boy who does not quite fit in (as might happen in many other societies), may instead see it all as evidence that he is indeed not really a true boy at all. Another label is close at hand. He is a *kathoey*. His family, neighbours, friends, and schoolmates may use the label without any alarm. He may learn to, too. As the young *kathoey* grows up, she (I use the female pronoun here) will meet other *kathoey* who mentor her along a path towards her new gender. At every step of the journey, her choices (regarding what she is, and what she will do about it) have been validated by the social and cultural context in which she lives.

Now consider an identical boy, this time growing up in the English or Hong Kong Chinese cultures with which I am familiar. He, his parents, siblings, and peers may interpret his feelings quite differently, viewing them as evidence that he is a sensitive boy, perhaps an effeminate one—a sissy, but a boy nonetheless. Those around him may press him to do the things other boys do, and be like other boys are—to toughen up a bit. Family doctors, child psychologists, and psychiatrists may be called in to help. All those involved will adopt the same basic approach: they will see the boy, not as a female with the wrong body, but as a male with the wrong mental attitude, an attitude that needs to be changed. The end result is that he may live his whole life labelled as a male.

I am not suggesting here which road is right (although the large numbers of "late-onset" TGs gives cause for us to wonder about the Western way).

For the present, I am just trying to suggest that different roads are offered by different cultures.

Endnotes

1. For help in preparing this chapter, the author is grateful for a research grant awarded by the Clinic of Dr. Suporn Watanyusakul, Chonburi, Thailand.

2. All of these were features of life for TGs in the United Kingdom until recently. It was only when the United Kingdom Government was ruled by the European Court of Human Rights to be in contravention of the European Convention on Human Rights that it began to seriously consider how it might remove these and other difficulties facing TGs. Ironically, the United Kingdom Government's response to the ECHR judgment (United Kingdom Government, 2004) is probably the most far-sighted legislation anywhere in the world, leapfrogging ahead of the rest of the world in terms of rights to change legal status. It allows TGs who have lived in a cross-gendered role for at least two years to apply for a gender recognition certificate, and then, if they so wish, use that certificate to change their birth certificate. Note that they are able to do this regardless of what surgery or hormonal treatment they may *or may not* have undergone. It is the most avowedly social psychological legislation I know in this area.

3. Nowhere have I found any term that parallels the common English term, "transgendered male" (or its close relations), used to describe MtFs. The nearest to this I can find is (a) *kathoey phom yao* ("long-haired *kathoey*") and *kathoey tee sai suer pha phuying* ("*kathoey* dressing as a woman"), both of which, following on from the discussion of *kathoey* earlier, might imply the MtF is essentially a nonmale living as a woman, and (b) *ork sao* ("outwardly a female"), which might, I suppose, imply that she is not actually female.

4. Accepting that TGs are simply different, then what underlies this difference? We asked *kathoey* this question. The vast majority believed their transgender was something they were born with (84% of our sample). Around half (48%) went on to be more specific: it appeared to be *karma*; the accumulation of consequences for acts in previous lives (Winter, 2006b). A sizable number (51%) took a more sociogenic view, saying that they became *kathoey* at least partly because of friends, particularly other *kathoey*. However, apart from that, our *kathoey* admitted to very little other social influence: parents (30%), brothers or sisters (25%), and other relatives (23%). We are not yet in a position to say what ordinary (i.e., non-TG) Thais believe about the origins of transgender. Colleagues in Thailand are currently engaged in a study that should answer this question.

References

American Psychiatric Association. (1994). *Diagnostic and statistical manual of mental disorders* (4th ed.). Washington, D.C.: Author.

Bailey, J. M. (2003). *The man who would be queen: The science of gender bending and transsexualism.* Washington, D.C.: Joseph Henry Press.

Bartlett, N. H., Vasey, P. L., & Bukowski, W. M. (2000). Is gender identity disorder in children a mental disorder? *Sex Roles, 43*(11/12), 753–785.

Blanchard, R., & Collins, P. I. (1993). Men with sexual interest in transvestites, transsexuals and she-males. *Journal of Nervous and Mental Disease, 181,* 570–575.

Blanchard, R., Clemmensen, L. H., & Steiner, B. W. (1987). Heterosexual and homosexual gender dysphoria. *Archives of Sexual Behaviour, 16*(2), 139–152.

Conway, L. (2003). How frequently does transsexualism occur? Retrieved June 14, 2007, from http://ai.eecs.umich.edu/people/conway/TS/TSprevalence.html

Daskalos, C. T. (1998). Changes in the sexual orientation of six heterosexual male-to-female transsexuals. *Archives of Sexual Behaviour, 27*(6), 605–614.

Doorn, C. D., Poortinga, J., & Vershoor, A. M. (1994). Cross-gender identity in transvestites and male transsexuals. *Archives of Sexual Behaviour, 23,* 185–201.

Elliott, C. (2000, December). A new way to be mad. *The Atlantic Monthly.* Retrieved June 14, 2007, from http://www.theatlantic.com/doc/prem/2000012/madness

Green, R. (2000). Family cooccurrence of "gender dysphoria": ten sibling or parent-child pairs. *Archives of Sexual Behaviour, 29*(5), 499–507.

Jackson, P. A. (1995). *Dear Uncle Go: Male homosexuality in Thailand.* Bangkok: Bua Luang Books.

Money, J., & Primrose, C. (1968). Sexual dimorphism and dissociation in the psychology of male transsexuals. *Journal of Nervous and Mental Disease, 147*(5), 472–486.

Nuttbrock, L., Rosenblum, A., & Blumenstein, R. (2002). Transgender identity affirmation and mental health. *International Journal of Transgenderism, 6*(4). Retrieved June 14, 2007, from http://www.symposion.com/ijt/ijtvo06no04_03.htm

Rahula, W. (1959). *What Buddha taught.* London: Gordon Fraser.

Romjampa, T. (2003, August). *The construction of male homosexuality in the Journal of the Psychiatric Association of Thailand, 1973.* Paper presented at the Third International Conference of Asia Scholars, Singapore.

Skrapec, C., & MacKenzie, K. R. (1981). Psychological self-perception in male transsexuals, homosexuals and heterosexuals. *Archives of Sexual Behaviour, 10,* 357–370.

United Kingdom Government. (2004). Gender Recognition Act. Retrieved June 14, 2007, from http://www.opsi.gov.uk/acts/acts2004/20040007.htm

United Nations Educational, Scientific and Cultural Organization (UNESCO). (1992). *International statistical classification of diseases and related health problems* (10th ed.). Geneva: Author.

Winter, S. (2002). Counting *kathoey*. Web document on TransgenderASIA site. Retrieved June 14, 2007, from http://web.hku.hk/~sjwinter/Transgender ASIA/paper_counting_kathoey.htm

Winter, S. (2006a). Thai transgenders in focus: Demographics, transitions and identities. *International Journal of Transgenderism 9*(1), 15–27.

Winter, S. (2006b). Thai transgenders in focus: Their beliefs about attitudes towards and origins of transgender. *International Journal of Transgenderism, 9*(2), 47–62.

Winter, S., & Udomsak, N. (2002). Male, female and transgender: Stereotypes and self in Thailand. *International Journal of Transgenderism, 6*(1). Retrieved June 14, 2007, from http://www.symposion.com/ijt/ijtvo06no01_04.htm

Winter, S., Chalungsooth, P., Teh, Y. K., Rojanalert, N., Maneerat, K., Wong Y. W., et al. *What do people think about transgender? A six-nation study of beliefs and attitudes.* Manuscript in preparation.

9

GENDERED SELF-REPRESENTATIONS:
How the World's Successful Women and Men Speak in Journalistic Interviews

Maya Khemlani David
University of Malaya, Malaysia

Janet Yong
The Hong Kong Polytechnic University, Hong Kong

Introduction

The 20th century, especially in the last decade, has been marked with the rapid growth in the number of women in leadership positions. Today, more women have become powerful public figures in politics, business, and education.

What is the image of the modern powerful women in business and the professions? Edvinsson and Malone (1997) state that most people's utterances inform others of their personalities and identities. Recording the perspectives of the people in power, these interviews typically get at "the story underneath the story" of the intricacies of business decision-making, personal ambition, success, and family. Since knowledge is socially constructed and negotiated through dialogue, this research aims at analyzing the meanings underlying the discourse of well-known professional women who were interviewed.

The ultimate aim is to determine how powerful women constitute and position themselves in their discourse, and this will be compared to men's discourse in interviews published in popular magazines. Deconstruction of the dialogue will, it is hoped, present the image of women as seen by themselves. Women via their rhetoric construct their own realities. Talk gives us an idea of the value system. Consequently, the linguistic repertoire and its ideological implications will be discussed.

Previous Studies

Work by O'Barr and O'Barr (1976) and their associates (e.g., Conley, O'Barr, & Lind, 1978; Erickson & Schultz, 1978) on courtroom testimony with the purpose of investigating what kinds of talk were used by effective attorneys and witnesses, found that men and women expressed varieties of speech that were uncertain and trivial as well as less clear and forceful. Presence or absence of these features was associated not with sex but with social economic status and education, income, etc. Subsequent experiments with several populations of judges demonstrated that those with, what they came to call, "powerless" speech were judged less favorably on both credibility and measures of attractiveness, whatever the sex of the speaker. In these studies, therefore, sex was not the variable that influenced, affected, or impacted on discourse and power.

The Data

The data consisted of a total of 22 transcripts of individual interviews with 11 women and 11 men of different nationalities who work in top positions. Group interviews were not considered in this study in order to eliminate possible group influences in responses. The interviews were randomly selected from several Asian business and women magazines published between 1996 and 2002. Interviews with men in power were used to compare and contrast the two discourse types.

Power is easy to recognize but difficult to quantify. In compiling the second annual list of the 50 most powerful businesswomen outside and within the United States, *Fortune,* October 14, 2002, looked for women who run a major company or play a role at or near the top. Still, having power is not enough. To make the list, women also have to have operating responsibility. Thus, Oprah Winfrey, who many credit with hosting one of the most highly rated female talk shows, clearly has power by virtue of her position as one of the richest black women in the United States. In addition, some women are powerful in less conventional ways. Dato' Sharizat Abdul Jalil (Table 9.1, No. 2), who is the Minister responsible for women's affairs in Malaysia, and Nurhalida Dato' Seri Mohd. Khalil (Table 9.1, No. 6), who is a Malaysian professor of International Human Rights Law, belong to that category. So are influential men like the Prime Minister of Malaysia, Dr. Mahathir Mohammad (Table 9.2, No. 1), and the Sarawak Minister of Tourism, Dato' Dr. James Jemut Masing (Table 9.2, No. 6), whose political powers informed the way millions of Malaysians think and act. Also included in the definition of power is advancement made in information technology, high fashion, style, and creativity, which influence the way people work, dress, and spend their money and leisure.

Table 9.1 Titles and Identities of Women Interviewed

1. Raja Zamilia Raja Dato' Mansur. (Malaysian Malay). Public Relations Director of the *Ritz-Carlton, Pangkor Laut Resort, Tanjung Jara Resort, Malaysia.*

2. Dato' Shahrizat Abdul Jalil. (Malaysian Malay). Minister of Women's Affairs, Malaysia.

3. Lena Olving. (Swedish). Managing Director of *Volvo Malaysia.*

4. Oprah Winfrey. (American). Television Talk Show Host.

5. Dr. Jannie Tay. (Malaysian Chinese). Managing Director of *The Hour Glass.*

6. Nurhalida Dato' Seri Mohd Khalil. (Malaysian Malay). Lecturer of International Human Rights Law, University of Malaya.

7. Winnie Loo. (Malaysian Chinese). Artistic Director of *A Cut Above.*

8. Kai-Yin Lo. (Singaporean Chinese). Owner of *Neolithic Jewellery Store.* Also a jewellery designer, historian, film producer, writer, and chef.

9. Catherine Lam. (Singaporean Chinese). Executive Director and Owner of *Fabristeel.*

10. Laletha Nitiyanandan. (Singaporean Indian). Owner of *Business Trends,* a personal consultancy firm that recruits executives and provides staffing support to companies and organizations.

11. Ivy Tan. (Singaporean Chinese). Co-founder and Owner, and Deputy Managing Director of *Noel Gifts International.*

Mode of Analysis

We selected the interviews of men and women of different working age groups (35–76 years), professions and businesses, ethnicities, and nationalities to gain the perspective of a cross-section of business and professional people. All the interviews were conducted in English by both local and foreign male and female interviewers, which were published in the various magazines. Interview topics included both internal work environment and external work environment. The former consists of issues, which include business practices, training, finance, profits, productivity, clientele, products, and market growth. External work environment includes the impact of work on marriage and career, role definition, family and children, recreation, and social issues. The contents of the interviews were analyzed according to mention of major themes and their frequency of mention in the two sample groups. Not all the mentions made by the interviewees were questions asked or comments initiated by the interviewers. The data were obtained from an equal number of direct interviews (questions and answers) and interview reports (paraphrases).

Table 9.2   Titles and Identities of Men Interviewed

1. Dr. Mahathir Mohammad. (Malaysian Malay). Prime Minister of Malaysia.

2. Tony Gott. (British). Chief Executive of *Rolls-Royce Cars and Bentley Motor Cars.*

3. Ramakrishnan Govindasamy. (Malaysian Indian). Co-founder and CEO of *ivoli dotcom sdn bhd.*

4. Chan Boon Yong. (Malaysian Chinese). Managing Director of *Carat Club.*

5. Ow Chio Kiat. (Singaporean Chinese). Five-star hotelier, and Chairman of *Hai Sun Hup Group.*

6. Dato' Dr. James Jemut Masing. (Sarawakian). Minister of Tourism, Sarawak.

7. Richard Hoon. (Singaporean Chinese). CEO of *MRI Asia.*

8. Georges Gagnebin. (Swiss). CEO of *Union Bank of Switzerland Private Banking.*

9. John Glajz. (Australian). Managing Director of *Mondial.*

10. Bernard Chandran. (Malaysian Indian). Fashion Designer.

11. Benjamin Tan. (Malaysian Chinese). Owner of *SWOT Interior Consultancy Firm and Blue Dot.*

Findings

Following is a summary of some of the most significant findings of the study. The major themes mentioned by those interviewed, and their frequency (also in percentage) are indicated in Table 9.3.

This study identified eight major themes in the responses of both women and men business executives. Overall, there is a significant difference in the two responses in the eight categories. Our findings indicate that 54.5% of the women and only 17.2% of the men mentioned significant others such as spouse, children, mother, parents, and siblings in the course of their conversation. The six women either talked about husband, daughter, or father. Of the 11 men interviewed, only one younger male executive talked proudly of his wife who he said "made him what he was," while another acknowledged his family background and connections, and passion for his work were an advantage. He also attributed his success to common sense, or what he called EQ (emotional intelligence).

Meanwhile, 100% of the women claimed that their success at work was credited to other people in their lives. This was not the case with their male counterparts. Only 2 out of 11 men considered that success at work was attributed to someone other than themselves. When interviewees were asked the secret of their success at work, 3 of the 11 women executives (27.3%) said it was luck or circumstances. These were mentioned in addition to the inspiration and empowerment they received from parents, spouses, and/or siblings.

Table 9.3   Themes and Frequency

Major themes	Women Total 11	Men Total 11
1. Mention of significant others	6 (54.5%)	2 (17.2%)
2. Attributing success to others (e.g., family, friends, domestic help)	10 (90.9%)	2 (17.2%)
3. Attributing success to luck/ chance/circumstances	3 (27.3%)	0 (0%)
4. Attributing success to self/vision/hard work/intelligence	11 (100%)	11 (100%)
5. Multifaceted sense of self/function/role (e.g., spouse, parent)	7 (63.6%)	2 (17.2%)
6. Priority for family	7 (63.6%)	2 (17.2%)
7. Priority for work	8 (72.7%)	10 (90.9%)
Focus on people other than family (mainly employees and clients)		
(Business executives only)	9 (100%)	9 (100%)

One hundred percent of the women attributed their success to a male figure in their lives. One credited her achievements in business to the Prime Minister, Dr. Mahathir, whom she called her role model and mentor. All the 11 men executives did not believe luck or circumstances were the driving force that made them top in their respective companies. Instead, they claimed that self, vision, and hard work, or one of the three pointers was responsible. Significantly, all the interviewees ranked their self-ability and intelligence, work savvy, forecast, vision, and diligence as their most important characteristics. There were no differences by age or gender in perceived positive impact of commitment and dedication on promotion to top positions.

Nearly all of the people in power who were interviewed (72.7% of the women and 90.9% of the men) said that their priority in life was to work hard, *to put in the hours* as *nothing is easy*. However, two of the women would have to sacrifice a little more of their time at work when they have children and when their children grow up, and one said she was spending more time with her 11-month-old baby and had entrusted her responsibilities to her capable managers. Only one self-made male executive admitted that his dream of building a boutique hotel would have to wait as his newborn daughter took first priority.

In addition, while both sexes put in long hard hours at work (otherwise they would not be holding those top positions naturally), this claim was verbalized differently. Richard Hoon, CEO of MRI Asia, regarded the merger of MRI and Humana International as, "You couldn't find a better marriage." Glajz's (Managing Director of Mondial) latest "baby" is the launch of the Ms. Mondial Collection. When John Glajz said he was fortunate that he wore two hats, he meant "I buy and I supply" in contrast to having dual roles as breadwinner and spouse/parent. When one male executive said, "I couldn't have done this all alone," he meant that he owed his success in the workplace to his good common sense and EQ and not to his wife or family. Women tended more frequently to attribute their success at work to other things or other people.

It cannot be denied that most women executives in the interview possessed a multifaceted sense of self, function, and role. That theme echoes through the corps of executive and professional women. In our data, 7 out of 11 women bosses divided their time between work and home. The Chinese women entrepreneurs especially considered the family as the core unit. The assumption that family is paramount and that a happy family situation contributes to job success and job satisfaction was not shared by the men in the interviews. Of all the men who claimed that "the biggest challenge for them has been financial, nothing else comes close to (their work)," and they "have no time to stop and think about their obstacles," only two (17.2%) responded to family needs. One would devote his weekend—Friday dinner through Sunday bedtime—to his wife, his three daughters, and their grandparents, in between "squeezing" in a Saturday morning game of golf while his daughters are at ballet class, as well as a few hours of badminton on Sundays for his own enjoyment and recreation. The other, the Sarawak Minister of Tourism, despite being totally committed to his political career, saw himself as a family man who enjoyed "taking the family out, including the cats and the dogs, off into the wilds." On the contrary, Malaysia's Prime Minister's idea of spending time away from work was not doing it with family, but inspecting building sites because he loved to "see his people work." Any opportunity away from his top position in authority is spent in Argentina where he goes "riding morning, noon, and night."

All the women and men executives put employee welfare as their most important business aim. The Summary of Topline Results (2002) found that successful companies focus on people issues. A wide variety of different research studies have proven the link that the more satisfied employees are with their jobs, the better the company is likely to perform in terms of productivity and profitability. Concern for employee welfare is, hence, today acknowledged as a significant predictor of company performance. The CEO of MRI Asia wanted every staff member, who he considered his assets, to also eventually own the company. He also wanted to create "an environment where people appreciated one another." According to the Executive Director of Fabristeel, her role is "to bring out the best in people." She thinks "women have that particular capacity as they're able to listen and be more sympathetic."

Second, focus on people included focus on customers or clients, which ranked higher than significant others. Predictably, all the women and men executives valued the customer highly. Georges Gagnebin (CEO Union Bank of Switzerland Private banking and traditional watchmaking business) stressed that work "is all about values we share with (our clients). You have to understand that every client is somebody special." Bernard Chandran, a fashion designer, said more than his family, "people inspire him." Like the satisfied employee, a satisfied customer cannot be compromised because he recognized that "you can only fail a customer once."

Finally, more than the women, men focused on how great they were or how great their companies were in their lives. All the nine male executives talked about how great their companies were, which indirectly reflected on how great they were also. Tony Gott, British chief executive of Rolls-Royce Cars and Bentley Motor Cars, had this to say: "The dealers are crying out for cars." Ramakrishnan Govindasamy, CEO of a computer network company called ivoli dotcom, was proud they had "offers from six public-listed companies."

Nearly all the executive males in the interviews recognized the competitive market conditions in which they operate. In order to stay ahead in the company and their career, they claimed that they needed to constantly advance and take risks. Tony Gott said: "I took a risk but I hedged my bets, and I want to change current norms. I can be outwardly calm but I'm restless in business. I don't like status quo. Once you get into that, everyone else is overtaking you." His ambition was that "every level must be pushed, to move forward into something better." Tony obviously enjoys his role at work, which he said was a "hell of a challenge." While meeting challenges head on seemed to be the way to success at work, one billionaire Singaporean Chinese hotelier and company group chairman also believed in "being prudent and doing things right. I'm not comfortable taking risks and making money in the short term."

Male and Female Choice of Language

To make their point, the men executives used superlative adjectives and definitive words that have positive meanings more frequently, 99% of which are related to their work, not family (Table 9.4). Compared to men, women, on the other hand, tended to use less "forceful" adjectives and more hedges, diminutives, and words that carry emotions (Table 9.5). This gender split in language choice reflects the different perceptions men and women hold in regards to the same things or issues. In this case, these are work, family, and ambition.

Table 9.4   Men's Choice of Words and Adjectives

Managing a million things; it was horrendous; we dominate it; tremendous chance; successful future; biggest challenge; definitely a success; (success) is inevitable; need not develop an inferiority complex; doing things right; double back flips; perform miracles; want to build Asia's biggest company; can take Asia easily, a total of 15 to 20 offices; major IT player in the U.S.; broken records; utmost importance; being the biggest mean; a clear and focused solution; my absolute priority, undivided attention; we were taken seriously and now we are major players; great team; we do what we do best; a brave move; I hedged my bets; a global presence; equally crucial; a few good years; work hard and play hard.

Table 9.5   Women's Choice of Words and Adjectives

My work was taking a lot of my time; start on a small scale; I could manage; my responsibilities are less now; I can afford to travel more now; as long as you believed in what you did; make the best of; success is how you feel in the heart; to make a difference; to touch people's lives; I chatted with my staff and made coffee; having a vision but spiced with lots and lots of perseverance and teamwork; I love being a woman; I loved it, just loved it; I'm very happy; it gives me great joy; I was reduced to tears; just make me sick; so many horrible things.

Explanation and Elaboration of Findings

Women's Responses

Connections with others   The findings presented above indicate that women's own discourses are sites for the production of practices in which their identities are formed. There is a complex interrelationship between the self and others in women's identity development. Woman is not itself a unitary category but relates to different positions such as wife, mother, and daughter. Conversations with women about their lives were always related with all or a number of their significant others like their spouse, children, mother, father, siblings, etc. This connected self is encapsulated by a relational mode of discourse. A network of relationships offering connection to others is a constant topic in the talk of these female executives (Table 9.6).

Attributing success to others   In connection with these close networks is the fact that the various successes the women in the interviews have achieved were attributed to their significant others, primarily the spouse, or another close male member of the family like the father, brother or cousin, or relatives and friends. One aspiring individual praised the Malaysian Prime Minister who she has chosen as her role model and mentor for life. The various quotations are contained in Table 9.7 below.

At least four examples of successes, which were credited to significant others including mother, maid, relatives, and friends, were expressed as follows:

- I credit it (success) to others (e.g., husband, kids, mother, maid).
- My mother helps me by overseeing everything for me.
- Friends and relatives extended loans to keep the business going.
- Friends proved to be amazingly supportive.

Table 9.6   Mention of Significant Others

Take my husband for a holiday.

I'm very proud of (my husband) as he is of me.

I wouldn't mind hanging around my kids for a day.

My father is very recognized in Sweden but to me he is just my father.

Table 9.7   Attributions

The man in your life is very important for the woman whether its your father, brother or husband.

If this man is willing, he can empower you.

My father sends me books of famous speeches.

My success is due to having a supportive husband and family.

(My brother) said we could start on a small scale and then work up. He would provide the technical support and I would manage the company.

(My father) said it doesn't matter if you lost, as long as you believed in what you did.

(My father) and his business cronies tell me stories laced with integrity. ... I think I have absorbed their philosophies.

In the first three years, I would borrow from my father and friends to pay my staff.

At the suggestion of my brother, Alfred.

(My role model) is the Prime Minister. Dr. Mahathir Mohammad is my mentor for life.

Briefly, supportive spouses and parents were claimed to be the sine qua non of a successful woman. Women's discussions about their lives often focused on building a sense of self, which is dependent on the help of significant others who they acknowledged and appreciated throughout the interviews.

Attributing success to luck   Deaux and Emswiller (1974) found that girls and women would attribute what success they do achieve to chance rather than ability. At least 3 out of the 11 women interviewed said that they credit their professional success to luck or chance, or both.

- I credit it (success) to luck.
- I feel I'm lucky in that way.
- It is a path not based on choice but rather on circumstance.

Multifaceted sense of self, roles, and priorities   In this study, the women's gendered identities were found to be so deeply engrained that they surface frequently throughout their talk. A multifaceted sense of themselves, which are wives, daughters, and mothers, dominates the discourse. For the women in our study, their families took precedence over their work. One example is seen in this statement: "If my husband is fed, my children are fed only then I can go to work happy."

In addition, these women would also devote themselves to their professions. It is their desire to not only excel in their professional careers but in most cases also to care greatly for their families, as was expressed in the words of one top-ranking financial expert: "I want to be successful in my career but I also want to be a good wife and mother." This, according to one woman executive director "maybe … selfish but I would like to leave something behind for my children, something I have built." Although at the beginning she admitted that "I'm not cut out to be a homemaker. I really couldn't stay at home. I felt very restless," she also recognized that "at 50 my maternal responsibilities are less now that the children are grown up, I can afford to travel every other month." This superwoman was quoted as "having nerves of steel" in a company that ranked highest in the industry.

However, when it comes to competition between work and family, a younger executive would spend more time at home with her children. The owner of Business Trends, a fast-growing company in Malaysia, said: "I expect I'll have to take a slower pace at work when I have kids." She now works three half days and two full days a week because "her 11-month old baby takes priority now." Another example of the awareness of having to prioritize and juggle time due to the twin roles of career and wife/mother is captured in the words of a managing director: "Juggling my role as MD and being mother and wife. I never work on the weekends though."

Role of mother

The constant juggling between home and office demands comes through very often in the interviews. An awareness of this multifaceted role with its many and, at times, conflicting demands makes them realize that career women "always have to make time for the things (you) love." This sentiment is expressed in various ways, such as:

- "I get to work very early because I drop my daughter off at the International school in KL first which means I'm in the office by 7:15."
- "Trying to get my kids to wake up in the morning."

Men's Responses

Minimal mention of family   All the men, except two, did not appear to give credit to family for their success at work. One of them, Benjamin Tan, credits his wife, Anna, as the one who changed him for the better by encouraging him to take his career to a professional level. He says he wants to conceptualize a boutique hotel in Kuala Lumpur, but this has to wait because of his new baby daughter who he says is "my absolute priority and the only project that requires my constant, undivided attention now." The other, Richard Hoon, works between 12 to 14 hours daily, from Monday to Thursday, but he devotes his weekend "Friday dinner through Sunday bedtime—to his wife, his three daughters and their grandparents." During that time, he "squeezes in a Saturday morning game of golf, while his daughters are at ballet class, as well as a few hours of badminton on Sundays." With reference to work and leisure, the single men, more than their married counterparts, would put work first above pleasure. In other words, they are literally "married to their jobs" as the following statements testify:

- I work all day and most of the night. My office is my home, complete with sleeping bags. I go home on Saturday nights and return on Sundays.
- Without passion (for the job), it's so easy to get distracted.
- Nothing else comes close to it (computers). Out of 24 hours in a day, I probably spend something like 23 hours on it.

Focus on employees and clients   Without fail, all of the men in the interviews acknowledged that their work colleagues, employees, and clients are important assets in business and they wanted the world to know this fact. If their families were ranked the same, the message was certainly not expressed in quite the same overt and strong terms as those shown in Table 9.8 and Table 9.9.

Table 9.8 Focus on Employees

I want to create an environment where people appreciate one another.
I encourage my employees to work hard and play hard, too. They shouldn't bring their work home, and they shouldn't bring home to work.
I want every staff member to own the company. They are my assets, not brick and mortar. We're a people business.
In a good time, we need good people. In a bad time, we need better people.
Being the biggest means that we can have dedicated people on location serving their clients on the ground.
My philosophy is placing people first. My staff are not employees.
We love going for long drives, and we move as a group.

Table 9.9 Focus on Clients

As a commercial designer, one does not design for oneself … but to be appreciated by the public and quality built for the client.
Not only did I want to sell a product, I wanted to sell its integrity as well. I wanted to educate the customer.
It is still a people business and personalized service is still the utmost importance.
Only when a client advisor knows the economy, culture, social life, and business of the client will he be able to provide a clear and focused solution to his client's needs.
You have to understand that every client is somebody special.
We do have a long-standing clientele, we try to keep our customers happy, we keep in touch on a regular basis, and we have built up a good, solid relationship over the years.
People inspire me.
You don't design clothes for the media or your own image; you design them with a client in mind.

Mention of how great they and their companies are in their work lives   More often than not, the men tended to talk about their own self importance and/or the success of their companies, as seen in the examples given in Table 9.10.

Need to constantly advance and take risks   On the whole, the men in the interviews said they had to strategize their business moves constantly in order to stay ahead of other competing corporations. In the more competitive international and global businesses such as expensive cars, jewelery, food chains, hotels, and property market, the various CEOs have proudly proclaimed that they have had to take big risks and invest abroad so that their companies could expand and grow to giant heights (see Table 9.11).

Table 9.10   Focus on Companies

Last year we were in a state of flux, managing a million things at once. It was horrendous, wondering what was next. This year, everything's in place. The dealers are crying out for cars.

Plough the extra money into pearls. Almost immediately, people in the pearl business started to notice us. We were taken seriously and now we are major players.

I enjoy my role now. It's a hell of a challenge. I can see quite clearly a successful future for the company. It's not only possible, it's inevitable.

We had offers from six public-listed companies.

We were getting returns of $2 million from one of the five-star hotels that we bought. Now three and a half years later, we're past $7 million, and improved profits by 350%, but we still don't want to pretend that we're there yet.

We've broken records for the last three months so everyone's had an extra three days off.

I was dealing with 80 suppliers from all corners of the world. It became a challenge to turn at least 50% of them to customers.

Over the last six months, our business has grown in a tremendous way; more syndicates and more partnerships and a global presence.

Table 9.11   Risk-taking

When I took over the name and business, the liabilities were greater than the assets. I suppose it was a brave move. I took a risk but I hedged my bets.

I may be outwardly calm, but I'm restless in business. I don't like status quo. Once you get into that, everyone else is overtaking you. Every level must be pushed, to move forward into something better.

I want to change current norms.

We have a major IT player in the U.S., looking for 1,000 managers around the world in the next 12 to 18 months. They have set a budget of $30 million just for that. Which company can fill that? You need speed, accuracy, and global reach. In the past we couldn't do it.

We need not develop an inferiority complex in relation to any of (the global chains), we proved we can match them, and later actually outperformed these global brands.

I think we can take Asia, easily, a total of 15 to 20 offices. I want to build Asia's largest company.

Discussion

While feminists argue that we should stop dichotomizing behavior by sex (Bern, 1981), these interviews with "powerful women" reveal that women's own discourses are sited for the production of such gendered identities. It is clear that women, by their discourse, can render themselves powerful or powerless. If their success is credited to others or to chance and luck, are women not demeaning their own successes? The women in these sample interviews have a sense of self, which is dependent on other people in their lives. Men, on the other hand, inhabit an impersonal milieu where there is little talk about spouse and where the focus is on work, risk-taking, clients, and themselves. In contrast, women inhabit a personal world of family and friends. The multiple positions that women accord themselves result in crediting success to these important others in their lives and insisting that their priorities are both work and family, properly apportioned. Women see themselves in many roles as wives, partners, and mothers and as career women and homemakers, too.

These women hold in common various ideas and values, which dictate their actions, rules of behavior, and beliefs. We have also noted their concerns about balancing work and family. Their concept of power and success means a balanced, healthy family, and love relationship. Their power and status in the job market are not trivial achievements but are comparable to those of their male counterparts, and yet we do not encounter the same weight given to family commitments by men in power.

In the last 20 years or so, there have been some changes in the image of women in business. Indeed a new set of women has emerged in the business world in the new millennium, yet their roles have remained the same. The modern career women are presented as superwomen, who have managed to do all the work on the job and at home, sometimes with the services of paid professional domestic maids, which they arranged and organized to perfection. These women have portrayed themselves to be powerful, liberated, independent, and successful in running a business as well as a happy home.

In the corporate world, the men strongly believe that to succeed "they shouldn't bring their work home, and they shouldn't bring home to work." Why then do these individual women conform to the normative expectations of their roles and positions? Why do they simultaneously concentrate attention on love and family? Although in all the interviews these questions were not asked of them, it is obvious that these women see conformity with institutionalized expectations of their social and family roles as a moral duty. Any conflict of interests between work and family or violation of the standard norm would be met with guilt or shame on their part. Society still accepts men who devote themselves wholly to work but not women who are expected to put their family first or on the same priority as work.

Conclusion

In this study, we have developed an adequate understanding of the nature and language of the two genders. What have the interviews in this study told us about the language of powerful women and that of powerful men? It will require that we learn to think differently about them and see the world through their categories. We will have to learn to pay close attention to their language, their attitudes, and their behavior and ask what values and forms of relationships are being created and maintained, both consciously or unintentionally. In short, we ask what and whose interests are served through the choice of language used. We acknowledge that there are real differences in their choice of language, which reflect differences in priority and attitude. The cause is social upbringing and social roles and expectations. We believe that this socialization pattern leads to prevailing conceptions of masculinity, manhood, head of household, breadwinner, and many of the qualities defined as "feminine," which social realities condition women to see themselves in. Women harbor a sense of worth and pride in their jobs and families, which are supposed to inspire other working women, while men portray a sense of pride in their work and proud that they are part of a successful company. This is conveyed in statements that are meant to inspire themselves and other men.

This study does not claim that men use more powerful or masculine language while women employ more powerless or feminine varieties of speech, but that both are used by both men and women and that distribution is related primarily not to sex or positions of power in the workplace, since both the men and women interviewed held equally high positions of power, status, and authority, but to their social orientation and roles. The women in the interviews perceive that home, family, and love are important attributes that go hand in hand with powerful jobs, and men perceive themselves as breadwinners who leave such matters to their wives, no matter how successful and busy they are in their workplace and career.

A survey of 500 women and 132 men in 20 countries by the Conference Board (Catalyst, 2002) research organizations based in New York, suggested that women believe stereotyping is the biggest roadblock to advancement in business in Europe. Just a year ago, when Catalyst asked 3,000 women in their mid-20s to mid-30s to name the biggest barriers to women's advancement, 68% cited personal and family responsibilities. That compares with 50% who blamed lack of mentoring, 46% who said lack of experience, and just 45% who cited stereotyping of women's roles and responsibilities. Betsy Morris (2002) in her interview article called "Trophy Husband," about a househusband/stay-at-home dad/domestic engineer (call him what you will), published in *Fortune*, October 14, 2002, p. 60, remarked that "A precondition to having more women in positions of power is to have more sharing in the burden of parenthood." For all the progress women have made in the workforce, and men have made in accepting them there, many people of both sexes are uncomfortable with the outright reversal of gender roles. More and more women are wrestling with gender roles as high-powered jobs come within their reach. The dividends for these working wives—peace of mind, no distractions, the ability to focus single-mindedly on work—are precisely the ones their male counterparts have always had.

References

Benjamin Tan, the visionary. (2001). *The Peak, 12*(6), 107.

Bern, S. L. (1981). Gender schema theory: A cognitive account of sex-typing. *Psychological Review, 88,* 354–364.

Bernard Chandran, portrait of a perfectionist. (2001). *The Peak, 11*(6), 91–97.

Burke, J. (2001). John Glajz: Managing Director, Mondial Jewellers Pte. Ltd. *The Peak, 11*(6), 30–36.

Catalyst (2002). Women of color in corporate management: Three years later. Catalyst, New York.

Chan, W. K. (2002). Managing director of the Carat Club. *The Peak, 13*(1), 91.

Chandran, K. (2001). Tony Gott: Chief executive Rolls-Royce Motor Cars & Bentley Motor Cars. *The Peak, 11*(2), 14–20.

Conley, J. M., O'Barr, W., & Lind, E. A. (1978). The power of language: Presentation style in the courtroom. *Duke Law Journal, 6,* 1375–1399.

Deaux, K., & Emswiller, T. (1974). Explanations of successful performance on sex-linked tasks: What is skill for the male is luck for the female. *Journal of Personality and Social Psychology, 29,* 80–85.

Emerson, A. (2000). Lena Olving: Parked at the top. *Working Women Asia. Inaugural Issue.*

Edvinsson, L., & Malone, M. S. (1997). *Intellectual capital.* London: Piatkus.

Erickson, F., & Schultz, J. J. (1978). *Talking to the man: Social and cultural organization of communication in school counseling interviews.* New York: New York Academic Press.

Foo, M. Z. (2001). Ow Chio Kiat: Chairman, Hai Sun Sup Group. *The Peak, 12*(3), 24–32.

Foo, M. Z. (2002). Georges Gagnebin: Chief Executive Officer, UBS Private Banking. *The Peak, 13*(1), 20–24.

Guyon, J. (2002, October 14). The 50 most powerful businesswomen outside the U.S. *Fortune, 146*(6), 58–66.

Hermann, D. (2001). Lo and behold. *The Peak, 11*(4), 32–36.

Hjelt, P. (2003, October 13). The power 50. *Fortune, 148*(8), 44–50.

Investors in people. (August, 2002). People @ the heart of business. Retrieved November 17, 2004, from: http://www.investorsinpeople.co.uk/NR/rdonlyres/ ecuq3es3v4kauop3fuzhhi7ggcmcpapvepsw6e5juctszhg75yh5gbi4fn2m2ts- m4vykhm74djmbgzyj5grpe36gw2a/people+%40+heart+of+business.doc

Kolle, C. (2001, November). Breaking into the boy's club. *Asian Business*, 44.

Lee, J. (2002, February). Risk-takers. *Asian Business*, 12–13.

Lim, J. (1999, April). Top of the lot. *Female.*

Lugun, N. (1999, December). Dato' Dr. James Jemut Masing: Tour of duty. *Malaysian Tatler.*

Menon, S. (2001). Richard Hoon. CEO, MRI Asia. *The Peak, 11*(4), 26–30.

Morris, B. (2002). Trophy husbands. *The Peak, 146*(6), 71–81.

Nadarajah, S. (2000a). Raja Zamilia Raja Dato' Mansur: A myriad of journeys. *Working Women Asia, Inaugural Issue.*

Nadarajah, S. (2000b). Dr. Jannie Tay: Woman in time. *Working Women Asia, Inaugural Issue.*

Nathan, M. D. (2000a). Women in power suits. *Working Women Asia, Inaugural Issue.*

Nathan, M. D. (2000b). The glass ceiling. *Working Women Asia, Inaugural Issue.*

O'Barr, W. M., & O'Barr, J. F. (1976). *Language and politics.* The Hague: Mouton.

Ong, T., & Parrott, S. (2002, May). Exclusive interview—Dr. Mahathir. *Asia MC.*

Ramakrishnan Govindasamy, the software genius. (2002). *The Peak, 11*(5), 89.

Sidhu, S., & al-Attas, S. (2000). Y. B. Dato' Sharizat Abdul Jalil: A woman of style, elegance and power. *Working Women Asia, Inaugural Issue.*

Stevens, H. (2000). Oprah Winfrey: The mighty O. *Working Women Asia, Inaugural Issue.*

Up close with Nurhalida Dato' Seri Mohd. Khalil: Taking motherhood in her stride. (2002, May). *Ezyhealth.*

Woman of distinction. (2002). *The Peak, 3*(1), 69–75.

10

THE IMMIGRANT WO(MAN) AND GENDERED ACCESS TO SECOND LANGUAGE USE AND DEVELOPMENT:
The Case of a Vietnamese Couple in the States

Jette G. Hansen Edwards
The Chinese University of Hong Kong, Hong Kong

Defining and Researching Gender: From Biological to Social Spaces

Traditionally, the study of gender and second language acquisition (SLA) has located gender in a fixed, unchanging, and often biological space with the primary focus on differences between men and women with regard to the following: bias in second/foreign language textbooks (Lesikin, 1998; Rifkin, 1998), test bias (cf. Kunnan, 1990; O'Sullivan, 2000), learning styles/strategies (cf. Goh & Foong, 1997; Young & Oxford, 1997); teacher-talk and student-talk in the language classroom (Shehadeh, 1999), and different skills such as listening (Bacon, 1992; Markham, 1988), reading (Brantmeier, 2001; Carrell & Wise, 1998), and verbal skills (Losey, 1995). The findings from some of these research studies have contributed to a widespread belief that women are superior in L2 learning (cf. Boyle, 1987; Burstall, 1975; Ehrman & Oxford, 1989). However, as Ehrlich (1997) states, the research in this area often confuses gender and sex, and "exaggerate(s) and overgeneralize(s) differences between women and men in addition to ignoring the social, cultural, and situational forces that shape gender categories and gender relations" (p. 426).

A more promising area of research on SLA and gender defines gender as "social practice" (Ehrlich, 1997), locating it within a social, historical, and cultural space that is dynamic across time and space. In this view, gender is

"a system of culturally constructed relations of power, produced and reproduced in interaction between and among men and women" (Gal, 1991, p. 176).
One strand of research in this area has focused on how gender constrains the
level of access that L2 learners have to linguistic resources, with the majority
of the studies examining how women are denied access to linguistic resources,
both at school and at work (cf. Blackledge, 2001; Cumming & Gill, 1992;
Ehrlich, 2001; Goldstein, 1995, 2001; Losey, 1995; Kouritzin, 2000; Teutsch-
Dwyer, 2001). Findings indicate that both the first language (L1) and L2 community may constrain the language development of immigrant women. In
many cases, women may be denied access to English as a second language
(ESL) classes or workplaces where the L2 could be practiced due to L1 cultural
norms (cf. Cumming & Gill, 1992; Goldstein, 1995, 2001; Kouritzin, 2000).
Additionally, when they do attend the courses, they may not get as much attention in the classroom as men (Losey, 1995).

   While research has begun focusing on *how* these actions, activities, and behaviors are encouraged differently for women and men, and the
resulting access to L2 use and development opportunities, there has been
little research to date (cf. Teutsch-Dwyer, 2001) that directly examines the
impact of the differential access to L2 use and development opportunities on
the *acquisition* of an L2. Recent research, though, in the acquisition of an L2
phonology, has begun suggesting that the degree of accent in the L2 may be
influenced by extent of L1 use—the greater the L1 use, the greater the degree
of foreign accent (cf. Flege, Frieda, & Nozawa, 1997; MacKay, & Flege, 2001).

Background to the Study

The focus of this chapter is on a husband and wife, providing a unique opportunity to examine how a man and woman from the same sociocultural background, with the same family social networks, and similar age, incoming
English language proficiency, and educational background, have gendered
access to L2 development through workplaces. This research study explores
how the participants react to differing types and levels of access to L1 and L2
use, as well as establish and maintain this access within the family. The study
also examines how these differential levels of access to L2 use impact the
participants' acquisition of English, focusing specifically on the acquisition
of syllable final consonants and consonant clusters (codas).

   Data collection began in February of 1999, lasted two years, and continued until April of 2001. During the first year, data were collected at weekly
intervals for one to two hours at the participants' home, at their request,
and in various social settings for over 60 hours of data; thereafter, data were

collected at tri-monthly intervals. The meetings at the participants' home were tape-recorded and consisted of conversations between the two participants and me about their L2 use opportunities, social networks, and interactions at home and work. Ethnographic observation data were also collected across different social contexts in order to observe the participants' interaction patterns with other individuals and across various social activities and contexts. Extensive and detailed notes were made of these observations, which were not tape-recorded for confidentiality reasons.

Three times during the first year of the study, at approximately four-month intervals, one of the interviews was analyzed for the production of syllable final codas. A total of 4,440 codas were collected. The speech samples were transcribed using the International Phonetic Alphabet (IPA). Each data set was transcribed twice by the researcher, with an average intra-rater reliability of 93%. Additionally, approximately 20% of each of the researcher's transcriptions were randomly checked by an IPA-trained researcher, with an average inter-rater reliability of 94%. When discrepancies arose, a third rater evaluated the word in question, and the transcription that was selected by two individuals was chosen as accurate. In the rare cases (less than 1%) that a disagreement arose among all three transcriptions, the word in question was eliminated from the data set. Each token was coded for the target English word; if the target was unclear, the word was also eliminated from analysis.

A loglinear analysis was employed to test statistical significance of accurate production by time, participant, and coda length. The interview and ethnographic observation data were analyzed for emerging themes and patterns based on Grounded Theory (Strauss & Corbin, 1990).

The Nguyen Family

Nhi and Anh Nguyen (pseudonyms) immigrated to the United States in March 1998 in order to be reunited with family members already residing there. Nhi comes from a family of twelve, of whom he is the oldest. Nhi's family members left Vietnam shortly after the Vietnam War and as there was a great uncle in Nhi's family who lived in Germany, Nhi's family elected to go to Germany. At this time, Nhi's father was in prison, where he stayed for seven years as he had been high-ranking official in the South Vietnamese army. The oldest son, Nhi, could not leave Vietnam as he had to take care of his father in prison.

Anh comes from a family of five brothers and sisters, of whom she is also the oldest. The family began immigrating to the United States in 1975 after one of Anh's brothers and sisters was sponsored by an American woman who lived in Tucson, Arizona. This brother and sister were able to sponsor other relatives, and eventually all of Anh's siblings, as well as her mother, came to the United States.

Anh's family has integrated into their new life very successfully, attaining college degrees and middle-class incomes. All of Anh's brothers and sisters attended the University of Arizona. The first brother and sister who came to the United States became engineers and work for the government, one as a satellite engineer and the other as an electrical engineer. Anh's other brother also went to the University of Arizona and works as a technician for a weapons factory in Tucson. One of Anh's sisters went into the Navy after getting a degree in computer science from the University of Arizona and finished with the rank of captain. She works as a computer trainer in the Navy and lives in Virginia. A third sister is an engineer for IBM.

While their families were adapting to and becoming successful in their new countries, life was very hard for Nhi and Anh. In Vietnam, Nhi had been a high school chemistry teacher and Anh had been an elementary school teacher. After immigrating to Tucson, Anh found work inserting ad pages into the daily newspaper before it was delivered. She worked at this for several months before saving enough money to attend nail technician school. Nhi found a job in a factory as an order filler. At the beginning of the study, both Nhi and Anh were trying to take as many ESL classes as their work schedules would allow so that they could increase their English language proficiency. Both hoped to eventually attend college, Anh to study computer science and Nhi to study electrical engineering, in order to find work outside the nail shop and factory, respectively.

The Caretaker Identity, Gender, and Language Use and Learning

A First Glance

At a first glance, it appears that Anh had greater access to social and English language use opportunities than Nhi, and that these greater opportunities were acknowledged and supported within the family. For example, Anh had several opportunities to travel within the United States, taking a 10-day drive from Virginia Beach through Florida and Texas and back to Arizona with one of her sisters. She also went on a long weekend trip to Las Vegas with her coworkers. In contrast, Nhi did not take any trips due to difficulties in getting time off from work. As Nhi stated, "she always have ... many many chance travel ... I have no chance." Anh also had more social opportunities; she had made friends with a Chinese student and an Indonesian student in her ESL course during her first semester of study at a local community college and frequently met them for social gatherings. As Nhi often said of his wife, "she have many friends ... I am no friends." Finally, at work, Anh had to use English to interact with her customers in the nail shop while Nhi primarily worked without speaking at his job as an order filler. This is also acknowledged by Nhi: "my using English is ... less than her ... because I have few chances to practice English. ..." Anh could also be said to be highly successful in her job; even though she started working as a nail technician in March 1999, just two short years later, in April 2001, she opened her own nail salon. She was no longer an employee, but rather the "boss." In fact, in a move to support her and the family, Nhi changed his work schedule at the golf factory from five days of eight hours each day to four days of ten hours each so he could take classes in order to become a nail technician and to help out in the salon. Eventually, Nhi did get his nail technician's license and now works as an employee in Anh's nail salon part-time.

A Second Glance

Based on this initial analysis, the story of the Tran family seems to have little in common with the stories told by Goldstein (1995, 2001), Kouritzin (2000), Cumming and Gill (1992), Peirce (1995, 1997), and Losey (1995), among others. Anh did not seem to have any barriers in L2 use and development; in fact, the opposite appeared true: Her language use appeared to be facilitated across social and work settings while her husband's seemed to be hindered. Her husband not only supported her ESL coursework, but also supported her travel and social networks outside the family. In fact, he aspired to become like her, positioning her in a lead role within the family, as the "go-getter," "traveler," and "leader," and, eventually, as his own boss. As he stated, "I believe I believe ... she will study good ... she will go ... she very hard work very hard study ... but I don't believe me ... I follow I follow I follow her." However, while Anh appears to be facilitated in L2 use, her "contexts" of L2 use are in actuality more reduced than Nhi's, and the access to various L2 use contexts both Anh and Nhi have is gendered due to the positioning of Anh within the family as the caretaker as well as the leader. Due to the circumstances of the Trans' immigration to the United States, and the fact that they are residing in a community with Anh's brothers and sisters, the role of caretaker gets redefined from being a housekeeper, nurturer, wife, and mother, to being the financial caretaker for the family.

There are a number of factors that have affected this redefinition of caretaker: First, Anh is responsible for her immediate family being in the United States as they immigrated there because her family members were already established in the United States, whereas members of Nhi's family had immigrated to Germany. Once in the United States, Anh feels responsible for her immediate family's financial well-being, especially as she realizes that the norms of extended family financial support are different from those in Vietnam: In Vietnam, it is common to share financial and other resources among extended family members, whereas in the United States, this is typically not the case. As Anh finds out, her brothers and sisters have become Americanized to the extent that they expect Anh's family to become financially independent as soon as possible; initially, this was difficult for Anh to understand and accept:

My culture ... Asian ... we are everybody I my family he always life together ... in here ... I understand that everybody one family one person ... my brother and my sister ... they are live in here twenty year ago ... they are ... different me ... ago two year ... I can't understand ... my brother and my sister ... they life.

Anh's realization that each family is financially independent of each other, and that her own sisters and brothers expect Anh's family to become financially stable and less reliant on the rest of the family, combined with her status as the oldest sister, which in Vietnamese culture signifies responsibility for younger siblings, compel Anh to find work as quickly as possible in one of the most accessible workplaces for Vietnamese women in Tucson: the nail shop. As Anh says:

I study nail technician because my [friend] ... she work nails long time ... she ... encourage me study nail ... I start think I don't study nail because I don't understand everything and she encourage the if you study in Vietnamese you can study in here ... I study nail three months ... after I try in class ... because I don't understand my teacher explain everything ... I always read book and watch television and video ... I study my friend come back home ... I translation dictionary everyday ... after three months I pass the test.

As Anh's statement illustrates, getting a nail technician's license and gaining employment in a nail shop is one of the easier (relatively speaking) options available to Vietnamese women in Tucson because of the pre-established networks within the Vietnamese community. Another Vietnamese nail technician helps Anh get her license and find employment, and even though Anh is initially unable to read and fully understand the English texts used in the nail courses, she is able to become certified due to the help of her Vietnamese friend. Meanwhile, Nhi finds employment in a golf factory as an order filler, a job that is more acceptable for men within the Vietnamese community. Although women are employed in the factory, they are typically American or Mexican and not Vietnamese.

On the surface, the nail salon appears to be a site of many L2 language-use opportunities—and thus many chances to develop English skills—especially in contrast to work in a factory setting, where Nhi only has opportunities to use English is during short breaks and the lunch hour. As stated previously, Nhi perceives that his wife does have greater opportunities to practice her English than he does as she has to interact with customers all day long, and as her customers are usually American or Mexican, the interaction has to be in English.

In actuality, however, the nail shop proves to be an unsupportive English language-use environment for Anh for a number of reasons. First of all, the majority of Anh's customers are Mexican, and like Anh herself, have limited English communication skills. While she talks with her customers, her communication is restricted as she has difficulty expressing her ideas and also understanding the English her Mexican customers speak. Secondly, Anh also initially has an additional difficulty: As she is new at being a nail technician, she also experiences problems in performing her job well and has a difficult time concentrating on her work as well as on her English at the same time. Finally, she is also under increasing pressure from her boss to speak more English with her customers, and this pressure fuels her anxiety, culminating in her switching nail shops after three months in the first shop. As she says:

I have just nail technician because my owner talk talk me and why why you don't talk customer ... are you nervous ... are you afraid customer ... because I am talk a little bit ... speaking English with customer ... I make no good ... no good ... I ... control machine ... yes because I worry ... I nervous in talk customer.

A common theme throughout the period of the study, and across the three nail shops Anh works in before opening her own shop, is her sense of frustration at work because of her limited English skills. This frustration is due partly because of the pressure from her boss to have "small talk" with the customers. Additionally, she must talk to her customers about nail diseases and fungi, but does not feel that she has the vocabulary or the grammatical structures to communicate her ideas. She forces herself to try to communicate with them, but her experiences are not usually successful because as she states:

I talk ... vocabulary no sentence no structure ... I can't explain I can't explain their understand nail and disease ... I speak vocabulary ... no sentence no structure sentence ... customer don't understand and I don't understand them ... I think it is bad experience.

These experiences are very depressing and discouraging for Anh, and she breaks down crying when she relates them.

Anh craves a supportive and stable work environment so she can relax and spend her energy on improving her English and learning more about life in the United States. She switches to a second nail salon in the hope of finding this environment, but finds that the situation is similar to the first salon. Eventually, she finds work at a third salon—the third in a period of nine months—but finds that although she has more confidence in her abilities as a nail technician, she still lacks the English skills she needs to communicate with her clients successfully. The pressure to communicate with her customers is still present:

I I always ... their name name and ... what do you work work? You you live around live around ... yeah I ask ... their ... mmm ... family family ... and children ... sometimes ... because in the salon ... only one me talk ... talk a little customer and my owner attention me ... she and he ... and they are always ... complain ... complain me ... why you don't speak English. ...

When she does talk with her customers, she understands only about half: "my my customer always ask me ... I I understand about fifty or seventy ... yeah ... but I answer ... a little." Her difficulty, she believes, is in part because of her restricted opportunities to interact with native speakers in English as she only communicates with speakers of Spanish in English:

I feel confident in my my job ... yes ... mmmm ... the the difficult in ... with me are now pronunciation my my ... the ... my pronunciation ... is harder ... because I always ... communication with with customer Mexican....

She tries to speak English everyday "but ... customer Mexican ... sometime they are don't speak English ... or speak a few English ... I very hard to speak ... customer ... I I I feel I speak ... slow slow slowly yeah ... cause I I I want contact with Americans ... I can speak a lot of. ..." Because of her work hours, she is unable to continue attending ESL classes, and therefore feels frustrated because she has few opportunities either in the present or in the future to learn English. It is in part because of her frustrations about her English language skills, and the pressure put on her by the bosses of all three nail shops she works at, that she decides to open her own nail salon, even though this will eventually make it even more difficult for her to pursue her dream of attending college so she can become a computer programmer. However, she sublimates this desire to her family's well-being as she perceives that financial caretaking is the primary and immediate goal even at the expense of her own future.

In contrast, Nhi has fairly limited opportunities to practice English if measured time-wise—his only chances are during short breaks and his lunch hour. However, while Nhi also wants more opportunities to speak English, he does have a fairly supportive work environment in terms of English language practice. He has four good friends at work, two American and two Mexican men. He talks with them everyday during their break times and lunches, and as he says, "they teach English ... if I if I speak wrong they correct for me." They teach him job terminology and they often joke during breaks, as he says, "when ... break time ... we have we talk we talk together funny." He understands everything when he speaks with his friends at work as they tend to speak very slowly so he can follow and join their conversation.

Across time, this situation improves for Nhi, as the addition of an American woman to his work group enables him to get even more opportunities to practice English: "my my factory ... my group have ... a new friend a new friend ... woman... she she talk all the way." He credits her talkativeness to his English improvement: "I I I speak English with my my workmates better ... better yes ... because my my friends ... she is talks very talks a lot." His workmates teach him new words as well as correcting his mispronunciations:

when I ... I speak wrong ... they ... correct for me ... example I ... I say {pA.l′t}... they correct {pœ.l′t} ... and sometimes sometimes ... I misunderstand ... their ... misunderstand ... their description yeah ... I I I I ask again ... they speak slowly ... slowly I understand.

In fact, he feels that he is relying less on Vietnamese to understand English; while he was translating his ideas from Vietnamese into English before speaking, which slowed him down, he now feels he can think in English: "I am practicing because before I speak English ... I guess ... I guess my Vietnamese so I speak slowly ... now I I I try ... speak English ... I guess by English ... yeah ... I I feel I feel I feel ... I feel easy ... easily improving." His English improvement has also been noticed by his boss, who has given him a different job assignment nine months later at a time when Anh is switching to her third nail salon. Instead of pulling orders inside the warehouse, he now directly interacts with customers, taking orders to give to the person inside the warehouse to pull.

Language Use and Language Acquisition

By the end of the study, Anh and Nhi have different perspectives on their English language abilities and how their ability has changed over time. As Nhi states:

I begin to work at company ... I didn't hear and didn't speak ... English everybody ... and now ... I speak English everybody in my department ... in my company ... and I speak they are understand ... they understood I speak ... because study English ... with workmates. ...

Nhi perceives that his English has improved significantly across time because when he began working in the factory, he was unable to communicate in English and he now understands and is understood by everybody. He credits his co-workers with helping him—in fact, he states he studies English with them.

In contrast, while Anh's listening skills have improved, she still feels that her speaking skills, especially in the area of pronunciation, are weak. As she states:

Now I think I can hear ... I can hear my customer speak ... I understand ... fifty or sixty percent ... my customer talk long sentences ... sometimes I don't understand ... sometime I talk with customer understood but I try because not confident ... because my customer Mexican ... few customer they speak English very well ... almost they speak English very poor ... they are always speak short sentences yes I understood but I answer I answer sometime ... they don't understand ... they don't understood because I pronunciation very bad.

In order to examine the effects of the differential opportunities for English language use impacted Anh and Nhi's L2 phonological development, their production of syllable codas were analyzed. There were a total 4,400 syllable codas for analysis. Descriptive statistics of Anh and Nhi's production of final syllable codas by length (C means singleton codas as in the final consonant in *hat*, CC means two-member codas as in the final two consonants in *word*, and CCC means three-member codas as in the final three consonants in *words*) and time are given in Table 10.1.

As Table 10.1 illustrates, Nhi had a higher accurate percentage for both C and CC codas across time, except for C codas at time 3. The difference in accurate production is greater for CC codas. Neither Nhi nor Anh were able to accurately produce any of the CCC codas across time, and, therefore, there were no differences in production percentages for this type of coda. However, while the number of CCC attempts for Anh and Nhi at time 1 were very close (Anh had 22 attempts while Nhi had 20), Nhi's number of attempts increases to 31 and 30 at times 2 and 3, respectively, while Anh's drop to 21 and 6 at times 2 and 3, respectively. Therefore, while neither of the two participants were able to produce these codas accurately, Nhi does have a greater number of attempts for this coda than Anh.

A loglinear analysis was also conducted in order to determine whether the differences in accurate production between the two participants were significant, and whether differences in production by coda length and time were significant; it was found that all three factors, participant, time, and coda length, were statistically significant at $P < .025$ ($df = 4$, total $\chi^2 =$ 11.4385).

Table 10.1 Production of Codas by Participant, Time, and Length

Time	Time 1		Time 2		Time 3	
Participant	Anh	Nhi	Anh	Nhi	Anh	Anh
C						
Accurate	281	276	232	219	369	356
	45%	53%	40%	48%	49%	47%
Inaccurate	345	249	347	241	391	397
	55%	47%	60%	52%	51%	53%
Total	626	525	579	460	760	753
CC						
Accurate	6	11	3	5	3	11
	5%	9%	4%	7%	2%	11%
Inaccurate	111	115	70	63	118	91
	95%	91%	96%	93%	98%	89%
Total	117	126	73	68	121	102
CCC						
Accurate	0	0	0	0	0	0
	0%	0%	0%	0%	0%	0%
Inaccurate	22	20	21	31	6	30
	100%	100%	100%	100%	100%	100%
Total	22	22	21	31	6	30

The Impact of Gender Roles on Language Learning

As the story of the Nguyen family illustrates, gender may be a factor in which work roles are available for immigrant men and women. Because of Anh's perception that she had to bear the burden of the responsibility for the financial well-being of her immediate family, she took a job in a nail salon as this was a relatively easy job to find for Vietnamese women because of Vietnamese social networks. Though she was unhappy in her job, she stayed in that profession in order to continue earning money in order to help her immediate family become financially independent. In order to assuage the unhappiness she felt and the pressures on her to speak English in the salons, she moved from salon to salon, three in the space of one year. However, the situation did not change across each of these salons, and eventually Anh took the only option open to her: She opened her own salon and became her own boss.

At a first glance, this may appear to be an immigrant success story; however, a deeper analysis of the Nguyen's story indicates it is not. Anh is unhappy as a nail technician and being a boss, but has sublimated her own desires in order to guarantee the financial well-being of her family. The work context does not give her the opportunities she feels she needs to practice her English so she can pursue her real dream of becoming a computer programmer. As the data shows, the nail salon is highly restrictive in the types of opportunities Anh had to practice English. This has impacted Anh's perceptions of her ability to speak English and her ability to receive the types of input and opportunities for interaction to help her develop her L2 and her ability to pursue her aspired profession.

As the analysis of the linguistic data indicates, Anh's limited access to L2 use opportunities affected her acquisition of English. Her production of English syllable codas is statistically significantly less accurate than Nhi's across time and length. Nhi was also able to acquire more complex coda structures before Anh, as illustrated in his much greater accuracy in production of CC codas. Finally, Nhi appeared to be exposed to more complex coda structures—as evidenced by his greater attempts at words with CCC codas. This is perhaps not surprising given the greater opportunities for interaction and correction that Nhi had in comparison with Anh, and the fact that Nhi was scaffolded and corrected by his co-workers while Anh typically interacted solely in Vietnamese and had difficulty communicating with her clients, who were often also non-native speakers of English. Conversely, Anh's greater L1 and lesser L2 use makes it more difficult for her to develop linguistic knowledge and receive the opportunities for complex language use and scaffolding that may aid L2 acquisition. As Flege et al. (1997) and Piske et al. (2001) found, and this research study supports, it does appear that the greater the native language use, the greater the degree of foreign accent.

Conclusion

Very little research has been done on how gender roles—both within the L1 and the L2 community—affect the acquisition of an L2 (cf. Teutsch-Dwyer, 2001). This study examines this issue by focusing on the opportunities for L2 language use, both in terms of quality and quantity, by a husband and wife, and the acquisition of English syllable codas by these two participants. Findings from this study suggest that gender roles may impact the type of occupational opportunities available to some immigrant men and women due to L1 norms and social networks, and that workplaces can serve as facilitators or debilitators of L2 development in terms of supporting L2 and

L1 use. Additionally, outcomes of the workplace support for L2 use and development may ultimately impact the acquisition of the L2, as it illustrated in the differential production accuracies for syllable codas for the woman and the man in this study. Finally, the study raises a number of questions that bear further examination as the relationship between gender, the social context, and language learning continues to be explored: To what extent does the L1 and L2 culture limit work roles for immigrant women, and how do these limited roles impact language learning and subject positions? Do women's self-internalized moral and cultural values (e.g., to sacrifice one's aspired career to take up the financial burden of one's family) lead to their self-limiting job decisions? These questions require further research as the social construction of gender and the impact of this construction on L2 development becomes an increasingly important area of research in SLA.

References

Bacon, S. M. (1992). The relationship between gender, comprehension, processing strategies, and cognitive and affective response in foreign language listening. *The Modern Language Journal, 76*, 160–178.

Blackledge, A. (2001). Complex positionings: Women negotiating identity and power in a minority urban setting. In A. Pavlenko, A. Blackledge, I. Piller, & M. Teutsch-Dwyer (Eds.), *Multilingualism, second language learning, and gender* (pp. 53–75). Berlin: Mouton de Gruyter.

Boyle, J. (1987). Sex differences in listening vocabulary. *Language Learning, 37*, 273–284.

Brantmeier, C. (2001). Second language reading research on passage content and gender: Challenges for the intermediate-level curriculum. *Foreign Language Annals, 34*, 325–334.

Burstall, C. (1975). Factors affecting foreign language learning: A consideration of some recent findings. *Language Teaching and Linguistic Abstracts, 8*, 5–25.

Carrell, P., & Wise, T. (1998). The relationship between prior knowledge and topic interest in second language reading. *Studies in Second Language Acquisition, 20*, 285–309.

Cumming, A., & Gill, J. (1992). Motivation or accessibility? Factors permitting Indo-Canadian women to pursue ESL literacy instruction. In B. Burnaby & A. Cumming (Eds.), *Socio-political aspects of ESL education in Canada* (pp. 241–252). Toronto: OISE Press.

Ehrlich, S. (1997). Gender as social practice: Implications for second language acquisition. *Studies in Second Language Acquisition, 19*, 421–446.

Ehrlich, S. (2001). Gendering the "learner": Sexual harassment and second language acquisition. In A. Pavlenko, A. Blackledge, I. Piller, & M. Teutsch-Dwyer (Eds.), *Multilingualism, second language learning, and gender* (pp. 103–129). Berlin: Mouton de Gruyter.

Ehrman, M., & Oxford, R. (1989). Effects of sex differences, career choice, and psychological type on adults' language learning strategies. *Modern Language Journal, 73*, 1–13.

Flege, J. E., Frieda, E. M., & Nozawa, T. (1997). Amount of native-language (L1) use affects the pronunciation of an L2. *Journal of Phonetics, 25*, 169–186.

Gal, S. (1991). Between speech and silence: The problematics of research on language and gender. In M. Di Leonardo (Ed.), *Gender at the cross-roads of knowledge* (pp. 175–203). Berkeley: University of California Press.

Goh, C., & Foong, K. P. (1997). Chinese ESL students' learning strategies: A look at frequency, proficiency, and gender. *Hong Kong Journal of Applied Linguistics, 2*, 39–53.

Goldstein, T. (1995). Nobody is talking bad: Creating community and claiming power on the production lines. In K. Hall & M. Bucholtz (Eds.), *Gender articulated: Language and the socially constructed self* (pp. 375–400). New York: Routledge.

Goldstein, T. (2001). Researching women's language practices in multilingual workplaces. In A. Pavlenko, A. Blackledge, I. Piller, & M. Teutsch-Dwyer (Eds.), *Multilingualism, second language learning, and gender* (pp. 77–101). Berlin: Mouton de Gruyter.

Kouritzin, S. (2000). Immigrant mothers redefine access to ESL classes: Contradiction and ambivalence. *Journal of Multilingual and Multicultural Development, 21*, 14–32.

Kunnan, A. J. (1990). DIF in native language and gender groups in an ESL placement test. *TESOL Quarterly, 24*, 741–746.

Lesikin, J. (1998). Determining social prominence: A methodology for uncovering gender bias in ESL textbooks. *College ESL, 8*, 433–446.

Losey, K. M. (1995). Gender and ethnicity as factors in the development of verbal skills in bilingual Mexican American women. *TESOL Quarterly, 29*, 635–661.

Markham, P. L. (1988). Gender and the perceived expertness of the speaker as factors in ESL listening recall. *TESOL Quarterly, 22*, 397–406.

O'Sullivan, B. (2000). Exploring gender and oral proficiency interview performance. *System, 28*, 373–386.

Peirce, B. N. (1995). Social identity, investment, and language learning. *TESOL Quarterly, 29*, 9–31.

Peirce, B. N. (1997). Language, identity, and the ownership of English. *TESOL Quarterly, 31,* 409–429.

Piske, T., MacKay, I. R. A., & Flege, J. E. (2001). Factors affecting degree of foreign accent in an L2: A review. *Journal of Phonetics, 29,* 191–215.

Rifkin, B. (1998). Gender representation in foreign language textbooks: A case study of textbooks in Russian. *The Modern Language Journal, 82,* 217–236.

Shehadeh, A. (1999). Gender differences and equal opportunities in the ESL classroom. *ELT Journal, 53,* 256–261.

Strauss, A., & Corbin, J. (1990). *Basics of qualitative research: Grounded theory procedures and techniques.* Newbury Park, England: Sage Publications.

Teutsch-Dwyer, M. (2001). (Re)constructing masculinity in a new linguistic reality. In A. Pavlenko, A. Blackledge, I. Piller, & M. Teutsch-Dwyer (Eds.), *Multilingualism, second language learning, and gender* (pp. 175–198). Berlin: Mouton de Gruyter.

Young, D. J., & Oxford, R. (1997). A gender-related analysis of strategies used to process written input in the native language and a foreign language. *Applied Language Learning, 8,* 43–73.

11

CO-CONSTRUCTING PREJUDICED TALK:
Ethnic Stereotyping in Intercultural Communication between Hong Kong Chinese and English-Speaking Westerners

Winnie Cheng
Hong Kong Polytechnic University, Hong Kong

Negotiating Prejudiced Talk

In conversation, the participants collaboratively contribute towards both the topic subject contents and the direction and organization of the topical framework, both informed by the goals for conversational interaction and reflecting the physical, social, cultural, and linguistic contexts of interaction. Conversations are dynamic and each contribution from a speaker has to be seen as part of the ongoing business of negotiating what is being talked about. Discourse topics are a direct product of the speakers' cooperative effort. In social interactions such as conversations, the speakers' immediate concerns are very often to have a pleasant and mutually satisfying talk with each other, to keep the conversation going and developing, and finally to close it smoothly. Nevertheless, in contexts of interaction where topics are culturally sensitive and pragmatically face-threatening, such as those concerned with racial and ethnic stereotypes, prejudice, or even discrimination, the participants as social actors can often find themselves engaging in the invocation, formulation, and expression of gendered and ethnicized identities and subject positions that are mediated through language, discourse, and social interactions.

In the modern society, of which Hong Kong is an example, where egalitarianism is upheld and racial equality is promoted, social actors in causal conversations who openly construct, contest, or reproduce beliefs, attitudes, and perspectives that contradict social conventions and ideologies are engaged in symbolic struggles that forge differential membership categories (Sacks, 1966, 1972a, 1972b) for themselves and others in these struggles. The Membership Categorization Device (MCD) developed by Sacks (1966, 1972a, 1972b), and later on termed Membership Category Analysis (MCA) (Hester & Eglin, 1997), serves as an "apparatus" for identifying people by placing them in categories and their associated "category-bound activities" (Sacks, 1966, 1972a, 1972b) and "category-bound features" (Jayyusi, 1984). In other words, when interacting with each other, social actors continuously relate themselves and others to various categories, dependent on the context of interaction, and also to activities and features that characterize the categories.

At the pragmatic level, the conversational participants may also find such sensitive topics potentially face-threatening in at least two ways. First, when a speaker is constructing and delivering racial and even discriminatory prejudiced talk, his or her own positive face and the addressee's negative face are being threatened simultaneously (Brown & Levinson, 1987; Goffman, 1967). The positive face of the speaker is being threatened as he or she may be seen as mean and prejudiced, and hence falls short of being likable and respectable. The addressee's face may also be threatened as the speaker is imposing socially undesirable ideational messages on him or her. Second, the degree of face-threat becomes greater when the race or ethnicity to which one, or both of the participants, belongs is being discussed. In other words, the face threat is greater when participants can identify themselves with what is being remarked upon or even criticized. The participants very often adopt politeness strategies (Brown & Levinson, 1987) to compensate for face loss. As Hernández-Flores (1999, p. 37) puts it, "Politeness is based on a social ideology, i.e. on a set of ideas about behaviour which are shared by a community and, hence are recognized as appropriate in the community." van Dijk (1984) adopts a sociopsychological discourse–analytical approach (Reisigl and Wodak, 2001, p. 21) to examining prejudice[1] and defines prejudice as

> … not merely a characteristic of individual beliefs or emotions about social groups, but a shared form of social representation in group members, acquired during processes of socialization and transformed and enacted in social communication and interaction. Such ethnic attitudes have social functions, e.g. to protect the interests of the ingroup. Their cognitive structures and the strategies of their use reflect these social functions. (1984, p. 13)

Hence, according to van Dijk (1984), when participants are engaged in prejudiced talk, their verbal behaviours are influenced by a complex system of social constraints, rules, norms, information, and situational variables (van Dijk, 1984), and they tend to adopt a range of pragmatic and interactional strategies to fulfill various social and communicative functions of the discourse (Kleiner, 1998; Shi-xu, 1994; van Dijk, 1984). Face-to-face conversations between participants from different racial and sociolinguistic backgrounds, such as those examined in this paper, constitute an even more unique and richer interactional context for examining the ways in which participants deal with culturally sensitive and face-threatening topics, as the conversations will often enlist a range of norms, beliefs, values, attitudes, perspectives, and background knowledge deriving from and embedded within more than one sociocultural and linguistic world.

A Critical Discourse-Analytical Approach to Studying Culturally Sensitive Topics

This chapter describes a critical discourse analysis of two conversational exchanges on sensitive topics, each between a Hong Kong Chinese (HKC) and an English-speaking Westerner (ESW) in Hong Kong. Specifically, it describes the respective strategies employed by the HKC and ESW speakers to invoke cultural knowledge, and to engage in the symbolic struggles that forge membership categorization when they are constructing and contesting ideational messages related to cultural stereotypes and prejudice in discourse.

The data set, from which relevant excerpts were identified and analyzed in this chapter, comprises 25 dyadic conversations, totalling 13 hours of audio-taped and transcribed data. The data set was carefully monitored in terms of the HKC participants' educational background, first language, place of residence, social status, and experience in their use of English. In the data set are 24 different Hong Kong Chinese (8 male and 16 female) and 25 different native speakers of English (19 male and 6 female). Each HKC-ESW pair is made up of friends or colleagues. Prior consent was obtained from both parties before their social interaction was recorded, without the researcher's presence.

In the data set, seven extracts have been identified to contain topical subject contents concerned with issues and ideologies of cultural identities, stereotypes and prejudice, and two of them are discussed in this chapter.

Managing Culturally Sensitive Topics: Analysis of Extract 1

In Extract 1 (Appendix 11.1), the Irish woman (ESW) is the private English tutor for the daughters of the HKC woman. The recording was made in the HKC's home. The participants exchange their ideological assumptions, beliefs, and attitudes about the relative statuses between women and men in various ethnic and racial groups, and the changes in the roles of and attitudes towards women and men in these groups over time. They also discuss reasons for these changes. Below, the analysis examines the interactional and pragmatic strategies employed by the participants to collaboratively develop and manage this discourse, negotiate ideologies related to gender and cultural identities, manage interpersonal relationships, and organize interactional pattern.

Extract 1 starts with the ESW initiating a new topic in which she asks the HKC about her views on the relative roles of husband and wife in the family in Hong Kong nowadays, which are different from those of the older generation. In response, the HKC indicates agreement: "I think the the fathers are playing a more er active role in the in the household responsibilities" (lines 364–366), and then supports the topic by offering an explication and by characterizing the different roles nowadays:

> ... and er (.) I I think this change of change of attitude is brought about by the economic er the yea the structure [it's because the woman are playing erm are taking more role in the financial er parts [and so they have er more say in the house [and they can then direct their husband to take more responsibility of the of the household [yea household business. (lines 366–374).

After this, the HKC has a long turn, which mainly presents the ideological assumptions that she holds regarding the relative roles, statuses, and responsibilities of Hong Kong men/husbands and Hong Kong Chinese women/ wives in the past and nowadays, before and after the change in attitudes (lines 377–386):

> In the past the concept is really the man is the er responsible for the financial side and so they are already working so (.) so hard outside and so it is fair for them to be the king er when they come back er er home and just lie down and relax and enjoy [so they they don't feel guilty if they just er they just do that (.) and the the wife will er will think it is really their duty to serve their [husbands yes but nowadays is so different the [the wives are also working like a dog outside [((laugh)) and so the when when when we come back er we should share our [our duties mhmm yea.

In this turn, she is describing some phenomena and, at the same time, negatively evaluating them, which can be seen in her choice of words. She uses metaphors "the king" (line 379) to describe the status enjoyed by the husband at home in the past, and describes the wife's role as "serving their husbands." She also uses "a dog" (line 384) to describe the working life led by the wife nowadays. These words imply a contrast in the view and perception that she has, or that she thinks people have, about gender status in the past and present. Further, her descriptions imply that in the past, there was a huge, unjust, and disapproved status difference between the working husband and the housewife, while today, women play two roles and lead a tough life both at work and at home.

In lines 388–402, the participants express and negotiate their own beliefs about the extent of change and differences in the roles played by men and women. The ESW thinks that the current generation is totally different from the previous one: "It's quite interesting actually to see how quickly in just in one generation how it's [just changed almost whereas it's totally equal [yea" (lines 388–390). The HKC supports her partially, saying "yea er not totally but nearly" (line 391). The ESW agrees by saying "nearly equal yea," but with reservation, "but it's been a big erm change for men," implying that generally men have changed so that they are very equal to women, but then softens her position by quoting exceptional cases, "I think it's been quite hard in some cases [for them to accept this change [and some of them are still quite traditional or old-fashioned I think" (lines 392–395). It is interesting of the ESW to use "still quite traditional or old-fashioned" (lines 393–395) to characterize those Hong Kong men who find it difficult to change their attitudes towards the role and status of women.

In the same utterance, the ESW drifts to a related topic about Japanese men. She is then interrupted by the HKC who offers an utterance completion. The HKC repeats the word "traditional" but adds "more" to intensify the extent to which Japanese men are traditional, as opposed to Hong Kong men. Apart from this, the HKC's completion offer indicates that she does not have difficulty inferring the meaning of the ESW's utterance. The ESW interrupts the HKC and keeps using "traditional," and this time uses "very" two times when she says "[traditional yes it's very very traditional they're they're holding on very much to the traditional values" (lines 401–402). The ESW uses this upgrade to intensify her negative evaluation of the values upheld by Japanese. The repetition of the word "traditional," which depicts a quality, by the two speakers across a few turns indicates the ESW and the HKC jointly constructing and presenting a discourse related to how one racial group compares with another. Effectively, they use the same word to link up two racial groups to indicate sameness between the groups, and even intensify the degree of a quality characteristic of one cultural group by using qualifying adverbs (*more, very*). Interruptions are a manifestation of an interactional pattern. The participants interrupt each other, resulting in the current speaker yielding her turn, and yet the interruption can be considered co-operative, as it is used to complete the current speaker's utterance and to provide supportive information to develop the current topic.

Invocation of identities of gender and ethnicity can be found in Extract 1. In line 404, the HKC identifies herself as a woman born in Hong Kong, for which she feels grateful. She also provides a reason for her view: "Yea yea so so I am always glad that er I am born in Hong Kong [which I think Hong Kong is a place er where woman er enjoy er quite high status." The ESW agrees with her and drifts the topic to comparing Hong Kong with America, saying that they are the same in terms of women's status: "That's right they do actually yea and it's it's almost equal and you know it's the same as the Americans very international Hong Kong [the (.) I I find" (lines 411–412). By saying this, the ESW is making a positive evaluation of the HKC speaker's identity. The HKC interrupts to indicate agreement, and thus emphasizing her identity. This time round, however, she identifies herself as Chinese and born in Hong Kong, "[um um um yes I am glad er that I am a Chinese and born in Hong Kong ((laugh)): (lines 413–414). The implication generated is that she is glad that she is Chinese and born in Hong Kong, and not Japanese. Her ESW interlocutor is able to infer the meaning, which is evident from her shifting the topic back to the strange situation in Japan.

Managing interpersonal relationships is also observed. In the case of the HKC, she uses *contradicting* (line 421) to supplement *strange* by the ESW (line 418), emphasizes her agreement with and support for the ESW's view regarding Japanese by means of exaggeration, when she says "I am always wondering" (line 421), crystallizes and contextualizes what the ESW says about "a very er old-fashioned idea of woman's role" (line 416) to become "they have wasted half of their manpower" (lines 421–422), and paraphrases the ESW's "in Japan I mean for one of the most powerful industrial nations in the world" (lines 415–416) to become "they get so advanced in their technology" (line 424). In the case of the ESW, she employs involvement strategies (Scollon and Scollon, 1995). She closes her utterance with a tag question, "… it seems [(.) quite strange doesn't it" (lines 416–418), spoken with a falling tone. This is a Type 3 tag question, based on its syntactic structure (Quirk, Greenbaum, Leech, & Svartvik, 1985, p. 811). The tag question spoken with a falling tone, nevertheless, indicates a communicative choice made by the speaker, namely that the speaker is certain of the assumption and the addressee is invited to agree with her (Tsui, 1994, p. 70). As expected, the HKC responds with "[yea yea" (line 419) to indicate agreement. Another example of involvement strategy is her echoing the HKC's words. In response to the HKC, who closes the utterance with an evaluative statement "that's something amazing" (lines 424–426), the ESW repeats the HKC's words "yea it is amazing" (line 427).

Another kind of interactional pattern is also observed in the relative roles taken by the ESW and the HKC in lines 429–442. The ESW takes a long turn to present her view about the inequality between men and women in Japan, which is attributable to "the power structure" (line 429). The HKC plays a supportive role and gives back-channel responses throughout. The ESW closes her turn by means of an evaluative remark, "I don't know if it will ever change I mean we're they're very erm they are very determined to keep these values I think yea" (lines 440–442). In response, the HKC says "yea yea I don't know," followed by laughter (line 437). In lines 429–442, the ESW is making most of the contribution to the proposition, while the HKC is playing a supportive role.

After the brief laughter, the HKC changes the propositional content of the racial talk away from the Japanese to herself. She identifies herself as having daughters, but not sons, and says "I would like the that'll ((laugh)) become more equal" (lines 444–446), implying that she can identify with and sympathize with the treatment extended to Japanese women, and so hoping that the situation in Japan will change in favour of women. Near equality in status is what the HKC is implying, and the ESW picks up on this, saying "you like Hong Kong attitude ((laugh))" (line 446). The HKC responds affirmatively, and starts to mention her daughters, but stops to talk in a general sense about girls in Hong Kong: "So daughters er so girls you know work harder so that's er when you grow up you can play a part too [(((laugh)) you know they'll play a part in the in the [society" (lines 447–450).

Support is extended to the HKC, which is part of the interpersonal relationship, when the ESW develops the topic by means of basically paraphrasing the HKC's utterance "[yea yea it's very important very very important I think [that they continue their education [and become a part of erm the working environment" (lines 441–453). Another instance of this interactional pattern is observed in lines 453–462. In the same utterance, the ESW drifts to a related topic and, that is, in China and other countries that are developing, women have just started to get better opportunities in education and work. The HKC contributes only in the sense of giving supportive back channels. The topic is then changed by the HKC (not shown).

To sum up, the participants in Extract 1 are involved in developing a topic framework that is concerned with the roles and statuses of women, as opposed to those of men, across several ethnic and racial groups. The analysis has shown a great deal of negotiation taking place in the discourse. The speakers present, exchange, discuss, develop, and mull over various ideas, assumptions, beliefs, values, and attitudes relating to the topic at hand. Also, through sequencing topics, the speakers jointly develop a series of logically connected topics, and this is represented diagrammatically as follows:

> Hong Kong (past) and Hong Kong (now) → Japan (now) → Hong Kong (now) → Hong Kong (now) and America (now) → Hong Kong (now) → Japan (now) → Hong Kong (future) → Hong Kong (now) → China and other countries (now)

Hong Kong, with which the HKC woman identifies, is the theme running through the conversational extract. As the conversation develops, the participants discuss the past, the present, and the future of Hong Kong. Acting as the focal point of reference, Hong Kong is discussed in relation to other countries, namely Japan, America, China, and other countries and their cultural values and beliefs.

In terms of interactional pattern, the two female speakers assume a variety of roles at different stages of the discourse. At times, their contribution to the talk is shared and equal in terms of content and turn-taking. At other times, the ESW is the primary speaker, while the HKC plays a supportive role. Their goals of interaction, nevertheless, are common, and have been realized in several ways. First, the participants share and exchange common ground in that both are being positive about women's status in Hong Kong and critical about the status of Japanese women and mainland Chinese women. Specifically, they share and exchange their personal and social knowledge and experiences related to propositions that can easily invoke basic human rights, gender discrimination, prejudice and injustice, involving various ethnic and racial groups, one of which the HKC identifies with. Second, each of the women presents herself as both an individual and a social being, embodying a set of values, assumptions, and beliefs relating to the topic framework being constructed and negotiated. Third, the participants may gain mutual and better understanding from the interaction that involves sharing and exchanging views, beliefs, and even emotions relating to the topic. Fourth, as a result of socializing about personal experiences and self-presentation of views and beliefs, the participants may feel a greater sense of camaraderie (van Dijk, 1984). Finally, and more importantly, the two speakers are engaged in symbolic struggles surrounding cultural stereotypes and discrimination, an analysis of which will be presented later in the chapter.

Managing Culturally Sensitive Topics: Analysis of Extract 2

Extract 2 (Appendix 11.2) shows the participants communicating and negotiating beliefs and attitudes along the line of ethnic and racial stereotypical assumptions and practices, namely the relation between man and animals in general, and that between man and dogs in particular, both within and outside the speakers' respective racial and ethnic groups. More specifically, they are comparing the eating habits of Hong Kong Chinese, mainland Chinese and Americans, as well as the views of these groups towards animals.

The HKC starts the topic, when he asks his American interlocutor whether he eats the insides of the animal, to which the ESW disaffirms, saying "Oh no I don't eat that" (line 86). In return, the ESW asks the HKC whether he does ("You eat that," line 86). The HKC gives an affirmative answer, followed by a reason "Yea because I'm Chinese." Giving a reason is a positive politeness strategy to involve the hearer as a participant in the conversation, which is a sign of interpersonal relationship management. More importantly, the response represents the HKC identifying himself with the Chinese and the associated stereotypical eating habits; that is, the Chinese eat the insides of animals, and is hence a case of invocation of identity.

Following that, in a half-joking and half-boasting tone, the HKC continues, giving his opinion that the Chinese, as a racial group, eat all animals with four feet, and giving dogs and cats as examples following an apology for being Chinese: "Sorry I'm Chinese I will eat this (.) all animals who is the with four foot sounds good we'll eat just like dog er cat er" (lines 88–89). Hearing that, the ESW asks in a surprised tone for clarification and confirmation ("You eat the dog," line 90).

Invocation of cultural identity is at work in the turns that follow. In relation to eating dog, the HKC, however, clearly distances himself from the ethnic mainland Chinese by means of a number of discourse strategies. He uses strong denying "No no no" (line 91), saying that he does not eat dog. He agrees with the American's view towards the habit of dog-eating in mainland China by repeating the negative evaluation "[it's it's terrible [oh I don't know no no it's terrible" (line 105). When the ESW asks whether dog is sold in Hong Kong (line 109), the HKC denies that and provides an explanation "No it's illegal" (line 110) to sell dogs in Hong Kong, implying that selling dog is not illegal in mainland China and confirms the ESW's allegation that mainlanders "eat anything" in China (lines 115). The HKC clearly distinguishes between Hong Kong and mainland China: In Hong Kong it is illegal to eat dogs but in Mainland China you can find food stalls selling dogs, with dogs hung up. At the same time, he is distinguishing the mainland Chinese who eat dog and cat from Hong Kong Chinese who do not. Through doing so, he is categorically dissociating himself, a Hong Kong Chinese man, from mainland Chinese.

The verbal exchanges that follow illustrate the collaborative process undertaken by the speakers to manage the topic. The ESW drifts the topic, and jokes about what might happen to somebody eating out in mainland China "You have to be careful (.) they could call it beef and and put dog in your food (.) right (.) over in China if you ordered [er" (lines 119–122). The HKC shows full support to his ESW interlocutor by collaboratively developing the topic, agreeing that people need to "be careful" (line 123). Each of the participants contributes to creating the story about the terrible kinds of food that somebody eating out in mainland China might possibly be given to eat by means of quick overlapping talk, building on the previous utterance to increase the absurdity in the jointly constructed proposition of the talk. When the ESW suggests that beef "could be somebody's cat" (line 126), the HKC interrupts and makes the ESW's story even more horrible, saying "well mix up er" (mixing up beef, dog, and cat) (line 127). Building on that and making the story even more vividly disgusting, hideous, and ghastly, the ESW adds more details "They can mix it up with some [cat and [dog and some noodles and call it er pork call it chick" (lines 128 and 130). The HKC supports the topic by giving back-channel responses (line 129), and collaboratively develops it by suggesting "You must ah V__ you must ask V__ don't eat don't eat those things" (line 131).

The participants have a good laugh while engaged on this topic. Then the American man drifts to a related topic. After an evaluation, "That is nasty" (line 134), he follows up by saying that Americans regard the dog as "man's best friend," and that killing a dog is a very serious offence. Here, the American is contributing to this prejudiced discourse by comparing the behaviours and practices of various racial groups. He then expresses his aversion to the mainland Chinese, saying "You don't kill it for for food that's that just downright crazy [(.) crazy people across the border" (lines 140 and 145), to which the HKC agrees and supports with "mm mm I think so" (line 142). Then the participants are ready to close the topic, as each of them says "yea" and laughs but neither contributes further to the topic. The ESW then changes the topic (line 147, not shown).

Discussion and Conclusion

This chapter has identified and analyzed, from a data set comprising 25 dyadic intercultural conversations, two conversational exchanges relating to negotiating culturally sensitive and face-threatening topics, and specifically the strategies employed by the interlocutors to collaboratively develop topical frameworks, negotiate ideologies, organize interaction, and manage interpersonal relationships. As analysis of Extract 1 shows, the nature of the topic framework is highly likely to invoke cultural knowledge, attitudes, ideologies, and most importantly of all, cultural identities specific to individual participants. The HKC woman and the ESW woman have effectively employed a range of devices and strategies to collaboratively manage not only the ideological, but also interpersonal, aspects of the topic. Invocation of cultural identity and membership is also apparent in the interaction.

Compared to Extract 1, the HKC man and the ESW man in Extract 2 appear to hold stronger and more critical ideological positions regarding ethnic and racial stereotypes and prejudice. Neither of them, however, seems to feel intimidated by or uncomfortable about constructing the racist discourse. In fact, they seem to be enjoying this joint construction of prejudice talk. They collaboratively develop it and concoct absurd scenarios, appearing to derive a lot of fun out of doing so. A change in the stance of the HKC has been observed when the conversation unfolds. In line 88, he apologizes for being Chinese, but as the topic develops, he starts to differentiate between mainland Chinese and Hong Kong Chinese. After the HKC man has explicitly "announced" that he is different from people in mainland China, and made it clear that Hong Kong is different from mainland China in terms of eating habits and practices, he can be seen to be as unrestrained as the ESW in cracking racist jokes about mainland China and the mainland Chinese. Indeed, by exaggerating the offensiveness and pervasiveness of these habits and practices, the HKC is trying to distance himself more from his fellow countrymen born and living in mainland China, and thus disclaiming membership from the group of mainland Chinese who feed on such animals as cats and dogs.

In both extracts, the HKC accommodates the prejudiced talk of the ESW. As the talk develops, the HKC collaborates with the ESW in constructing and contesting essentialized, disapproving, ethnic and gender stereotypes of "other less civilized" peoples in Asia, namely the "traditional" Japanese woman and the "dog-eating, horrible" mainland Chinese. At the level of discourse analysis, the chapter demonstrates that the interactional processes are central to the ongoing production and development of meaning (Lee, 1992, p. xi). Such processes have revealed both the underlying cultural assumptions held by the participants, and the strategies the participants employ for the formulation and presentation of such stereotypes. These strategies include turn-taking organization, speech acts such as agreeing and evaluating, repetition, overlapping talk, completion offer, pauses, hesitations, backchannels, nonlinguistic signals (such as intonation and laughter), lexical choice, upgrade, face work and politeness, and so forth.

Regarding interactional patterning, the topics of stereotypes, identities, and prejudice are introduced and developed spontaneously. A range of topic-management strategies has been observed, including topical initiation and continuity, topical sequencing, topic changes, and so on, which show the way in which racial and ethnic stereotypes (and at times prejudiced discourse topics) are introduced, discussed, changed, and finished by the participants. The analysis also shows that conversational topics can be initiated and finished by either of the participants as the conversation unfolds, instead of being predetermined and then assigned to particular participants.

The discourse relating to ideologies of race and ethnicity realizes interpersonal and social functions (van Dijk, 1984). The communicative and social functions of prejudiced talk described in van Dijk (1984) are socializing personal experiences, self-presentation, identity and social integration, persuasion, informal mass communication, a mode of conflict resolution, amusement, and social precepts. The participants described in this chapter are aware of the face-wants and the identities of both themselves and their interlocutors while expressing racial and ethnic ideologies. Some of the discoursal and pragmatic features observed play an important role in the construction, reinforcement, and dissemination of the ideological assumptions relating to race and ethnicity in intercultural conversations. Many of the ideological messages presented by the participants are invoked as the conversation unfolds, serving such functions as socializing personal experiences, self-presentation, management of delicate opinions and persuasion, and finally, amusement.

One interesting observation, which is worth pursuing in future studies, is the "conversation-style differences" (Tannen, 1994, p. 24) between the female and the male participants in the prejudiced talk. In Extract 2, prejudiced talk is like a poker game. As one player increases the level of racial or ethnic stereotyping, the other player meets or increases the level. Presumably, if prejudiced talk is not met or exceeded, the player making the running will back down to assume harmony. The female participants in Extract 1, however, seem to be negotiating the topics in a less direct and vigorous way. They hedge their disagreements. They both make longer turns whereby they provide details and examples and personal views to support either one's own or the other's propositions. In general, the female talk in Extract 1 shows the participants trying to maintain a balance in the force of their contributions. Their conversational style can succinctly be described as "maintaining an appearance of equality, taking into account the effect of the exchange on the other person, and expending effort to downplay the speakers' authority" (Tannen, 1994, p. 23). The conversational style of the men in Extract 2 involves "using opposition such as banter, joking, teasing, and playful put-downs, and expending effort to avoid the one-down position in the interaction" (Tannen, 1994, p. 23). While the conversational-style differences described by Tannen (1994) are supposed to be common across genres and contexts of interaction, such differences have been observed to take place in the prejudiced talk in two extracts of intercultural conversation.

At the level of critical discourse analysis, this chapter has shown that by "othering" remote others, the HKC participants have claimed for themselves a relatively modern, civilized, and superior identity, compared to the "others." By so doing, on the one hand, the HKC themselves from the "traditional" Japanese woman identity and the barbarian "dog-eating" mainland Chinese identity. On the other, the HKC have claimed an affinity with the ESW. Using the strategy of identity fixing, that is, fixing the remote "Other," the HKC and the ESW have successfully negotiated and built common ground along the lines of racial and ethnic identities, stereotypes, and prejudice in order to establish rapport. This chapter has shown that the strategy of co-constructing and co-contesting of essentialized and denigrated subject positions and identities for "the remote Other," and at the same time the superior "Self," seems to be working well as an intercultural communication strategy in the context of prejudiced talk.

To conclude, the data analyzed in this chapter is too small for even an attempt to draw any tentative conclusions. A direction for future studies in prejudiced talk could be to investigate the relationships between gender mix and cultural backgrounds of the conversational participants on the one hand and the direction, organization, and negotiation of the topic framework on the other. As an intercultural communication strategy, the co-constructing of denigrated subject positions and identities for "the remote other" seems workable and successful, as can be seen in the analysis in this chapter. Future research work should, however, also address the question of how different participants of different gender mix and cultural backgrounds can have interacted differently, how face-threatening topics can be dealt with without adopting such a strategy of othering remote others.

Endnote

1. van Dijk (1984) does not neatly distinguish between racism, ethnicism, and discrimination as he believes that these are fuzzy and overlapping concepts (Reisigl and Wodak, 2001, p. 21).

Appendix 11.1 Extract 1

(009)

A: female Irish	**a: female Hong Kong Chinese**

359.A	how do you think er nowdays do you think men in Hong Kong are taking more of an
360.	active role in raising the family than before like maybe in your parents' time it was
361.	mainly your mother that took the active role [do you think fathers now are taking much
362.a	[yes
363.	more of an active role
364.a	er for those er families er (.) yes which I know [I think the the fathers are playing a more
365.A	[yea
366.	er active role in the in the household responsibilities [and er (.) I I think this change of
367.A	[yea
368.	attitude is brought about by the economic er the yea the structure [it's because the
369.A	[yea
370.	women are playing erm are taking more role in the financial er parts [and so they have
371.A	[yea yea
372.	er more say in the house [and they can then direct their husband to take more
373.A	[mm
374.	responsibility of the of the household [yea house household business
375.A	[yea
376.A	responsibilities
377.a	yea responsibilities but in the past the the concept is really the man is the er responsible
378.	for the financial side and so they are already working so (.) so hard outside and so it is
379.	fair for them to be the king er when they come back er er home and just lie down and
380.	relax and enjoy [so they they don't feel guilty if they just er they just do that (.) and the

381.A   [mm

382.   the wife will er will think it is really their duty to serve their [husbands yes but nowadays

383.A   [husbands yes

384.   is so different the [the wives are also working like a dog outside [((laugh)) and so the

385.A   [yea [that's yea

386.   when when when we come back er we should share out [our duties mhmm yea

387.A   [that's right yea

388.A   it's quite interesting actually to see how quickly in just in one generation how it's [just

389.a   [yea

390.   changed almost whereas it's totally equal [yea

391.a   [yea er not totally but nearly ((laugh))

392.A   nearly equal yea but it's been a big erm a big change for men I think it's been quite hard

393.   hard in some cases [for them to accept this change [and some of them are still quite

394.a   [yes [uh huh uh huh

395.   traditional or old-fashioned I think [so they like to still think that the woman should stay

396.a   [yes yes yes

397.   at home [like I was talking to some erm (.) students of mine who were Japanese

398.a   [yea

399.   [and they were [telling me that they

400.a   [uh huh [oh (.) Japanese are more er [traditional

401.A   [traditional yes it's very very

402.   traditional

403.   they're they're holding on very much to their traditional values

404.a   yes

405.A   but once once a woman gets married that she almost has to leave her (.) job [and stay at

406.a   [yea yea yea

407.   home [even though she has no children

408.a   [yea

409.a   yea yea so so I am always glad that er I am er born in Hong Kong [which I think Hong

410.A   [yea

411.   Kong is a place er where woman er enjoy er quite high status

412.A   that's right they do actually yea and it's it's almost equal and you know it's the same as

413.   the Americans very international Hong Kong [the (.) I I find

414.a   [um um um yes I am glad er that I am a

415.   Chinese and born in Hong Kong ((laugh))

416.A   so what do you think in Japan I mean for one of the most powerful industrial nations in

417.   the world they still have erm (.) a very er old fashioned idea of woman's role [it seems

418.a   [yea

419.   [quite strange [doesn't it

420.a   [uh huh [yea yea very

421.A   yea

422.a   and contradicting and er and er I am always wondering since they have waste half of

423.   their manpower

424.A   that's right yes

425.a   and er but still they they they get so advanced in their technology [and that's something

426.A   [yea

427.   amazing

428.A   yea it is amazing

429.a   and which I don't understand ((laugh))

430.A   yea maybe that's er maybe something to do with the way that erm the power structure

431.   [you know they try to keep the men erm (.) encourage the man to stay in the same

432.a   [yea

433.   position [all the way through in their career [they encourage the men to continue er to

434.a   [mm [mm

435.   work and (.) they don't seem to trust the women [they feel the woman is who has

436.a   [mm

437.   married er almost has erm her responsibilities are split [and she is not as loyal to her job

438.a   [mm

439.   [so they they encourage the man to keep on his job and he is the main breadwinner

440.a   [mm

441.   [whereas I don't know if it will ever change I mean we're they're very erm they are very

442.a   [mm

443.   determined to keep these values [I think yea

444.a   [yea yea I don't know ((laugh)) so the er I I I've only got

445.   daughters I don't have [sons so I I would like the that'll ((laugh)) become more equal

446.A   [sons

447.A   you like Hong Kong attitude ((laugh))

448.a   ((laugh)) yea yea so daughters er so girls you know work harder so that's er when you

449.   grow up you can play a part too [((laugh)) you know they'll play a part in the in the

450.A   [play a big part

451.   [society

452.A   [yea yea it's very important very very important I think [that they continue their

453.a   [yea

454.   education [and become a part of erm the working environment [I think it is very sad

454.a   [yes yes [yes

456.   when erm you have you know like in places like China you know they have and also in

457.   most erm countries that are not very well developed [the woman has to stay at home and

458.a   [mm

459.   very much erm keep the household together and she has she doesn't get a chance they

460.   don't give her a chance to get an education and have a choice (.) whereas men all

461.	through the generations always had choices [but now it seems like women are just
462.a	[yes
463.	getting the opportunity [to have an equal say [over their destiny

---

Appendix 11.2   Extract 2
(020)

b: male Hong Kong Chinese	**B: male American**

82.b	do you do you like to eat the inside body I mean the animal inside body do you get the
83.	meaning
84.B	do I eat meat
85.b	meat yea not inside body just like er brain er the the heart er
86.B	oh no I don't eat that [you eat that
87.b	[((laugh))
88.b	yea because I'm Chinese sorry I'm Chinese I will eat this (.) all animals who is the with
89.	four foot sounds good we'll eat just like dog er cat er
90.B	you eat the dog
91.b	no no no but
92.B	you don't eat dog
93.b	yea
94.B	but when you will when you will go to China you will see something (.) food stall you'll
95.	(.) you'll (.) eat the dog
96.B	yea
97.b	((Cantonese))
98.B	they sell dogs there
99.b	yea
100.B	it's hanging
101.b	yea hanging the dog
102.B	oh my god
103.b	yea
104.B	[you don't eat that
105.b	[it's it's terrible [oh I don't know no no it's terrible

106.B	[oh my
107.B	[wow
108.b	[you'll see ((Cantonese))
109.B	do they sell that in Hong Kong
110.b	no it's illegal
111.B	that's illegal yeah it's crazy
112.b:	it's very terrible
113.B:	oh my god
114.b	yea
115.B	they eat anything over there
116.b	yeap (.) anything
117.B	oh my god
118.	(pause)
119.B	you have to be careful (.) they could call it beef and put dog in your food (.) right (.)
120.	over in China
121.b	mm
122.B	if you ordered [er
123.b	[yea be careful
124.B	beef
125.b	[yea
126.B	[it could it could be somebody's cat
127.b	well mix up er
128.B	they can mix it up with some [cat and [dog and some noodles and call it er pork call it
129.b	[yea [yea
130.	[chick
131.b	[you must you must ah V__ you must ask V__ don't eat don't eat those things
132.	((B and b laugh))
133.b	maybe er V make a joke joking with you give you the (inaudible) just like that
134.B	that that that is nasty let me tell you (.) if that ever happened in the United States
135.	someone could get killed for that
136.b	it's very

137.B   for serving dogs someone would get really killed (.) that's like er in America dog is

138.   man's best friend

139.b   mm

140.B   [you don't kill it for for food

141.b   [I think so I think so

142.B   that's that just downright crazy [(.) crazy people across the border ((laugh))

143.b   [mm

144.b   mm mm I think so

145.B   yea ((laugh))

146.b   mm

References

Brown, P., & Levinson, S. (1987). *Politeness: Some universals in language usage.* New York: Cambridge University Press.

Goffman, E. (1967). *Interaction ritual: Essays on face-to-face behavior.* New York: Pantheon Books.

Hernández-Flores, N. (1999). *Politeness ideology in Spanish colloquial conversation: The case of advice.* Pragmatics, 9(1), 37–49.

Hester, S., & Eglin, P. (Eds.). (1997). *Culture in action: Studies in membership categorization analysis.* Washington, DC: International Institute for Ethnomethodology and Conversation Analysis.

Jayyusi, L. (1984). *Categorization and the moral order.* London: Routledge & Kegan Paul.

Kleiner, B. (1998). The modern racist ideology and its reproduction in "pseudo-argument." *Discourse & Society,* 9(2), 187–215.

Lee, D. A. 1992. *Competing discourses: Perspective and ideology in language.* Essex, England: Longman.

Quirk, R., Greenbaum, G., Leech, G., & Svartvik, J. (1985). *A comprehensive grammar of the English language.* London: Longman.

Reisigl, M., & Wodak, R. (2001). *Discourse and discrimination: Rhetorics of racism and antisemitism.* London and New York: Routledge.

Sacks, H. (1966). The search for help: No one to turn to. Unpublished PhD dissertation. Berkeley: University of California, Department of Sociology.

Sacks, H. (1972a). An initial investigation of the usability of conversational data for doing sociology. In D. Sudnow (Ed.), *Studies in social interaction* (pp. 31–74). New York: Free Press.

Sacks, H. (1972b). On the analysability of stories by children. In J. Gumperz, & D. Hymes (Eds.), *Directions in sociolinguistics: The ethnography of communication* (pp. 325–345). New York: Holt.

Scollon, R., & Scollon, S.W. (1995). *Intercultural communication: A discourse approach*. Oxford: Blackwell Publishers.

Shi-xu. (1994). Ideology: Strategies of reason and functions of control in accounts of the non-western other. *Journal of Pragmatics*, 21, 645–669.

Tannen, D. (1994). *Talking from 9 to 5*. New York: William Morrow and Company, Inc.

Tsui, A. B. M. (1994). *English conversation*. Oxford: Oxford University Press.

van Dijk, T. A. (1984). *Prejudice in discourse: An analysis of ethnic prejudice in cognition and conversation*. Amsterdam: John Benjamins.

12

OUT-PERFORMING IDENTITIES

John Nguyet Erni

Lingnan University, Hong Kong

Dear Friend:

I am black.

I am sure that you did not realize this when you made/laughed at/agreed with that racist remark. In the past, I have attempted to alert white people to my racial identity in advance. Unfortunately, this invariably causes them to react to me as pushy, manipulative, or socially inappropriate. Therefore, my policy is to assume that white people do not make these remarks, even when they believe there are no black people present, and to distribute this card when they do.

I regret any discomfort my presence is causing you, just as I am sure you regret the discomfort your racism is causing me.

Sincerely yours,

Adrian Margaret Smith Piper

Performance artist Adrian Piper passes out this "business card" at her show and, when necessary, to others who fail to detect her black identity in her everyday world. As a light-skinned African American, Piper resists the erasure of her racial difference by those who, in a way, subject her to "passing" without her consent. In African American history, the act of passing—mostly by the light-skinned—has been seen as a vital performance of survival in the hostile environment of racial persecution (e.g., Fabi, 2001; Pfeiffer, 2003). However, here, Piper reverses this survival act of passing as white so as to point to another necessary survival act for African Americans: the resistance to enduring the insider's racist jokes. In other words, consensual passing and non-consented passing are equally significant in the politics of identity, each unfolding a different dimension—and fragility—of performativity.

Piper's performance is relevant to this book in at least two ways. First, it heightens the theatricality of identity in everyday life. In Piper's case, this theatrical quality is registered in the politics of the visible. As Phelan (1993) suggests about Piper's work: "by marking her racial 'otherness' in the landscape of the Same, Piper points to the universalizing mimetic 'likeness' that the given to be seen attempts to secure. In denying that likeness, Piper makes the insecurity of vision and visibility apparent" (p. 98). In the various cases included in the present volume, the authors' performativity of identities also shares an anxiety in and of the visible (e.g., chapters by Eng and Connelly), while others register that performativity in relation to the politics of nationhood (e.g., Martinsson and Reimers), the discourse of professionalism (e.g., Khemlani David and Yong), the epistemological force of individualism (e.g., Skeggs), the politics of domesticity (e.g., Hansen), and so on. What clearly emerges in these cases is that whenever symbolic struggles over identity are played out, a potential to destabilize hegemonic arrangements in everyday life emerges. Vision, nationhood, professionalism, individualism, and domesticity are simultaneously asserted and disavowed through the theatrical performance of identities.

A second related relevance of Piper's performance to the purpose of this volume has to do with a new crisis that the declaration of identity can bring about. Piper's "I am black" is asserted against her own lived history of *becoming black*: a metamorphosis hinted at through her changing tactics, from provoking "pushiness" etc., to assuming an educated stance among whites, to acknowledging "discomfort" caused by her racial declaration. Put in another way, such a self-declaration is no simple discourse! "I am X" causes a ripple over the "realness" of X, particularly in an everyday world likely to be marked by an endless theatricality of microspeech acts.

A broader, and perhaps more unsettling, implication of the problem of "becoming X" (where X serves as a referent in the symbolic struggles over identity) is that it shines a spotlight on where our political projects are weak. This has been raised before: to what extent has feminism essentialized the woman, has critical race theory elementalized black identity, has queer theory canonized gay and lesbian identities, and so on? Where Marx in his times mistook the whole social formation as a sphere of antagonism organized around the subjugation of "the proletariat," who was theorized in singular, binaristic relations with the capitalist class, contemporary theorists have likewise organized their political projects around fixed and fixable identities, often to the detriment of those whose real lived experiences "spill over" the identity frames purportedly used to represent them. It is not until these critical political projects begin to "compare notes," so to speak, that we realize the trap of identity politics, such as when feminism meets queer theory and in the process enables new revisions of what constitutes "sexual difference," "the body," "the public/private split," and so on (see Butler, 1994; Erni, 1998; Griggers, 1996; Martin, 1994). Increasingly it has been realized that as the feminist movement intersects with the civil rights, sexual liberation, and postcolonial movements, the centrality of the rallying frame of "identity politics" obscures the particularities of oppressions based on gender, race, and sexuality in ways that are *not* manifestly gender-specific, race-specific, or sex-specific. The problems of global capital, technology, nationalism, citizenship, human rights, diasporic formation, to name only a few, apprehend gender, race, class, and sexuality in complex ways, deepening the ambivalence of a political theory that over-invests in an identity-based perspective. Needless to say, the same problems render any model that fails to think *across* identities at multiple discursive planes theoretically and politically limiting. Ultimately, the present debate in cultural studies over the multiple intersections among various domains of identity and difference turns on our ability to think in terms that are no longer universalizing or predestined, but are mobile, temporary, organic. It seems to be more appropriate to speak in terms of "identity networks" when theorizing about symbolic struggles in the everyday world. Yet, how can we reassemble this vision after we have pronounced the collapse of universalizing, predestined paradigms of knowledge and the inefficacy of the imperative to categorize, to set essentializing boundaries?

One of the ways of understanding the intricacies of the self is to consider the process by which the discursive technologies of the self (in Foucault's sense[1]) replicate for the continuous maintenance of truth-making. The repetition of those technologies and the norm that governs the repetition has led Butler to propose a theory of "performativity." Drawing on Foucault and speech-act theories, Butler reinforces Foucault's notion of the materiality of bodies and subjectivities by adding to it an emphasis on the processual and enunciative nature of materialization. She proposes "a return to the notion of matter, not as site or surface, but as a process of materialization that stabilizes over time to produce the effect of boundary, fixity, and surface we call matter. ... Construction not only takes place *in* time, but is itself a temporal process which operates through the reiteration of norms" (Butler, 1993, pp. 9–10). She argues that one acquires subjectivity through reiteration and the temporal logic that governs it. However, through the same process, one's subjectivity can be challenged, even destabilized. Accordingly, every identity is constituted by discursive formation as much as by deformation (p. 229). After "essentialism," then, we can reinforce Butler's theory of performativity by emphasizing those moments of performance of the self that are intense but not necessarily accumulative, energetic but not always constitutive, encountering but not formative, connecting but not congealing; but always consequential.

Deleuze's concept of "becoming" provides a complementary model to that of performativity. In *A Thousand Plateaus*, Deleuze and Guattari speak about "becoming" in this way:

> For us ... there are as many sexes as there are terms in symbiosis, as many differences as elements contributing to a process of contagion. We know that many beings pass between a man and a woman; they come from different worlds, are born on the wind, form rhizomes around roots; they cannot be understood in terms of production, only in terms of becoming. (cited in Braidotti, 1994, p. 111)

This figurative language provides not only the vehicle with which to describe the notion of becoming but also provides its radical potential for reconfiguring the self. Calling it "a materialist, high-tech brand of vitalism," Braidotti stresses that "becoming" represents a radical theory of difference, in which difference is imbued with a generative positivity capable of social transformation. Gender, as seen in the passage above, does not refer to empirical man or woman. Rather, gender refers to a network of symbolic and material planes that precipitates around and produces gendered forms of self and sociality. Already, this way of conceptualizing gender blends its contours with other social axes of difference, such as subaltern, dark skin, fair skin, lesbian, postcolonial, and so forth. Each form of difference is always capable of refiguring difference, because each difference is an emerging figure, becoming different. Many feminists have adopted the Deleuzian perspective and argued that gendered subjectivity was a matter of "becoming."[2]

"Becoming X" thus refers to the process of refiguring lives, texts, desires, institutions, behaviors, and various ways of being in the world, so that the transformation is continuous, specific, provisional, something not easily made stable. To echo Sedgwick (1993), we need to pay close attention to those spaces and times where things may be relentlessly "untidy," simply because their rules of emergence exceed social norms. Further, Braidotti approximates this kind of refiguration with the phrase "as if." The practice of "as if" registers those "untidy" surpluses of experiences. The practice of "as if" activates a stream of mobile bodies, affects, and signifiers, setting them into the orbit that surrounds closely connected zones of differences. It is "as if" gender, sexuality, race, postcoloniality, and class were evocative of one another, allowing us to flow from one zone of specificity to another in varying intensities. Braidotti refers to this kind of fluidity within the imaginary of "nomadic" refiguration as "emphatic proximity, intensive interconnectedness" (Braidotti, 1994, p. 5).

In sum, it is conceptually necessary for us to think about identity constructions not in terms of model, framework, or even theory, but in terms of operations/operationality. Ideas and identities are actual and actualizing entities; their existence depends on how, where, and when they operationalize (walk, move, poach, make do, rebel) along existing vectors of power and thus generate certain social and discursive effect. These effects may appear at the ideological, cognitive, bodily, or affective level, or a combination of some or all of these levels. These effects may not be permanent, root-taking, authentic, grounded, or deep; but nor are they without consequences. Most importantly, no identities or ensemble of identities operate in a vacuum; they always register and are registered by context, conjuncture, history. It is to this energetic possibility toward refiguration that we must strive when thinking about progressive politics.

Endnotes

1. Foucault conceptualizes the "technology of the self" as the validation— making true—of power through its production and reproduction of the governing knowledge about the body and subjectivity. For Foucault, knowledge is, in the deepest sense, practice. Drawing on Foucault's "Questions of Method," we can define discourse as an aggregate of the technologies of practices (how things operate) and the rise of rationality (what cultural and historical effects of dominance the practices engender). The technology of the self—assembled through the practices of, for instance, educational or legal discourses—thus reinforces governmentalist rationality that, in turn, validates those practices as true, normal, common sensical, good.

2. Feminist refigurations of "woman" have taken many forms, with varying degrees of theoretical abstractions, such as Teresa de Lauretis's figure of the "eccentric subject," Donna Haraway's "cyborg," Luce Irigaray's "two lips," Alice Jardin's "gynesis," Camilla Griggers's figuration of the "becoming-woman" in technological spaces, Rosi Braidotti's "nomadic subject," Elspeth Probyn's "outside belongings," and Elizabeth Grosz's lesbian volatility as a figure of intensities and flows. All of these feminist figurations represent defiant feminist plentitude. Not all of them draw on the Deleuzian framework, but they share the desire to re-invent gender and sexuality. Far from advocating a complete dissolution of all identities into a meaningless flux, they, in fact, rewrite gender and sexuality by tracing their multiple specificities in material contexts, such as in scientific technologies, at the scene of writing, in cityscapes, or in the transnational sphere.

References

Braidotti, R. (1994). *Nomadic subjects: Embodiment and sexual difference in contemporary feminist theory.* New York: Columbia University Press.

Butler, J. (1993). *Bodies that matter: On the discursive limits of "sex."* New York: Routledge.

Butler, J. (1994, Summer–Fall). Against proper objects. [Special issue: More gender trouble: Feminism meets queer theory]. *Differences, 6,* 1–26.

Deleuze, G., & Felix, G. (1987). *A thousand plateaus: Capitalism and schizophrenia* (B. Massumi, Trans.). Minneapolis: University of Minnesota Press. (Original work published 1987)

Erni, J. (1998). Ambiguous elements: Rethinking the gender/sexuality matrix in an epidemic. In N. Roth & K. Hogan (Eds.), *Gendered epidemic: Representations of women in the age of HIV/AIDS* (pp. 3–29). New York: Routledge.

Fabi, M. G. (2001). *Passing and the rise of the African American novel.* Chicago: University of Illinois Press.

Griggers, C. (1996). *Becoming-woman.* Minneapolis: University of Minnesota Press.

Martin, B. (1994, Summer–Fall). Sexualities without genders and other queer utopias. *Diacritics, 24*(2–3), 104–121.

Pfeiffer, K. (2003). *Race passing and American individualism.* Amherst: University of Massachussetts Press.

Phelan, P. (1993). The golden apple: Jennie Livingston's "Paris is burning." In P. Phelan (Ed.), *Unmarked: The politics of performance* (pp. 93–111). London: Routledge.

Sedgwick, E. K. (1993). *Tendencies.* Durham: Duke University Press.

13

MODERNITY, POSTMODERNITY, AND THE FUTURE OF "IDENTITY": IMPLICATIONS FOR EDUCATORS

Angel M. Y. Lin

City University of Hong Kong, Hong Kong

> I am a self only in relation to certain interlocutors: in one way in relation to those conversation partners who were essential to my achieving self-definition; in another in relation to those who are now crucial to my continuing grasp of languages of self-understanding—and, of course, these classes may overlap. A self exists only within what I call "webs of interlocution."
> (Taylor, 1989, p. 36)

The term "identity" has been developed and used in different disciplines with different meanings and senses. As a theoretical term originally emerging from the different, though related, disciplines of philosophy, psychology, sociology, and cultural studies, it has acquired a diverse range of usages. As a theoretical term that has spilled over into everyday language and become a common term used in people's everyday lives, it has acquired yet another set of ordinary usages overlapping with only some of its original theoretical meanings. In recent years, the term, "identity," has further acquired rising currency and capital in the research literature and discourses among communities of applied linguists, educators, and researchers. However, it also seems to have become one of the most commonly used, but under-theorized and often only partially understood terms, especially in the field of language education, where most scholar-researchers have not had the time and resources to delve into the diverse research fields from which the term has acquired its diverse meanings and theoretical import, some of which might be of relevance and significance to the work of the language educator-researcher.

In this chapter, I shall attempt to trace the use of the term "identity" in different fields and disciplines. I shall also seek to show how the discussion of identity issues is related to discussion of modernity and postmodernity, and then to propose some relevant and important senses of identity that can be used to facilitate the projects of educators and researchers.

Philosophical Debates on "Personal Identity" and Musings on the Non-/Unity of Self in Science Fiction

The usage of the term "identity" can be traced back to the use of the term "personal identity" in philosophical debates on what are the criteria of identity for persons. The debates revolve around the philosophical question of what the necessary and sufficient conditions are for us to say that, for instance, the person over there is identical to the person who was there yesterday; or, in more intimate terms, the person I called myself yesterday is identical to the person I call myself today. Personal identity is the identity of the self; but philosophers have traditionally debated whether the concept of personal identity matters. The key proponent of this view is Parfit (1986), who argues that brain-splitting plus transplants (at least in imaginary scenarios) will give what matters to us when we talk about personal identity (e.g., personal memory or self-consciousness of the unity or continuity of self) and yet because it generates two candidates, does not preserve the original person. An illustrative example can, perhaps, be provided in the main character played by Arnold Schwarzenegger in the 1990 Hollywood film, *Total Recall* (based on a science fiction written by Philip K. Dick, 1987), where the main character, originally a powerful and loyal member of the ruling dictatorship, was given a memory transplant that erased his previous memory of his identity, and then the events happening around him gradually led him to believe that he had been someone working for the underground revolutionaries. All of these were part of a plan to make him the perfect spy to penetrate the revolutionary groups. However, the memory transplant was so successful that in the end, Schwarzenegger, when given the knowledge of "who he really was," *chose* to be the person he had already become: someone who sympathized with the cause of the revolutionaries. He had *chosen* to become another person and not to revert back to his previous identity.

In our intuition about who we are, it seems that a sense of psychological continuity or our memory of who we were and what we have become is central to our sense of personal identity. Talks about psychological continuity, memory, and self-consciousness naturally lead us to the discipline of psychology, which has also devoted much work to the question of identity.

Perspectives from Interactive Social Psychology

What, then, is an identity? The common sense answer is that it has to do with who we, and others, think we are. But what does that consist of? When asked who we are, the research shows, most of us will respond with:

What one does—skills, vocations, roles (**competencies**)
Where one is from—locations, beliefs, groups (**communities**)
Who one is with—personal relationships (**commitments**)

—or, in Erikson's term, *mutualities*
(Hoover and Ericksen, 2004, p. 4; bold and italics original)

The above quote (let us call it the "3 Cs resources" of identity making; more on this later) was taken from Hoover's edited volume (2004) on the legacy of Erik Erikson, a prominent psychologist who had drawn on multiple disciplinary perspectives to study the development and achievement (as well as lack of achievement—crisis) of identity in people (Erikson, 1950, 1958, 1968). Erikson (and other psychologists inspired by him) adopted an interdisciplinary, "psychohistorical approach, in which he emphasizes the unique cultural circumstances (encompassing political, economic, social, and linguistic forces) that shape an individual's development" (Hoover and Ericksen, 2004, p. 6). The psycho-historical approach as described before would sound very akin to many sociologists' understanding of identity, namely, the social constructedness of identity. However, psychologists working in Erikson's tradition focus also on the developmental aspects or the process of identity formation. An important theory is provided in the identity status framework proposed by Marcia (1966, 1967; Marcia et al., 1993). In Table 13.1, I summarize Marcia's framework based on Kroger's delineation (2004).

Four identity statuses (or identity styles) can be classified by cross-tabulating the two variables of Identity Achievement and Role Confusion, which were understood as two dimensions or continuums. Those persons in the Moratorium quadrant and those in the Diffusion quadrant are both experiencing a high degree of role confusion (i.e., uncommitted to any social roles or values). However, the Moratoriums are very much in the process of active identity exploration, of examining different options available in their contexts for vocational, ideological, and relational and community commitments; whereas the Identity Diffuse are not. The Moratoriums can be said to be on their way to attaining the status of Identity Achievement. The Identity Achieved had undertaken serious vocational, ideological, relational, and community commitments after a process of active exploration among alternative possibilities and had found niches in society that seemed to really "fit" their own interests and abilities. The Foreclosures, in contrast, have formed

Table 13.1 Marcia's Framework of Four Identity Statuses (Styles) (summarized into a table by the author based on descriptions by Kroger, 2004)

Variable: Role confusion	Variable: Identity achievement	
	High degree	Low degree
High degree	Moratorium	Diffusion
Low degree	Identity achievement	Foreclosure

their commitments on the basis of identification by adopting the roles and values of their significant others (Kroger, 2004).

Among the most critical of identity's properties, as understood by Erikson, is its provision for a sense of continuity and self-sameness essential to a satisfying human existence (Kroger, 2004, p. 62) (more on the nature of this satisfaction when we discuss Taylor's theories about identity later). This description characterizes the person who has attained the Identity Achievement status in Marcia's framework described before (see Table 13.1). While linguistic philosophers and sociologists might disagree with psychologists in some of their basic theoretical orientations (e.g., in their understanding of "variables" and in their methodological paradigms), it is in the respect of understanding identity as a kind of achievement through active, conscious efforts (or construction) of the individual, who is seen as always socially situated and constantly interacting with (significant) others in her/his communities, that they seem to agree albeit theorizing from very different theoretical planes. This takes us to the theorizing work of Taylor (1989) about the sources of self and the making of the modern identity.

The Modern Condition, Loss of Horizon, and Identity

As a student of the modern human condition and a scholar who is simultaneously held in high regard and much cited in the fields of philosophy, anthropology, cultural studies, language studies, and sociology, Taylor holds special relevance to educators and researchers precisely because of his "philosophical anthropology" and his emphasis on the discursive constitution of the self and identities. Taylor (1989), drawing on the ordinary language philosophy of the later Wittgenstein (Kenny, 1994), stresses the social, discursive, and interlocutionary (i.e., conversational, dialogic) origins of one's sense of self and identities. This view is akin to Vygotsky's ontogenetic theories about the social, interactional origins of higher mental functioning (Vygotsky, 1978). Taylor points out that since birth we have been immersed in "webs of interlocutions" (Taylor, 1989, p. 36), interacting with significant others (our "conversation partners") in the community(ies) that we are situated in:

> I am a self only in relation to certain interlocutors: in one way in relation to those conversation partners who were essential to my achieving self-definition; in another, in relation to those who are now crucial to my continuing grasp of languages of self-understanding—and, of course, these classes may overlap. A self exists only within what I call 'webs of interlocution'.
>
> It is this original situation which gives sense to our concept of 'identity', offering an answer to the question of who I am through a definition of *where I am speaking from and to whom*. The full definition of someone's identity thus usually involves not only his stand on moral and spiritual matters but also some reference to a defining community. These two dimensions were reflected in the examples. ... [in which] I spoke of identifying oneself as a Catholic or an anarchist, or as an Armenian or a Quebecois. Normally, however, one dimension would not be exclusive of the other. Thus, it might be essential to the self-definition of A that he is a Catholic and a Quebecois; of B, that he is an Armenian and an anarchist. (These descriptions might not exhaust the identity of either.) (Taylor, 1989, p. 36; italics added)

It is important to highlight the dialogic, discursive, interactional, and interlocutionary, that is, *social* nature of identities. Who I am or what I make out my identity to be (to myself and others) at a certain moment (which can be relatively transient or lengthened) seems to be always situated in a consideration of *where I am speaking from and to whom*. This has important implications for educators and researchers (as we shall see in the discussion later in this chapter). The religious, ethnic, national, cultural, or other kinds of communities that one identifies with become one's sources of reference for one's values and commitments—one's moral, spiritual stances.

Apart from the emphasis on the dialogic, discursive, and social nature of one's sources of self and identities, Taylor's key arguments about the modern situation and loss of horizon (Taylor, 1989) are also worth our attention. To Taylor, Erikson's notion of identity crisis (see discussion before) is not just a transitional stage in an adolescent's development but also a general feature of the modern human condition. Erikson's (1958) argument of Martin Luther as a case illustrating a young man experiencing an identity crisis before settling as a protestant is quite beside the point, according to Taylor:

> Erikson has made a perceptive study of Luther's crisis of faith and reads it in the light of contemporary identity crises, but Luther himself, of course, would have found this description reprehensive if not utterly incomprehensible. Underlying our modern talk of identity is the notion

that questions of moral orientation cannot all be solved in simply universal terms. And this is connected to our post-Romantic understanding of individual differences as well as to the importance we give to expression in each person's discovery of his or her moral horizon. ... This is linked, of course, with the crisis for Luther turning around the acute sense of condemnation and irremediable exile, rather than around a modern sense of meaninglessness, or lack of purpose, or emptiness. (Taylor, 1989, p. 28)

Taylor argues that what characterizes the modern human condition is a general, widespread sense of what Weber called "disenchantment" or what Nietzsche described as "loss of horizon" (1989, p. 17). While the pre-modern person (e.g., Luther) could rely on some well-received tradition or religion for his moral frameworks and identities (until he replaced one universal system with another universal system, as in the Reformation movement), the modern man/woman has lost that definitive, universal assurance of moral frameworks. Thus "identities" of a diverse range (or identifications with different communities or groups defined in ways deemed significant to the person) become important sources and resources in their "quest" for a sense of where one stands and where one is heading to—providing value frameworks to make the kind of "qualitative distinctions" or "strong evaluations" (p. 31) that one is bound to be confronted with as a human being, according to Taylor's theorizing of the basic human need to ask the inescapable questions of: Who am I? What is the good life? Or what makes my life meaningful or worthwhile?

Taylor's claims about the basic human need to seek moral frameworks and horizons (which can be provided by various identities made available through a person's interactions with significant others and memberships in different communities and groups) might be in concert with Erikson and his colleagues' theories about identity crises (especially those experienced at the adolescent stage).

While Taylor and the psychologists seem to focus on the individual's active quest for, or negotiation and construction of, an identity (or identities) through interactions with significant others and communities, the sociologists seem to be more concerned about the (often unequal) distribution of resources or different kinds of "capitals" for the negotiation and acquisition of worthwhile identities (e.g., socially prestigious and well-accepted identities; identities that confer power and economic benefits, etc.) among different groups of people and their offspring. Their concern is more about the production and reproduction of people's differential access to the powerful identities in society. It is to this important body of literature that we shall turn now.

Sociology of Education: Capitals and Differential Access to the Societies' Valuable Identities

Sociologists seek to uncover the structures and mechanisms that produce and reproduce the social and economic stratification of different groups of people. Education and schooling systems in modern society are key sites of such socioeconomic and cultural production and reproduction. As British sociologist Crossley (2003) puts it:

> Class-based cultural advantages are passed from parents to children through the habitus, but as pre-reflective and habitual acquisitions they are generally misrecognized within the school system as 'natural talents' and are rewarded 'appropriately'. The school thus launders cultural advantages, albeit unwittingly, transforming them into the hard and clean currency of qualifications. (Crossley, 2003, p. 43)

In this "laundering process," key categories of students/children are constructed and used to both produce and reproduce differential types of identities and subjectivities, that is, to both classify students into different kinds of people and to produce their consciousness and willing acceptance of "who they are" (or what kind of students/people they are and will be).

In this context, it would be helpful to consider the work of French sociologist and anthropologist Pierre Bourdieu and his often-cited notions of *habitus, cultural capital, and symbolic violence* in our understanding of how schooling and education systems work at classifying, stratifying, and re/producing different social identities and subjectivities. In the following paragraphs, I shall annotate some of the useful notions from Bourdieu and show how they can help us to understand the ways in which different kinds of student identities are produced and reproduced in schools.

Cultural Capital

This is a concept from Bourdieu (1973, 1977, 1991; Bourdieu & Passeron, 1977) referring to language use, skills, competencies, and orientations/dispositions/ attitudes/schemes of perception (also called "habitus"[1]), that a child is endowed with by virtue of socialization in her/his family and community. Bourdieu's argument is that children of the socioeconomic elite are bestowed by their familial socialization with both more and the right kind of cultural capital for school success (i.e., their habitus becomes their cultural capital). A recurrent theme in Bourdieu's works is that children from disadvantaged groups, with a habitus incompatible with that presupposed in school, are not competing with equal starting points with children of the socioeconomic elite and thus the reproduction of social stratification (see Lin, 1996, 1999 for an analysis of such reproduction in some schools in Hong Kong). The notion of cultural capital has been used by education researchers (e.g., Delpit, 1988; Luke, 1996) to describe the disadvantaged position of ethnic and linguistic minorities and to problematize the notion that state education in modern societies is built on meritocracy and equal opportunity.

Symbolic Violence

Another recurrent theme in Bourdieu's writings concerns how the disadvantaging effect of the schooling system is masked, legitimized, or naturalized in people's consciousness. School failure can be conveniently attributed to individual cognitive deficit or lack of effort and not to the unequal initial shares of the cultural capital both valued and legitimized in school:

> ... the dominated classes allow (the struggle) to be imposed on them when they accept the stakes offered by the dominant classes. It is an integrative struggle and, by virtue of the initial handicaps, a reproductive struggle, since those who enter this chase, in which they are beaten before they start ... implicitly recognize the legitimacy of the goals pursued by those whom they pursue, by the mere fact of taking part. (Bourdieu, 1984, p. 165)

Symbolic violence, according to Bourdieu, is the imposition of representations of the world and social meanings upon groups in such a way that they are experienced as legitimate. This is achieved through a process of *misrecognition*. For instance, the recent "English Only" campaigns in the United States provide illustrations of the political struggles required to create and maintain a unified linguistic market in which only one language is recognized as the legitimate and appropriate linguistic marker of the American identity and this "English = American" symbolic representation has numerous consequences for schooling and jobs (Collins, 1993).

Specifically, Bourdieu (1984) describes four kinds of capital in the schema (see Table 13.2, taken from Luke, 1995), which I find particularly useful for language educators.

With differential kinds of initial capitals, school children from different social groups are soon classified into different categories and given different identity labels. However, as Crossley (2003; see quote before) points out, the different identity labels are assigned and legitimated by seeing this streaming and classifying as based mainly on children's "natural talents" or diligence,

Table 13.2 Types of Capital in Bourdieu's Framework (summarized by Luke, 1995)

Symbolic capital		
Institutionally recognized and legitimated authority and entitlement requisite for the conversion of cultural, economic, and social capital		
Cultural capital	Embodied capital	Knowledges, skills, dispositions of the bodily habitus
	Objectified capital	Cultural goods, material objects, and media physically transmissable to others
	Institutional capital	Academic qualifications, professional certificates, and credentials
Economic capital	Material goods and resources directly translatable into money	
Social capital	Access to cultural and subcultural institutions, social relations, and practices	

while their differential starting points (i.e., differential capitals in the form of different kinds of dispositions and competencies) are masked. Positive identities are constructed and reproduced for those children coming in with the right kind of cultural capital while negative identities are constructed for those coming in without such capital. Of particular relevance to language researchers is Bourdieu's discussion of *imposter* (Bourdieu, 1991). For instance, in the fields of second- and foreign-language education, a boundary is often drawn between the native speaker versus non-native speaker identity categories. A non-native speaker imitating the accent of a native speaker might be seen as an impostor; that is, an ESL student trying hard to speak in the accent of the host country (e.g., Canada) might often be seen as a linguistic minority student trying hard but never quite fully acquiring the identity of the native Canadian speaker (see Taylor, 2006). The society's valuable identities often require certain embodied cultural capital (e.g., certain prestigious accents), which might often be beyond the reach of those who have not been endowed with such capital in their habitus.

Creative, Discursive Agency

Bourdieu has often been accused of being overly deterministic and a theorist more of reproduction than transformation (e.g., Canagarajah, 1993; Jenkins, 1992), and thus a theorist of modernity rather than postmodernity. Lemke, however, points out that Bourdieu is not limited to reproduction; what he does limit is the effectiveness of single agents in changing whole fields of valuation in specific social fields (Jay Lemke, personal communication). For instance, the legitimate prestige and value attached to English in Hong Kong cannot be changed by single agents unless there are systematic changes in the social selection mechanism (e.g., the medium of the universities and the professions; the language of the job market; the globalization forces). While the above seems true, an area in which Bourdieu offers few analyses is the creative, discursive agency of social actors who find themselves caught in dilemmas. As linguistic anthropologist Collins (1993) points out:

> ... we need to allow for dilemmas and intractable oppositions; for divided consciousness, not just dominated minds; ... for creative, discursive agency in conditions prestructured, to be sure, but also fissured in unpredictable and dynamic ways. (p. 134)

Collins' focus on the efficacy of human discursive agency in inducing changes in social structures comes from poststructuralist thinking often associated with postmodernism and postmodernity. Later in this chapter, we shall turn to the postmodernist thinkers who theorize about, among other things, the individual actor's creative making of identities (e.g., drawing on mass mediated images and storylines) in the increasingly postmodern condition, characterized by increasing mass migration and electronic mediation.

Insights from Globalization and Cultural Studies: Electronic Mediation, Mass Migration, and the Role of Imagination in the Re-invention/Fashioning of Identities

Postmodernism is the umbrella term covering diverse strands of thinking that nevertheless share a common distrust of and shying away from the totalizing master narratives that characterize modernist thinking (one common modernist master narrative, for instance, is that of the progress of humans towards greater liberation and emancipation). Postmodernist writers announce "the collapse of universalizing, predestined paradigms of knowledge and the inefficacy of the imperative to categorize, to set essentializing boundaries" (Erni, this volume). Postmodernity, on the other hand, refers to the different features that mark out our contemporary situation as increasingly different from the times before us, and those times are different from the modern situation or modernity. Globalization and cultural studies scholar Appadurai (1996) points out that two such features are the rising global trend of mass migration and the growing pervasiveness and importance of electronic mass media in people's everyday lives.

With increasing mass migration taking place under forces of globalization, we see more bodies crossing national, cultural, and geographical borders. Large-scale de-territorialization of peoples is taking place. For instance, in contemporary North America, one will find huge communities of Chinese, Koreans, Vietnamese, or other groups of people having migrated from their original homeland and settled in different North American cities. To these diasporic communities and their children, their identities are very much an issue and result of active negotiation and struggle rather than natural conferring by virtue of either their place of abode or place of origin. The usual sense of ambivalence found in immigrant children about their cultural, ethnic, and linguistic identities can lead to positive viewing of their hybrid identities or negative stereotyping of their "nonpure" identities, often under the disparaging gaze of their compatriots both in their current host country and in their place of origin.

Parallel to the trend of increasing bodies crossing national and geographic borders there is also the phenomenon of more diverse images, fantasies, and story scripts embedded in the diverse popular cultural and media products crossing national and geographic boundaries, entering into people's homes and everyday lives through electronic mass media; namely, television, cinema, and video technology. Appadurai (1996) theorizes that this trend has led to the increasing importance of the role of the imagination in the everyday social life of people:

> ... In the past two decades, as the deterritorialization of persons, images, and ideas has taken on new force. ... More persons throughout the world see their lives through the prisms of the possible lives offered by mass media in all their forms. That is, *fantasy now is a social practice*; it enters, in a host of ways, into *the fabrication of social lives* for many people in many societies. (pp. 53–54; italics added)

The implication of this, to my mind, is that the habitus of any person is increasingly in flux, that is, no longer as predictable as before. For instance, a Chinese high school student located in Shanghai now can enter into the fantasy world of diverse video game scenarios from different places (e.g., South Korea, Japan, Taiwan) as well as enter into virtual communities with netizens crossing cultural, ethnic, linguistic, and national boundaries.

The implication for our consideration of identity is that the average person now has many more resources available to her/him for re/constructing, re/imagining, and re/fashioning her/his identities, some of which might exist mainly in the virtual world. If we draw on the 3 Cs resources described by Hoover and Erikson (2004; see before), then the range and nature of *competencies, communities,* and *commitments* that an average adolescent (at least for those inhabiting rapidly globalizing cities in the world) can develop, interact with, belong to, and draw upon have exponentially expanded more than for their counterparts two decades ago.

This kind of thing presents both possibilities and traps as global capitalism has made electronic mass media a powerful tool of shaping people's imagination of possible lives and possible identities. Entire urban tribes and their associated consumer identities (e.g., "the Pepsi Generation") can be created and maintained through sophisticated manipulation of visual images, music, songs, story scripts, linguistic metaphors, and fantasies by the marketing and advertising engines that are continuously pumping into people's imagination scenarios of possible lives, glamorous identities, and premier consumption lifestyles of the new urban, cosmopolitan elite tribes (e.g., the Bobo urban tribe; see Brooks, 2000). Cultural branding strategies (Holt, 2004) are successful precisely because they work at the cultural level by creating distinctive, prestigious identities or boosting up identities that are under threat. Advertising campaigns feed on people's identity anxieties and identity crises (e.g., skilled manual laborers being phased out in the 1970s in the United States found in the Budweiser beer commercials the positive image of their masculinity again; see Holt, 2004). With the pervasive electronic mass media reaching every aspect of people's everyday lives, prestigiously branded consumer identities (e.g., the Bobos) can be created and maintained to feed the insatiable appetite of global capitalism. Such is the contemporary, postmodern situation that many of us might find ourselves situated in, especially in the rapidly globalizing cities of the world.

Putting It All Together: How Do the Many Theoretical Lives and Senses of "Identity" Help Us Understand Our Work as Educators and Researchers?

While the philosophers, psychologists, sociologists, globalization and cultural studies scholars might all have different theoretical and methodological orientations, they do seem to share some common ideas about the making and working of identities. For instance, they all seem to agree that we must not see identities as essentialist categories based on what is usually misrecognized as primordia (e.g., gender, class, ethnicity, etc.), but as results of people's active construction of coherent accounts that help them to make sense of their lives and their position in relation to others and to the world. The three Cs identity resources outlined by the psychologists seem to summarize a large part of the consensus about the main kinds of resources for the making of identities: competencies, communities, and commitments, and of course, the three are also inter-related. While philosophers and students of modernity such as Taylor stress the importance of identities as providing the horizon and framework for the modern person to locate her/himself in the moral space, to rescue oneself from the kind of identity crisis characteristic of the modern condition, sociologists devote themselves to the study of different kinds of valuation mechanisms maintained in different social fields, which legislate about what kinds of identities count as valuable ones and what kinds of cultural capital count as tickets to and markers of these identities—all in the production and reproduction of the prestigious identities and privilege of specific social groups who are endowed with such capital in their habitus to start with. Postmodernist scholars in globalization and cultural studies, on the other hand, alert us to the radical cultural change taking place around and in us—the proliferation of imagined possible lives, lifestyles, and glamorous identities, at least for those who can afford the price. These images are pumped into people's homes by powerful mass media engines driven by global capitalism. We might summarize the common themes emerging from these diverse theoretical discourses about identity as follows:

Coherent accounts (or narratives/stories) of self are results of one's active construction, by smoothing over one's fragmented experiences and contradictory practices, beliefs, and desires to construct a sense of personal continuity and unity (see Connelly, this volume). The need to construct such a coherent account of self (personal identity) is debatable (see Parfit's ideas discussed earlier) and might be culturally and historically conditioned (see Skeggs, Chapter 2, this volume).

Identities are socially and discursively constructed; they are not naturalistic categories based on what people misrecognize as "primordial" features such as gender and ethnicity, as these are also regimes of difference socially and discursively constructed (e.g., see Winter, this volume).

Some philosophers believe that people have a fundamental, existential need to find meaning in their lives and to find their bearings with regard to what counts as the good life (Taylor, 1989). This echoes with many psychologists' observation that people, and especially adolescents, do seem to have a psychological need to construct for themselves identities that are positive and empowering (Erikson, 1950, 1958, 1968). One needs to feel that one has self-worth, by seeing oneself as having certain competencies that are valued and valuable in society or in some reference groups significant to them, by belonging to certain communities that one cherishes, and by sharing the values and commitments of these communities significant to them (Hoover & Erikson, 2004) (e.g., marginalized schoolboys taking up a hypermasculine identity to resist marginalization by school authorities; see Harrington, this volume). One can experience a sense of what the psychologists call identity crisis or the philosophers call loss of horizon when one fails to find such satisfying identities for oneself. Students of modernity argue that a feature of the modern condition is the pervasive sense of loss of horizon and a continuous quest of the modern person for reassembling one, as traditional frameworks with universal value claims gradually give way to multiple, diverse frameworks in which the modern person is immersed, and out of which the modern person finds resources to position her/himself in relation to the good and to others (Taylor, 1989).

Those who have the power to define and delimit identity categories in society or in specific social fields (often doing so in rigid, reductionist, essentializing ways; see Martinsson & Reimers, this volume) have both the symbolic capital (e.g., to define what kinds of competences are worthwhile or markers of valuable identities) and the cultural capital to produce and reproduce the privilege of their groups (see both chapters by Skeggs, this volume). Those who seek to resist such essentializing, categorizing, and positioning might engage in strategies of identity politics struggle, and might also take up essentialism as a strategy to redefine and reassert the value associated with their own identities (e.g., see the schoolboys described by Harrington, this volume).

Fixed identity categories and their essentialized contents are often naturalized, legitimized, and produced and reproduced in people's everyday discourse (e.g., powerful middle class women reproducing the discourse of stereotypical gender roles for women in Malaysia, see Khemlani David & Yong, this volume). These identity ideological contents might be willingly accepted and subscribed to by those marginalized by these identity categories themselves; for instance, an immigrant woman's identification with her role as a filial daughter and thus her decision to stay in a poor-prospect job (which limits her access to valuable communities, opportunities to acquire important competencies, and future professional identities) to earn the money to support her family (see Hansen, this volume).

Fixed identity categories and stereotypes might also be mobilized in people's everyday interactions to re/position (remote) *others* as debased or subhuman beings in a move to construct for oneself a superior identity in relation to (remote) *others* (see Cheng's conversation analysis of such identity positioning acts, this volume).

Social actors marginalized in a certain social field might mobilize other resources and capitals available to them to "turn the tables," to infuse new meanings and positive associations into their formerly marginalized identities (see Eng, this volume).

Under globalization forces with mass migration and the penetration of electronic mass media, the role of the imagination in people's social life has become ever more important. Cultural marketing strategies capitalize on people's identity needs/crises and provide people with powerful images and cultural resources to construct positive identities or boost up their identities, which have been under threat. Cultural capitalism also capitalizes on working-class people's emotions and affective energies, extracts them, and infuses these energies and emotions into white middle-class bodies—rebranding them as new powerful, marketable identities, while leaving the black working-class youth identity as stigmatized as before (see second chapter of Skeggs, this volume).

Postmodernist and poststructuralist scholars have sought to break away from the straitjacket of modernist, essentialist identity categories and point to the performativity theory of identity (Butler, 1993; see discussion by Erni, this volume).

Having summarized the trends emerging from different scholars' views on identity, what then are the implications for us, educators, located in different contexts of the world? Before carrying on with this heavy theoretical discussion, perhaps we can revisit the lyrics of John Lennon's (1971) song, "Imagine," in which Lennon expresses his dream world in which people live as one.

Can the world live as one? Should or can we do away with identity categories and boundaries? Can we live without having the need to engage in some kind of identity struggle and politics? It would be relatively less difficult to imagine such a scenario if one already occupies the privileged positions and possesses the prestigious identities in society. In fact, it would be to such a person's advantage to make everyone think that there are no such boundaries and that everyone is equal or has equal access to the world's goods, both symbolic and material ones; and, that if one does not have access, it is mainly due to his lack of efforts and industry (i.e., the meritocracy myth), and not because he has made certain cultural capital the essential criteria for acquiring those prestigious identities (and the privilege that comes with them). It is also to such a person's advantage to make everyone think that such capital is beyond the reach of people outside of their own groups/communities/habitus.

As long as there is social inequality and as long as the powerful groups of people in society continue to fix essentialist identities for others (or conversely, ignore or deny the existence of others who are different from them), there will still be the need for identity struggles and identity politics. However, can such a politics go beyond strategic essentialism? As cultural studies scholar Hall (1996) puts it:

> This does not make it any easier to conceive of how a politics can be constructed which works with and through difference, which is able to build those forms of solidarity and identification which make common struggle and resistance possible but without suppressing the real heterogeneity of interests and identities, and which can effectively draw the political boundary lines without which political contestation is impossible, without fixing those boundaries for eternity. ... But the difficulty of conceptualizing such a politics (and the temptation to slip into a sort of endlessly sliding discursive liberal-pluralism) does not absolve us of the task of developing such a politics. (p. 444)

Without attempting to offer any solutions (which is quite impossible, if not presumptuous, for any single researcher to embark on), I shall propose one possible way of showing how educators can draw on the postmodernist theory of performativity to help marginalized students (e.g., like the schoolboys described in Harrington's chapter, this volume) to create positive, fluid, hybrid, and multiple identities that can be accepted by themselves and others.

Learning from Postmodernist Cultural Strategies: Creative Performativity and Helping Students to Recreate Their Identities in Positive, Fluid, Dynamic, Hybrid, and Multiple Ways

Identities per se do not seem to constitute the problem. In fact, we all need some kind of identities, especially positive ones, which we can feel proud of and which are accepted by significant others. What is problematic, however, is the fixing, essentializing act (usually by the powerful groups in society) of using rigid identity boundaries and contents to label, stereotype, and limit the possibilities of groups of people/students, and to exclude them from the society's goods, or conversely, to deny their difference or existence and ignore their needs altogether.

If postmodernist cultural rebranding strategies have been successfully used by cultural capitalism to capitalize on people's identity needs/crises, and to create powerful consumer identities to feed the appetite of global capitalism (see discussion before), we can perhaps appropriate these cultural strategies and use them for helping students to recreate positive identities for themselves, but in much more fluid, hybrid, and dynamic ways than the cultural industries' rebranding strategies.

Teachers in the schooling system occupy functional roles that are imbued with authorities (though only in a relative sense and this is always subject to negotiation and renegotiation by students). Like it or not, teachers have been occupying powerful positions; and we can use our power to privilege certain groups of students (usually those who have come from similar cultural and social backgrounds as ours and have the cultural capital to respond positively to our demands and become likable to us) and denigrate certain other groups of students (usually those coming from a different social, cultural, or linguistic background from ours and not having the appropriate capital (attitudes and competencies) to respond positively to our expectations). We tend to create rigid, stereotypic identity categories for both groups of students and solidify the boundaries between them. However, if we draw on the postmodernist theory of performativity of identity (Butler, 1993), we would see the need to re-create identities in much more fluid, hybrid, multiple, and dynamic ways; as Erni (this volume) delineates Butler's theory below:

> ... [Butler] argues that one acquires subjectivity through reiteration and the temporal logic that governs it. But through the same process, one's subjectivity can be challenged, even destabilized. Accordingly, every identity is constituted by discursive formation as much as by deformation (p. 229). After "essentialism," then, we can reinforce Butler's theory of performativity by emphasizing those moments of performance of the self that are intense but not necessarily accumulative, energetic but not always constitutive, encountering but not formative, connecting but not congealing. But always consequential.

If language is the primary medium mediating the construction, deconstruction, and reconstruction of identities, then perhaps educators can explore ways in which language can be creatively used to provide more fluid discursive resources for students to achieve new, multiple ways of understanding themselves—to create new languages of self-understanding in more multiple, positive, and empowering ways. For instance, instead of following the traditional schooling values of classifying students (usually in binary ways) as "bright students" versus "slow students" (or "good students" vs. "uncooperative students"), we can propose new nonessentializing languages of self-understanding, for example, by creating multiple, positive vocabularies to describe the diverse range of resources and attitudes that students bring with them.

However, positive language alone is not sufficient if we do not relax our own value judgments by allowing students' voices, discourses, attitudes, and cultural and linguistic resources to enter into dialogue with ours, to interpenetrate and interilluminate ours in a two-way enrichment sense (vs. the one-way transmission model of traditional teaching): that is, to allow our own, as well as students', values, resources, and competencies to be mutually hybridizing and hybridized (see Luk & Lin, 2006 for some concrete classroom examples).

Similarly, teachers can also strive to create conditions (e.g., multiple "webs of interlocution," see Taylor, 1989 and discussion earlier in this chapter) under which students can create and belong to multiple communities in school, which offer them nurturing attention and positive identities but without solidifying their membership categories—for example, without iron-casting them in only one category (e.g., rigid binary identities of the masculine vs. the feminine), always opening up new, hybrid multiple identity possibilities for them to explore and develop their different potential interests and abilities in new arenas, interacting with different groups of peers and people. If cultural capitalism has capitalized on electronic media to provide new possibilities of creating new positive identities for people (albeit with the final aim of driving them to consume), teachers can also help students to draw on their imagination to reinvent, refashion, and re-create new, positive, multiple, fluid, and dynamic identities for themselves to overcome the straitjacket of the usual binary, static student, gender, ethnic, social class (or other essentializing) identities circulating in most school contexts. As Appadurai (1996) puts it:

> … the imagination has now acquired a singular new power in social life. The imagination—expressed in dreams, songs, fantasies, myths, and stories—has always been part of the repertoire of every society, in some culturally organized way. But there is a peculiar new force to the imagination in social life today. More persons in more parts of the world consider a wider set of *possible lives* than they ever did before. One important source of this change is the mass media, which present a rich, ever-changing store of *possible lives*, some of which enter the lived imagination of ordinary people more successfully than others. … (p. 53; italics added).

Songs, dancing, drama, and multimodality arts, including youth-popular cultural genres such as hip-hop and rap music, and artistic and discursive genres from different linguistic/cultural traditions, can be explored as means to help students to work together to imagine and create more empowering identities for both male and female students, linguistic minority students, and students with nonmainstream talents and needs. While these proposals are not new at all, it is hoped that by destabilizing the rigid identity categories and boundaries (that schooling usually imposes on students and teachers) that teachers and students can work together to explore new ways of imagining, creating, and living out fluid, multiple, and dynamic ways of being, speaking, relating, acting, and seeing in the world that defy the essentializing effects of labeling, stereotyping, iron-casting and self-negating identification practices. To end this essay, I shall quote urban hiphop artist and poet, Saul Williams:

> ... I was able to see that hip hop was still voicing a CENTURIES OLD DESIRE FOR RESPECT. ... (Williams, 2006, p. xxvii; capitals added)

Starting off as a source of countercultural African American youth resistant identities in the 1960s and early 1970s, American hip-hop culture has, however, been very much commercialized and rebranded by mainstream cultural industries, losing much of its youthful resistant and reflective power. Williams, in his 2006 collection of poetry, *Dead Emcee Scrolls*, seeks to rekindle our thinking about what hip-hop culture desires and can aim to achieve—respect, for self and others. It is hoped that our theoretical explorations into the many senses and meanings of identities and the processes of identity-making will help us achieve precisely this aim—respect, for self and others, and fluid, empowering, and dynamic identities for all.

Endnote

1. However, "habitus" stresses more the encompassing ecology that a person is immersed in from early age, while "capital" stresses more the currency in specific fields of those predispositions, attitudes, and skills acquired because of immersion in a particular habitus.

References

Appadurai, A. (1996). *Modernity at large: Cultural dimensions of globalization.* Minneapolis: University of Minnesota Press.

Bourdieu, P. (1973). Cultural reproduction and social reproduction. In R. Brown, (Ed.), *Knowledge, education and cultural change.* London: Tavistock.

Bourdieu, P. (1977). *Outline of a theory of practice* (R. Nice, Trans.). Cambridge: Cambridge University Press.

Bourdieu, P. (1984). *Distinction: A social critique of the judgement of taste.* London: Routledge and Kegan Paul.

Bourdieu, P. (1991). *Language and symbolic power.* Cambridge, MA: Harvard University Press.

Bourdieu, P., & Passeron, J.-C. (1977). *Reproduction in education, society and culture.* London: Sage.

Brooks, D. (2000). *Bobos in paradise: The new upper class and how they got there.* New York: Simon & Schuster.

Butler, J. (1993). *Bodies that matter: On the discursive limits of "sex."* New York: Routledge.

Canagarajah, A. S. (1993). Critical ethnography of a Sri Lankan classroom: Ambiguities in student opposition to reproduction through ESOL. *TESOL Quarterly, 27*(4), 601–626.

Collins, J. (1993). Determination and contradiction: An appreciation and critique of the work of Pierre Bourdieu on language and education. In C. Calhoun, E. LiPuma, & M. Postone (Eds.), *Bourdieu: Critical perspectives* (pp. 116–138). Chicago, Ill.: University of Chicago Press.

Crossley, N. (2003). From reproduction to transformation: Social movement fields and the radical habitus. *Theory, Culture & Society, 20*(6), 1–20.

Dick, P. K. (1987). *We can remember it for you wholesale (The collected short stories of Philip K Dick).* London: Millennium, Orion Books Ltd.

Delpit, L. D. (1988). The silenced dialogue: Power and pedagogy in educating other people's children. *Harvard Educational Review, 58*(3), 280–298.

Erikson, E. (1950). *Childhood and society.* New York: Norton.

Erikson, E. (1958). *Young man Luther.* New York: Norton.

Erikson, E. (1968). *Identity, youth and crisis.* New York: Norton.

Hall, S. (1996). New ethnicities. In D. Morley, & K.-H. Chen (Eds.), *Critical dialogues in cultural studies* (pp. 441–449). London: Routledge.

Holt, D. B. (2004). *How brands become icons: The principles of cultural branding.* Boston, MA: Harvard Business School Press.

Hoover, K. (Ed.). (2004). *The future of identity: Centennial reflections on the legacy of Erik Erikson.* Lanham: Lexington Books.

Hoover, K, & Ericksen, L. K. (2004). Introduction: The future of identity. In K. Hoover (Ed.), *The future of identity: Centennial reflections on the legacy of Erik Erikson* (pp. 1–14). Lanham, MD: Lexington Books.

Jenkins, R. (1992). *Pierre Bourdieu.* London: Routledge.

Kenny, A. (Ed.) (1994). *The Wittgenstein reader.* Oxford, UK: Blackwell.

Kroger, J. (2004). Identity in formation. In K. Hoover (Ed.), *The future of identity: Centennial reflections on the legacy of Erik Erikson* (pp. 61–76). Lanham, MD: Lexington Books.

Lennon, J. (1971, September 9). *Imagine*. An album released by Apple/EMI.

Lin, A. M. Y. (1996). Bilingualism or linguistic segregation? Symbolic domination, resistance, and code-switching in Hong Kong schools. *Linguistics and Education, 8*(1), 49–84.

Lin, A. M. Y. (1999). Doing-English-lessons in the reproduction or transformation of social worlds? *TESOL Quarterly, 33*(3), 393–412.

Luk, J. C. M., & Lin, A. M. Y. (2006). *Classroom interactions as cross-cultural encounters: Native speakers in EFL lessons*. Mahwah, NJ: Lawrence Erlbaum.

Luke, A. (1995, April 20). *When literacy might/not make a difference: Textual practice and capital*. Paper presented at the 1995 American Educational Research Association Annual Meetings, Symposium on Writing, Identity and Social Power in School and Community, San Francisco. Session Chairs: Kris Gutierrez & David Bloome.

Luke, A. (1996). Genres of power? Literacy education and the production of capital. In R. Hasan & G. Williams (Eds.), *Literacy in society* (pp. 308–338). London: Longman.

Marcia, J. E. (1966). Development and validation of ego identity status. *Journal of Personality and Social Psychology, 3*, 551–558.

Marcia, J. E. (1967). Ego identity status: Relationship to change in self-esteem, "general maladjustment," and "authoritarianism." *Journal of Personality, 35*, 18–31.

Marcia, J. E., Waterman, A. S., Matteson, D. R., Archer, S. L., & Orlofsky, J. L. (1993). *Ego identity: A handbook for psychosocial research*. New York: Springer-Verlag.

Martin-Jones, M., & Heller, M. (1996). Education in multilingual settings: Discourse, identities and power. *Linguistics and Education, 8*(1), 3–16.

Mehan, H. (1979). *Learning lessons: Social organization in the classroom*. Cambridge, MA: Harvard University Press.

Parfit, D. (1986). *Reasons and persons*. Oxford: Clarendon Press.

Pennycook, A. (1994). *The cultural politics of English as an international language*. London: Longman.

Taylor, C. (1989). *Sources of the self: The making of the modern identity*. Cambridge, MA: Cambridge University Press.

Taylor, L. (2006). Cultural translation and the double movement of difference in learning "English as a second identity." *Critical Inquiry in Language Studies, 3*(2&3), 101–130.

Vygotsky, L. S. (1978) *Mind in society: The development of higher psychological processes*. Cambridge: Harvard University Press.

Williams, S. (2006). *The dead emcee scrolls*. New York: Pocket Books.

CONTRIBUTING AUTHORS

Winnie Cheng
Professor
Department of English
The Hong Kong Polytechnic University
Hung Hom, Kowloon
Hong Kong

Winnie Cheng is a professor in the Department of English of the Hong Kong Polytechnic University. She is also director of the Research Centre for Professional Communication in English. Her current areas of research include corpus linguistics, conversational analysis, discourse analysis, discourse intonation, intercultural communication and pragmatics, and online education.

Jan Connelly
Senior Lecturer
School of Education
University of New England
Armidale, New South Wales, Australia

Dr. Jan Connelly has taught in primary classrooms, ESL/TESOL contexts, and tertiary institutions in Australia and Hong Kong. Her research and writing focuses on the issues that emerge when teaching and learning occur in contexts of linguistic and cultural difference in remote and rural locations. Jan believes that how these contexts and their related circumstances impact on teachers' pedagogy and students' learning are central to issues of justice and equity in education.

Maya Khemlani David
Professor
Faculty of Languages and Linguistics
University of Malaya
Kuala Lumpur, Malaysia

Professor Dr. Maya Khemlani David (Faculty of Languages and Linguistics, University of Malaya) is an honorary fellow of the Chartered Institute of

Linguists, United Kingdom and has a special interest in the role of language in establishing and maintaining national unity. David has written *The Sindhis of Malaysia: A Sociolinguistic Account* (2001, London, ASEAN) and co-written *Writing a Research Paper* (2006, Serdang: UPM). Her co-edited and edited publications are *Language and the Power of the Media* (2006, Frankfurt, Peter Lang), *Language Choices and Discourse of Malaysian Families: Case Studies of Families in Kuala Lumpur, Malaysia* (2006, Petaling Jaya, Strategic International and Research Development Centre), *Teaching of English in Second and Foreign Language Settings: Focus on Malaysia* (2004, Frankfurt, Peter Lang) and *Developing Reading Skills* (2002, Kuala Lumpur, Melta/Sasbadi).

Jette G. Hansen Edwards
Associate Professor, Department of English
Chinese University of Hong Kong
Shatin, New Territories
Hong Kong

Jette G. Hansen Edwards is associate professor in the Department of English at the Chinese University of Hong Kong. Her research interests include the acquisition of a second language phonology, second language variation, gender, and peer response in second language writing. She is the author of *Acquiring a Non-native Phonology: Linguistic Constraints and Social Barriers* (2006, Continuum Group), and the co-author of *Peer Response in L2 Writing* (2002, University of Michigan Press). Additionally, she has published articles in refereed journals such as *Applied Linguistics, ELT Journal, Studies in Second Language Acquisition, TESOL Quarterly,* and *Written Communication.*

Joseph S. Eng
Professor and Director, Writing Program and ASAP
California State University
Monterey, California

Joseph S. Eng is the director of the University Writing Program and Academic Skills Achievement Program, and professor of English and rhetoric. Eng teaches writing and oversees programs serving campus-wide faculty writing initiatives and first-generation college students. For seven years up to the summer of 2006, he had been director of composition and associate professor of English at Eastern Washington University in Cheney, Washington. He has taught undergraduate and graduate courses in writing, theories, pedagogy, and research methodologies for more than two decades. Recent publications include articles and book chapters on grading and assessment, composition pedagogy, and writing program administration.

John Nguyet Erni
Professor
Department of Cultural Studies
Lingnan University
Tuen Mun, New Territories, Hong Kong

John Nguyet Erni is professor of cultural studies at Lingnan University, Hong Kong. His books include *Unstable Frontiers: Technomedicine and the Cultural Politics of Curing* AIDS (Minnesota, 1994), *Internationalizing Cultural Studies: An Anthology* (with Ackbar Abbas, Blackwell, 2005), and *Asian Media Studies: The Politics of Subjectivities* (with Siew Keng Chua, Blackwell, 2005).

Ingrid Harrington
Lecturer
School of Education
University of New England
New South Wales, Australia

Dr. Ingrid Harrington teaches with the Special Education Team at the University of New England, Armidale, Australia. She has extensive experience as a teacher in K–12 schools, and has worked as a teacher with disadvantaged youth in community and institutional settings. She currently teaches the behaviour management and special needs units in the B. Ed award.

Her research interests include a range of gender issues in schools, including boy's participation, performance, and retention to Year 12, and supporting beginning teachers in their first five years of service. She is regularly invited to give presentations in Europe, Asia, and Scandinavia.

Angel M. Y. Lin
, Associate Professor
Department of English and Communication
City University of Hong Kong
Kowloon, Hong Kong

Angel M. Y. Lin received her Ph.D. from the Ontario Institute for Studies in Education, University of Toronto, Canada in 1996. She works in the areas of cultural studies, critical discourse analysis, urban ethnography, critical education studies, feminist media studies and youth cultural studies. With a background in ethnomethodology, conversation analysis and social theory, her theoretical orientations are phenomenological, sociocultural and critical.

Lena Martinsson
Associate Professor
Department of Gender Studies
University of Göteborg
Göteborg, Sweden

Lena Martinsson is associate professor at the Department of Ethnology, University of Göteborg. Her main field of research is intersectional analysis on rhetoric on gender equality and diversity management in school and working life. From a post-Marxist angle, she is also conducting studies about constructions of class in everyday life.

Eva Reimers
Associate Professor
Department of Social and Welfare Studies
University of Linköping
Norrköping, Sweden

Eva Reimers is senior lecturer and associate professor at Department of Social and Welfare Studies, University of Linköping, Sweden. Her research interests are discourse analysis of norms and normality pertaining to areas such as rites and rituals, media, death and bereavement, and education.

Beverley Skeggs
Professor
Sociology Department
Goldsmiths, University of London, New Cross
London, U.K.

Beverley Skeggs' research interests include class, cultural formations, feminist and poststructuralist theory, Pierre Bourdieu and Marx, sexuality, space and violence. Bev is interested in the relationship between the most intimate and the most structural, between who we think we are and global capitalism. Her latest book *Class, Self, Culture* (London: Routledge 2004) explores these interests by examining how class is produced across a range of sites. In another book (which was produced as part of the ESRC funded Violence, Sexuality and Space project) *Sexuality and the Politics of Violence,* co-written with Les Moran, Paul Tyrer and Karen Corteen (London: Routledge 2003), she also shows how judgments about culture have become similarly pertinent to how people are assessed through law and how they can make justice claims. Both these books emerged as a result of interests generated in an ethnographic research project, published as *Formations of Class and Gender: Becoming Respectable* (London: Sage 1997). This book questions the assumptions of post-structural theories on gender and class by applying them to the lives of 83 white working-class women. Again, it explores how personhood is produced through the inhabitation of the categorical positions of class, sexuality, and gender.

Sam Winter
Associate Professor
Division of Learning, Development and Diversity
Faculty of Education
University of Hong Kong
Hong Kong

Sam Winter worked as a teacher and a psychologist in his native England, before moving 23 years ago to work in Hong Kong, where he is currently in the Faculty of Education at the University of Hong Kong. For the last eight years Sam has researched and taught in the area of transgender in Asia. He has also been involved with a group working for transpeople's rights in Hong Kong. He believes that transpeople are different, not deviant, and that the only gender identity disorder worthy of the name is society's inability to accept that difference. He is director of the Transgender ASIA Centre, the aim of which is to encourage research, education, and social action for transpeople in Asia (http://web.hku.hk/~sjwinter/TransgenderASIA/index.htm).

Janet Yong
Associate Professor
School of Accounting and Finance
Hong Kong Polytechnic University
Hung Hom, Kowloon
Hong Kong

Janet Yong was an associate professor on the Faculty of Languages and Linguistics at the University of Malaya in Kuala Lumpur before joining

The Hong Kong Polytechnic University. She now writes, coordinates, and teaches the English Enhancement and Business Communication programs at the School of Accounting and Finance. In addition to ESL/EFL teaching and testing and curriculum development, Janet specializes in phonetics and phonology, research methods, sociolinguistics, and language and conflict resolution. Her Ph.D. research is on Malay word prosody. She has recently completed a study on slang ways of Mat Rempits in Malaysia and is starting work on a book on language and conflict resolution. Her current research includes a systematic study of phonological relationships among Han-Viet-Yue dialects.

AUTHOR INDEX

SUBJECT INDEX

A

Aboriginal Student Support and Parents
   Association (ASSPA), 90, 93–5
anatomania, 120, 123, 127, 132
androcentricity, 75
apotemnophilia, 131
apparent retention rate (ARR), 102
appropriation of culture, 44
ARC/SPIRT, 105
ARR. *see* apparent retention rate (ARR)
ASSPA. *see* Aboriginal Student Support and
   Parents Association (ASSPA)
Australia's National Goals for Schooling,
   101
authorisation, 15–20, 28
authority, 14

B

becoming X, 196
being-for-the-self, 1
borderland, 71
bourgeois perspective, 16–17, 27, 45

C

capital
   cultural, 20–21, 37, 40–43, 205–7, 211–15
   economic, 207
   national, 21
   social, 207
   symbolic, 205–7
capitalism, 29, 37, 52, 60–61
capitalist semiotisation, 18
caretaker identity, 158–63
categorical typification, 13
categorisation, surveillant, 18
category-bound activities, 172

category-bound features, 172
CDA (Critical Discourse Analysis), 91–7
citizenship, 57–8
class
   as moral-cultural property, 38–9
   as neoliberal resource, 44
   changing formations of, 39–43
   entitlement of, 44–7
   formation and reproduction, 19, 27, 44
   gender and, 39–40, 51, 61–2
   relations of, 36
   spatialisation of, 40–41
   transference of, 41–3
co-inquiry, 79, 81
codas, syllable, 164–6
coherent self, 27
community, 21–2
complete self, 14, 19
composition theory, 69, 71
confession, 13
conscience, 13
consciousness, 13, 205, 208
contact zone, 71, 74
contract theory, 14–15
contractual recognition, 14–15
conversation-style differences, 182–3
counterhegemony, 75
creative performativity, 214–17
creativity, induced by social diversity,
   56, 59
Critical Discourse Analysis (CDA), 91–7
cultural capital, 20–21, 37, 40–43, 205–7,
   211–15
cultural diversity, 53
cultural identity, 178–9, 181
cultural marketing strategy, 213
cultural practice, 39
cultural studies, 208–11
cultural turn, 45
culturally sensitive topics, 173–80
culture
   appropriation of, 44
   ethnic teacher and, 73–4

P

performance management, 53, 59
personal identity. *see* identity
personal values, 99
personality
development of, 13
personhood, 11
American, 20
European, 15
negative, 23–5
production of, 13–14, 17
perspective, as central component of
identity, 15–16, 18
pluralism, disharmonious, 51–2, 54, 60–63
politeness strategy, 172, 179
politics
equality, 51
identity, 12, 16–19, 26–8, 37, 46, 51,
195
of difference, 51–2, 61
of feminism, 67
of location, 69
of recognition, 12, 51
of redistribution, 12
of social diversity, 61
polyvocality, 71
popular culture discourse,
school-based, 110
positioning, process of, 106–7, 113
positive identity, 211–17
possessive individualism, 2, 13–16, 20
postmodern self, 76–7
postmodern theory, 76–7
postmodernism, 208–11, 214–17
poststructural analysis of identity and
subjectivity, 91–2
power, definition of, 138
powerless speech, 138, 150
practical nationality, 20–21
pragmatic signs of CDA, 93–5
prejudiced talk. *see also* language; speech
approach to studying culturally
sensitive topics, 173
dialogue of, 185–91
discussion of, 180–83
management of culturally sensitive
topics, 174–80
negotiation of, 171–3

product use, 42
psycho-historical approach to identity, 201

R

race, 42, 69
racism
culturally essentialized, 22–5
mobilised, 25–6, 41–2
teacher and, 90–91, 99
trauma of, 85
real-life test, 123
rebranding strategy, 214–15
recognition, 12
reflexive self, 78–80
reflexive solidarity, 52, 62–3
representation, struggles around, 13
resourceful self, generation of, 13–16
resources, access to, 18
rights discourse, 12
role confusion, 201
rural culture, 101–2

S

savage other, 15
school-based popular culture discourse, 110
scientific management, 53
second language acquisition (SLA). *see also*
English as a second language (ESL)
caretaker identity, gender, and,
158–63
defining and researching gender,
155–6
impact of gender roles on, 165–6
language use and acquisition, 163–5
study on, 156–8
self
coherent accounts of, 211
discourse of, 11–16
fractions of, 19
irreducible difference of, 20
middle-class, 38, 47
multifaceted sense of, 146–7
reflexive, 78–80
resourceful, 13–16

social psychological perspective of,
121–2, 129–31
Thai perspective of, 122, 124–5, 128–32
traumatic telling of self, 19–20

V

value
attribution of, 39–40, 46
labour theory of, 45
marketisation of, 46
of citizens, 20–22
of cultural practice, 39
of culture, 38–9, 102
of education, 103
of identity, 25–6, 28, 211–12
transference of, 35–6
visibility, 26–8

W

webs of interlocution, 199, 202–3, 216
women
and speech (*see* speech)
as powerful public figures,
137–9, 150
language choice of, 143–7
multifaceted sense of self, 146–7
role of, 150
women's culture, 19, 22
work conditions, 69
working class
culture of, 43–4
evaluation of, 38
fragmentation of, 46–7
value and, 38–44
wounded attachment, 17, 27–8
writer, ethnic teacher as, 71–2